About the author

I was created by Indian parents in a British colony of East Africa in 1939. Despite some disasters in my early life, I was able to progress and experience the joy of existence. After starting work as an engineer in Kenya, I ended up spending most of my working life in Britain. For fifty years I travelled around our fabulous globe both for my work and for my pleasure. Delights, disasters and revelations in my life have prompted me to relate my life experiences to current and future people on our unique planet.

A LIFE POST-1939

AUTOBIOGRAPHY PART I

Rajinder Sharma

A LIFE POST-1939

AUTOBIOGRAPHY PART I

Vanguard Press

VANGUARD PAPERBACK

© Copyright 2019
Rajinder Sharma

A CIP catalogue record for this title is

available from the British Library.

ISBN 978 1 784653 93 3

Vanguard Press is an imprint of
Pegasus Elliot MacKenzie Publishers Ltd.
www.pegasuspublishers.com

This edition published in 2019

Vanguard Press
Sheraton House Castle Park
Cambridge England
Printed & Bound in Great Britain

Dedication

The lives of my Indian parents and grandparents were affected by the British colonization of India. My own life was influenced by British education in an African colony. My employment by the British Armed Forces resulted in me having the delight of going around the globe and experiencing the delights of our existence on a wonderful planet. My autobiography is dedicated to the British people for having created those delights for me.

Contents

Preface

After the age of seventy, I was struck by a head problem that forced me to retire from my working life. During recovery, I had been doing a lot of walking and cycling around the beautiful countryside. On a walk along the Exe estuary I met up with a man. We ended up walking and talking all the way to Exmouth, where I might have told him about a disaster that I had experienced in my life at the age of five. During our parting on that beach, he suggested that I should consider writing a book about my life. That was something that had never entered my mind as I had not had any achievement in my life, but there had been terrible failures.

My recollection of the 1945 disaster was limited as I was only five years old at the time. Still, it did stimulate me to continue recollecting my life in India at the age of five and six. I could never have imagined that recollections of my early life, during my later life, could have had a stimulating effect on me. Even the ordinary life of my great grandfather would have been interesting to me if he had left behind some recollections of his ordinary life. Also, none of us have any idea of the early life experiences and education of our father. As I had already been through the main functions of my life, there was plenty of free time for me to start recollecting all my life experiences, which I am leaving behind for later generations. I am very grateful to the man who triggered me into writing a book about my life, but I cannot recall his name.

I am thankful to my father and mother who brought me into existence out of almost nothing; to the people of Kutch in India who saved my life in 1945 and to my uncle who brought me up after the death of my father in 1949. I am also thankful to all the people with whom I have been sharing my limited life on a most wonderful and unique planet.

mmxix

Chapter 1

My early life in Africa and India

Mombasa

My coming into existence has been no more than the formation of a drop of water on a planet for a fraction of time. It was in the town of Mombasa that I popped into an existence. Mombasa used to be an island tucked in the East African coast just south of the equator. For centuries the Arabs had colonised it. In 1492, Vasco de Gama was the first of the Europeans to have sailed around Africa and at Mombasa he could see the town from his anchored position beside the port on his journey to India. The Portuguese took over the town in the 16th century and built the castle of Fort Jesus by the sea at the east end of the town in 1593. At the end of the 17th century the Arab rulers of Zanzibar took over Mombasa and held it for 140 years. Then the British and the Germans gained control of East Africa and just before the 20th century the British proclaimed Kenya as a protectorate.

The original island of Mombasa was tucked inside the mainland. The British built a causeway to the mainland for laying down a railway line for steam trains to go all the way to Uganda. Mombasa stopped being an island, but the sea tides still went both ways around the town to the causeway at the west end. A new harbour was built at the south end of the island after the tricky route out to the sea had been suitably opened for steamships. A ferry that had earlier been used for the transfer of people and vehicles between the island and the mainland on the south side continued to do so. The dhows (sailing ships) continued to use the old port on the north-eastern end of the island. On that north side at Nyali, the connection with the mainland was an unusual floating bridge. The very long bridge went up and down with daily tides which made the crossing of the channel quite tricky and exciting for cars, cyclists and pedestrians.

I was born at home in the early morning of 7th of December 1939. That was after the start of World War II and I could not be blamed for starting it. However, that war nearly resulted in the termination of my life in 1945 before it was over. I was the fourth child amongst the surviving children of my parents, father Som Nath Sharma and mother, Dhan Devi who came from the Prashar family. My paternal grandparents, Polo Ram Sharma and Puran Devi lived in the village of Shamespur in the Ludhiana district of the state of Punjab in India. My father was born there on 9 October 1904. He was the oldest child of his parents and got married in India around 1930 to my mother from the nearby village of Sialva. After that he moved to Mombasa in the British colony of Kenya in East Africa in 1932 to work as an electrician on the steam ships in the port. The first child of my parents was a boy who did not survive at an early age. Then the next four of us children did survive. I arrived on 7 December 1939 and am the youngest of the surviving children. My brothers are Baldev Kumar and Krishan Dev and my sister is Krishna. My parents named me Rajinder Kumar Sharma. Our Hindu names have some special indications. The middle name Kumar stands for bachelor and should be dropped after marriage. The outer two names should be dropped completely when a Hindu becomes a yogi so that there is no connection with the family. Modern birth registration resulted in me keeping the full name. After me, there were two more children who did not survive. They were my two younger sisters and I remember playing a lot with the older one called Bholi. I also played with my youngest sister on my mother's bed when she was a baby. I vaguely remember that baby having passed away from life, but I cannot recall my playful sister Bholi passing out of her existence. Both of my younger sisters had passed away by the time I was five years old. So, out of a total of seven children in the family, only four of us have survived. The three older ones have already lived past the age of eighty.

My first five years

My father worked in the electrical field for African Marines on the south side of Mombasa town. My birth and my growing up period occurred in the bungalow situated on a dust lane off the main tarmac of Makupa Road that ran between the western mainland causeway and the old town centre on the east side. My mother told me of an attempt by a robber to steal the sheet from her bed at night through a flap in the window. She stopped it being pulled away because I was wrapped up in it. We lived on a lane that had concrete houses that were occupied by Hindu, Muslim and Sikh Indians and a white Seychelles family who were Christians. The Christian house was directly opposite us and was the same as ours. Behind us, there were thatched mud houses used by Africans.

Our home was a detached bungalow that had a tin roof, four main rooms with a hall in the middle, a front veranda and a kitchen outside the back of the house linked by a roofed corridor. A flush toilet inside the house had a seat and the other toilet outside was level with the floor. There were two coconut trees in front of the house and one outside at the back. In our backyard, there were two pawpaw trees and in the area around our houses there were many mango and guava trees. At the back of the house there was a garage, but we had no car. My father had a motorcycle with a sidecar and sometimes the whole family jumped onto it to go to the beach. One day he took us to the beach for a swim on the mainland side of Nyali beach on the north-western side of the island. On arrival, the exciting attraction of the sea made me take off my shoes and run into the water in my shirt and shorts.

I have a slight remembrance of window blackouts that were arranged in a front room at night because of a world war that was going on during those early days of my life, but I never heard any enemy aeroplanes. Later, I also remember the danger of the sight of the Hindu swastika symbol on somebody's outside wall because enemy Germans had started using the old Hindu symbol as their symbol for war.

Start of 1945

I had just reached the age of five just before the start of the year 1945 when I was sent to the White Sisters Convent School where my brothers already were. Our normal school year was from January to December. My sister was at a school which taught in Hindi. At the convent school we were taught in English. As I knew nothing of English, my communication must have been in Swahili which I had picked up from our *aya,* an African woman carer. It was completely perplexing for me to be in the school environment where we were taught by nuns in their white robes. I can only remember what happened to me one day at the new school environment. To get away from the classroom I stepped out towards the toilets but was accompanied by the nun who waited outside for me. Whilst returning, I walked behind her and then ran away into the nearby classroom of my eldest brother. The nun caught up with me and took me back to her classroom. My brother was annoyed with me and told me never to do it again. I was in the school for just a little more than a term during which I must have picked up some English.

During the war period, my father had decided to take all of us to India where he had come from, together with our mother. In Africa, he was coming up to a period in his job when people from overseas could take a paid leave of about six months. However, the world war was still on at that time and there was a problem of finding a steamship to take us to India and my father was waiting for the war to end. Strangely, the answer for an alternative mode of travel was provided by the traders who used to bring items for sale at our doorstep.

Dhow sailing across Indian Ocean in 1945

Dhows usually sailed along the coast between Mombasa and the ports on the African and Arabian coasts. However, they even occasionally sailed across the ocean between India and Africa. The Indian sailors of similar dhows in Malindi had given guidance to Vasco de Gama for sailing across the ocean to India at the end of the 15th century. The dhows built in India were using a simple set of sails and required suitable wind direction for crossing the Indian Ocean. My brother Krishan tells me that there were Indian sailors who used to bring goods from India for sale to our doorsteps. When they realised that our father was trying to get to India, they offered to take us there in their dhow. My father was not comfortable about crossing the Indian Ocean in a dhow, but eventually decided to take the adventure of sailing across the ocean in the only available means of transport at that time.

There was only a set period for sailing to India with the monsoon winds and it would require about two weeks of sailing. In May 1945, we boarded the dhow for our journey to our grandparents living in the north of India in a Punjabi village. There were some other Indian families on that dhow which would sail to a port on the coastal area of the Kutch province in the state of Gujarat. That was closer to the Punjab than Bombay, which was in the middle of the east coast where the steam ships usually went.

When we got on board the dhow, my brother, Krishan, cracked his head on one of the low wooden bars and started the journey with a bleeding head. Then the dhow set out sailing and all I saw was the sea all around us and the sky above, but different colours of sea and sky appeared as we sailed. A few days after setting sail, we were caught up by a smaller dhow which had sailed the day after us. The two dhows got close to each other to enable the crews to talk. The only mode of communication between the dhows was by word of mouth. The crew managing our dhow must have struggled with navigation in the vast sea area which is why the other one was overtaking us.

We had great fun fishing off the side of the ship and managed to fill a tin with little fish that had been swimming beside us. We must have been using bent pins to catch them. There were other times when some small fish were flying over the ship and some were landing on the deck. After they had stopped flipping about, we would pick up those little fish. One day it was fascinating to see a large sailfish being pulled in onto the deck by the crew and it continued to flip about for a while. After it stopped flipping about, I went close to it and was pulled back and warned that the fish only looked dead and might still have flipped and knocked me into the sea. Later, I went to the front of the ship and watched one of the crew chopping up the fish into small pieces.

There was no toilet inside the ship. What we had for a toilet was a hole in the floor of a little box, outside the back of the ship, to enable us to dump our waste straight into the sea. It petrified me to sit on the hole with the sea in view underneath. Initially I dumped my waste off the hole and then had to make sure that it was washed clean off the ship.

There were beautiful views of the sea of different colours. Some days we would be moving very slowly as the wind would be very low. One day my worried father couldn't find me anywhere on the ship and went to see the captain, only to find me sitting with the captain and steering the ship. We were supposed to get to our destination after about two weeks, but we were still at sea for nearly three weeks. The chap steering at night had either fallen off to sleep or had no idea of star navigation. We required re-steering in the morning to get back on course. One evening the Indian coast was sighted near the Bay of Kutch. People started getting ready for getting off the next day. Together with our dad, we were washing two bicycles that were being taken for use in India. Our sailing would be coming to an end the next morning. We settled for the night, which was going to be the last one on the sailing trip. At night, we had been gently sailing away from the main port entrance to do our entry the next morning.

Sinking dhow 1945

In the morning, I was woken and moved out to the top of the deck. From there, I noticed that the dhow was leaning over to the left. There were many people on that side and I wondered why they did not go over to the right side to make the dhow get level. Then I noticed that the dhow was not sailing and some people were throwing off cereal sacks into the sea. The leaning dhow was taking in the sea water from the front and sinking. We must have been sailing close to the coast, but I cannot remember sighting land. Either the dhow had hit a rock under the sea surface or it may have had some leakage from the front. There was no sight of any other boat around us. There were no lifeboats on the dhow. In those days, there were no means of communication from the dhow. Everyone on board was in despair.

While still dumping everything off the ship the crew also launched the little boat on the dhow which would have to be rowed to get help from the coast to save the passengers. The boat was rowed by some crew members and anyone else who could row. An active passenger who had a disabled father got on the boat to help with the rowing. The crew then offered to take only some small children with them for rescue. One family put their child on the boat and my father did the same by putting me on the boat. I remember being on that boat. As soon as my mother realised what was happening, she screamed and got me off the rescue boat so that we would remain together whatever the prospects for our lives. I remember being taken off that boat and back onto the sinking dhow. My mother tied all four of us children together with her sari. The boat from the ship was then rowed off to get help for us before the dhow would take all of us down into the sea.

Our sinking dhow was on either the north side or the south side of our destination port of Porbandar, which is south of the Gulf of Kutch. After the boat from the dhow had disappeared there was a sighting of a small fishing boat. From our dhow, there was a lot of shouting for help, but the fishing boat disappeared away from us. We waited and thankfully later saw a large rowing boat coming up to our sinking dhow. People were greatly relieved to see the saving boat arriving just in time to help us get off the dhow before it had completely gone down into the sea. The families were taken first and after them the rest of the men. Thankfully all of the people left on the sinking dhow were rescued. We were on land at last without any of our belongings, but we were greatly relieved to have had our lives saved.

From our rescue location near Porbandar we were taken to Jamnagar in horse-drawn carriages. Then at Jamnagar we learned that the rescue boat from the dhow had also sunk before reaching the shore and most of the sailors had managed to swim to the beach. However, an adult passenger and a small child ended up drowning because they could not swim. Had I not been taken off that boat before it was rowed out, that could have been the last day of my life. We can never be sure of what might be coming our way during our lives. At Porbandar, the Maharaja of Kutch had provided us with relief and put us up in flats in Jamnagar. At the flats, I remember seeing the only clothing recovered from the sunken ship to be hanging out to dry. It was the wedding clothing of someone on our sinking dhow. For the rest of us, no belongings had been recovered from the ocean, but thankfully our lives had been saved. It was great to have been provided with relief in Jamnagar for about a week by the Maharaja of Kutch

Indian village life 1945-46

From Jamnagar, we then set off on a steam train to the Punjab to be with our grandparents. We travelled to our original destination, the village of Shamespur near Samrala in the Ludhiana district of Punjab province. In that small village, we met up with our grandparents, Polo Ram and Puran Devi, in a big mud house. At the entrance to the house there was a small, gentle, white cow that was providing milk for the family. Around the open centre of the house there were three divisions with one set of steps going to an open roof. My grandparents were in the section on the right and the other related families in the other sections. There was no electricity in the house; lighting was provided by oil lamps and cooking was done with heat from burning wood.

I did not realise then that we had been sailing to India for good when we left Africa. Now I see why my father was taking bicycles to India. He had planned to start working in Punjab and trying to give us a more suitable life than what we had been experiencing in Africa during the world war. However, the dhow sinking in the sea had resulted in making it very difficult for our father to settle into a new life in India, which was also suffering from the war effects. We had lost all of our possessions and there was going to be another problem for us children. We boys had been taught only in English in the convent school in Mombasa. In the Punjab province, the schools taught in Punjabi, Urdu or Hindi. Although we spoke Punjabi and Hindi we could not read or write them. My father was going to have difficulty in sending us boys to a school that taught in English because he needed to have some money. That is why he decided to return to his company in Africa to enable us boys to be able to do what he had earlier managed to do with his education in English in India.

The world war had not ended until later in 1945 and still there were no ships available for us to travel back to Africa. We just had to stay there until my father could return to his job and find a steamship to take us back. There was no way that we would ever sail in a dhow again. We spent about a year in India and none of us went to school during that period. For me it had been a great time and I remember a lot of events and experiences during that time. One day a barber came to our village to give us boys a haircut, something which we did not have for a long time. At the end of the haircuts we all had a clump of hair uncut at the back of the head. The barber had done that because we were Brahmins who normally had a little tail at the back of their heads which they tied into a knot. That was the *bhodi,* which was a religious symbol worn by the dedicated Hindus. As soon as we got home, we boys couldn't wait to chop those tails off our heads.

What amazed my grandfather and other relatives, was that at the age of only five I could speak English. Also, they thought that I was misbehaved and didn't listen to them. Being the youngest, I was my father's favourite and got a lot of freeway from him. We got on well with the people in the village as my grandfather was the senior of Hindus in the village. Around us there also were some Sikh families. A little way off from our house we also had a small brick-built hall by the archway in the village where we spent time as well. There were large ponds in several places in the village. The family cow that provided the milk for us had to be taken to the field. Later, that white cow was replaced by a big black buffalo to provide more milk required for the bigger family. Every time I walked past behind that buffalo it turned its big horned-head towards me and frightened me. I dreaded going near it. My elder brother went with the lads who took the animals out for feeding. He even got to sit on the buffalo for a ride. When they were passing the pond, the buffalo went into the water before my brother got off its back. There used to be a visit to the village by a holy white ox. He would turn up on his own and had a bell around his neck. The greatly admired ox had great stature and was fed by the village. After feeding he would wander off to other villages. It was amazing to see great love and respect that the villagers showed to a beautiful animal.

One day, we gathered around in an area beside the village where a lot of wood was being piled. Then, a wrapped human body was brought and put on top of the pile. The wood was lit with fire and the flames started covering the body. That was the process of a cremation of a body that took place out in the open. Seeing a dead person being cremated was for me an unusual experience when I was only five years old. Another day at home, I remember seeing a strange little insect crawling up the door frame of my grandparents' house. It was fascinating to be seeing it and when it was turning away from me, I decided to pick it up by the tail it was curling above itself so that it would not bite me. Wow! The pain in my thumb nearly knocked me out. That day I learnt what a scorpion is and what it could do with its tail.

In the Indian village, I saw that things were very different to what I was used to in Africa. The houses did not have toilets and in the early morning we had to wander off into the fields outside the village carrying a little pot of water for washing our bottom. There was a well outside the front of the house from which water could be taken, but we also had a water hand pump in our yard from which water was drawn out from the ground for all purposes. Bathing was done in a little common cabin room with water that we carried into the room in a bucket. We picked up and poured the water on the body with a bowl in one hand and cleaned the body with the other hand. The waste water flowed to the outside open drain that must have ended up in the village ponds.

In some places, I saw cows walking round a well. That was done to draw water for the fields by pulling a line of large cans rotated down to the bottom. Sometimes, young lads would grab the rope and stand on a tin to get down to the bottom. I didn't have the courage for doing that. Some cows were also walking round to drive a machine to make it squeeze the juice out of sugar canes. The juice was channelled into a large, flat metal plate over a fire to convert it into brown sugar. From there the liquid sugar would be channelled into a large wooden plate and the people allowed us to sit on the edge of that wooden plate and scoop out onto our hand a little of the cooling sugar. In India, we were doing things that we had never done in Africa. Another unusual activity in India for me was to eat my plate. The food of *aloo-saag* (potato and green vegetable) was presented to me on a plate that I also had to eat. The plate had been created by cooking maize flour into a stiff chapatti. We held the plate in one hand, broke off small parts of the plate and then used that to scoop up some *aloo-saag* to put into our mouth. As we had eaten our plate as well, there was no washing up required.

We also stayed with the family of my mother's brother in the village of Sialva. Those maternal uncles were the Prashars who were my *Mamajis*. There we had to pass our stools in the sandy fields outside the village. At those locations, there turned out to be wandering pigs that would come to eat our stools just as we were passing them. That made me be quick with the job and not to let some pig smell my waste during that time. The village of Sialva was near a small river where I had picked up a pebble with a ring on it. When we got back to Shamespur, my grandfather was happy to keep it and to use it as a religious symbol.

My father took us on a pilgrimage to the temple of Nana Devi at the foot of the Himalayas. We walked and struggled along the path up the hill to the temple. Donkeys were carrying the loads for the many people going up and down. The donkeys would walk on the edge of the path, which had a big fall down the mountain. There were many monkeys around in Nana Devi. Monkeys were treated by local people with respect. The Ramayana holy book states that it was the monkeys that had helped the God incarnation Rama to go and recover his captured wife Gita from Sri Lanka. The monkeys scared me as they tried to snatch things away from us when we were out in the street. Our accommodation was in a large room at the top with windows that opened out to the roofs of other buildings. From there we saw monkeys that would be running and jumping around on the tin roofs and made a lot of noise. There was the large male monkey that controlled the area. One day he jumped onto our open window and came into the room. We were scared and ran to the back of our mother. That monkey strode around the room, picked up the chapattis that our mother had cooked and wandered out. My mother didn't mind the actions of the holy creature.

Return to Kenya in 1946

Due to the difficulty of settling down after the loss of all our possessions in the sea, my father had decided to go back to Kenya. He was still getting paid for the long holiday that overseas people were given after five years work to sail to their home lands and have a good break. The steamships would have taken about eight days each way between India and East Africa. To return to Kenya, my father had to go back first to his company job and then we had to find a steamship to take us back. World War II was over later in 1945 but it was still difficult to find a steamship sailing to East Africa. So, we all ended up being out of school for a whole year.

It was in the early period of 1946 that we travelled by train to Bombay (Mumbai) to a catch a steamship for Mombasa. There we waited for about a month to get on a steamship. We stayed in a storeyed building on a busy street with sight of the traffic and people below. I remember hearing alarms in the street and my brothers told me that was because British warships had a navy problem with Indian sailors who had been complaining about the treatment they had been receiving from the English crew. Eventually, we got on the steamship *SS Amra* that sailed across the Indian Ocean to Mombasa during the second week of March and arrived in Mombasa on 17 March 1946. Strangely, I cannot remember anything about that voyage across the Indian Ocean, whereas my dhow voyage taken a year earlier had remained in my head.

Back to life in Africa

On returning to Mombasa, we went back to the same house that we used to be in before. My father returned to his job with African Marines and used to cycle to work as he no longer had a motorcycle. I joined my brothers to go and start again at the White Sisters Convent School. My sister went to the Arya Samaj School that taught in Hindi. At the convent school, we had white shirts and blue shorts and wore a school tie. The start of school was normally at the age of five, but the first two classes were labelled as nursery classes. My first class was Nursery 1 at the west end of a building which had the school hall in the middle of that building. There were several classes on both sides of the great hall. My classroom had several steps going up to its entrance. Outside our class there was a big play area.

At home, we often had our father bringing lots of fruit and other things for us. It used to be a great time for me when he was at home. During the following years, my father took me to his workplace and into the small ships that he worked on. One day at home I remember seeing a crowd of people around a car that had gone off the road near our house. To my dismay I learnt that my father was in it. As we did not have a family car, that one had been borrowed from someone at work. Thankfully he was not badly injured and was brought home okay. I understand that he had been drinking. At home, we had a servant called Ali. He stayed in the garage and would go away on some days to be with his family in the mainland countryside. To me it felt that he was like a family member to us and I used to spend time talking with him in Swahili in the garage.

Lions in Mombasa

Although Mombasa was almost an island tucked into the coast, we once had the most unusual visitors to our town. Three wild lions came to Mombasa from the mainland. They must have come across the causeway at night and then found no way out. Decades earlier, the railway line builders had encountered lions a hundred miles inland near the town of Voi. The appearance of lions in Mombasa was a mystery and some people did not even know that they were lions, never having seen one. The poor beasts couldn't find any food at night and ended up in the morning chasing people for a meal. People who sighted the lions ran for their lives and some even climbed up coconut trees with the lions trying to get up to them. When the police were alerted, they got some hunters to go and shoot the lions. A hunter called Khan, who lived only a couple of hundred yards from us, managed to find and shoot the three lions in the Ziwani area that was also near our house. The lions' bodies were then brought to the front of their house. On hearing this, my brothers and the other children in our street rushed off to see the lions at the house of the hunters. I had started to follow them, but then I got scared. What if the lions were not dead? That fear might have arisen from the event on board the dhow when I had been pulled away from the seemingly dead sailfish. I crept back into my own house and stayed there. All I saw were the photographs in the *Mombasa Times* of the three lions lying on their sides. They were called *Simba Tatu* meaning three lions in Swahili.

1947 Significant events

At the start of 1947 my eldest brother moved to another school as he had passed the age of twelve which was the oldest age for the boys in our school. I moved to my next class in the room adjoining the hall that had two more classrooms beside the other end of the hall. On 15 August 1947, a big event occurred in our lives. India got independence after the long British rule of about a hundred years. The sad thing was the split in the country and the creation of a new Muslim country named Pakistan. The letter P in Pakistan comes from the state of Punjab which was split between the two sides. (The letter A stands for Afghan, K for Kashmir and I for Indus.) There were terrible mass killings in the province of Punjab in India. That also resulted in a split in our friendships with Muslim neighbours in Mombasa. We even ended up fighting. One day I was horrified to see a Hindu being bitten on the face by a Muslim. It took a few years before our friendships with Muslims were restored. Our life linkage was with India although we lived in Africa in a British colony. Despite that, my education was in English: I knew nothing about real life in England. In my third year at school I got to Class One in a classroom that was inside the middle hall. I remember very little of my classroom activities during the first three years.

Age of nine experiences

In 1949 I moved to Class 2 in a room beside the hall with a nun as our teacher. She had a list of our names on the side of the board on which she would add points for various achievements and behaviour. I sat on the bench at the back of the class on the left side. There were religious classes during which I was taken out of the class and taken to another room together with other non-Christians and given some other lesson. One day in our normal class, our teacher posed the question about the verb from which the words "is" and "was" are derived. The class was unable to provide the answer, but I put my hand up because I remembered something that had been taught to me during my non-Christian periods. To the surprise of the class I gave the answer "to be" and the nun was pleased with the correct response. She added an extra point to my name on the board. I felt great with doing something well in class and enjoyed the learning periods. Our nun teacher was a very loving person and I was very pleased to be in her class.

In that classroom, bits of folded paper were being thrown to me by the two girls sitting to the right of me. They were older girls because the rules of the school were that those students who did not make the grades at the end of the year did not get promoted to the next class up. They were sending me love messages. That was a new experience for me and I did exchange looks and smiles with them. At the start of the second term we had assembled outside the hall. My nun teacher came over and took me out of the class group. She told me that she was taking me out of that class and putting me into another one. My heart sank. Had she found one of the bits of paper that the two girls had been throwing to me? She took me over to the other group with whom she was putting me. I was told that was the group of Class 3! I couldn't believe it. She was promoting me to the next class after I had spent only one term in her class. Wow, that was a real surprise to me. My new classroom was on its own in the middle of many others. I found that in the new class there was an extra lesson for French. This burdened me to learn more to catch up with the rest of the class. That was hard for me, but I just had to keep working. Sometime that year the numbering of the classes was changed. The kindergarten numbering was removed from the school and my new Class 3 ended up being labelled as Class 5. Then I was at the age of nine.

I used to have a great time with my father when he was home. We had a radio we could listen to and we also had a record player that had to be wound up manually for playing big records, with the sound coming out of a spiral horn. He would regularly bring home fresh fruit which he picked up from Arab stalls in town. Being the youngest, I was my father's favourite and would always run to him whenever I had hit someone during our quarrels at home.

Life sadness and recovery in 1949

Halfway through the year of 1949, I was to have the most saddening experience in my life. I did not even know it at that time, but my father seems to have had a stroke in May and had been taken to a hospital. Then, we later learnt that he had passed away. I could not believe it. After we got the news, we sat around silently. One of our neighbours came to our house. She put us children together in our front room and made us start crying at the loss of our father. My father's body was brought into the house. I was being led to the room where the body lay, but then someone else stopped me from entering the room and seeing my dead father. The body was then taken out to a cemetery. I remember being in an open area where logs of wood were being piled up, just as I had seen in India in 1945. There is nothing in my mind about what happened next. There was then a void in my life for quite a while. I just could not talk to anybody about that loss of life. One day my mother was bringing in some washed clothing from the outside washing line. Strangely, I asked her what clothing she was carrying. She told me that it was my father's clothing and I grasped the clothing close to me and hugged it. I was missing him tremendously, but my feelings for the loss of my father could not be passed to anyone. One day one of my friends expressed his sorrow at the passing of my father. The reminder made me come to tears and leave the group. The loss of my loving father, at an early age was the biggest disaster that I have experienced in my life.

My mother's brother, Chanan Ram Prashar, was the one who took over the task of looking after our family. Being the brother of my mother, he was my *Mamaji* and he was to become our saviour. He owned a cycle shop and had recently got married. I am eternally grateful to him for having taken on the task of bringing us up. Shortly after he had got married, he and Bimla *Mamiji* moved in with us in the rented house. Our whole family was then brought up by a very gentle and loving man. That then became my new family and I was very happy with it. However, one day I upset him. I had hit my sister for some silly quarrel when *Mamaji* came angrily towards me for seeing a boy hitting a girl. I ran out of the house and he ran after me although he had a limp due to a faulty ankle. That enabled me to run away from him. That is when I realised that my behaviour should be controlled by me to show respect to all around me. After that, I never created any tension with him. He never had any tension with anyone else in the house. My *Mamaji* was the one who pulled us through our weak state of existence and saw us all through our lives to engage in our careers. He was a truly gentle person.

In school, I worked hard to catch up with the others in my new class. At home, we also were joined by our cousin Jagan Nath from my mother's side, who got married in India and then came to Africa. He said that he would give me a bicycle if I managed to get to the top of my class at the end of the year. I did well to get to fifth place in a class that I had joined in the second term, but that was not enough to win a bike. However, my learning to ride a bicycle was done on a big bicycle that my brother had. As it was not possible for me to sit on the seat, I rode with my right leg going through the frame to the right pedal and my left leg on the near pedal. The handle above me would be grasped from a hanging position and I managed to ride the big bicycle. That form of riding a bicycle was also done by other small boys.

In December 1949, there was a delight in our new family when my *Mamiji* gave birth to her first child. I remember being called in to touch the new born baby for my goodwill and blessing. That baby boy later became great fun for us. I tried to keep him with me, away from the others and sometimes we would end up pulling him in opposite directions. We loved having a baby in the family. During our younger days, most of us had experienced chicken pox. However, I was also hit by the disease of smallpox. That required me to lie on some leaves on a stretcher bed without clothing, with painful spots appearing on my body. I had to refrain from touching the spots and somehow managed to recover. After that incident, my body was never to be troubled by smallpox again.

In the school, there were only a small percentage of non-Christians and we would end up as teams against the Christians in sporting activities during our breaks. We had Hindus, Khojas and Chinese in our group against the Christians group who were mainly Goans and some Seychelles. The Khojas were the special sect of Muslims led by the Aga Khan. It didn't occur to me then that the school was only for Asian students. Our school was being run by white sisters. There were no black or brown sisters, but there were some Christian Goan women as teachers. White children went to different schools and not all black children went to a school. Our parents had to pay school fees to enable us to go to a good school. However, after the death of my father the school did not require any fees for me.

On our doorstep at home, we had African sellers bringing various things including fruit. Sometimes women sellers would also be carrying their babies on their backs. During the whole of the day our front door would be open. Trade people would attract our attention by calling "*hodi hodi*" outside the open door. They would lay their products on our front steps. In a cage at the front of the house we had a green parrot with a red head. He was great fun and made lots of sounds. He would even make the *hodi hohi* call which would get us to go to the front entrance. One day the parrot was let out of its cage within the house and managed to get out and flew onto a mango tree. We failed to bring him back and lost that lovely parrot for good.

Last years at Convent School

During the period through the primary classes 6 and 7 in a block, we used to go to the hall for class singing. One day, a nun was walking and listening to our individual voices. She had stopped beside me and later called me to come to singing sessions for select groups for school singing. There were times when I had to be away from my classroom to participate in group singing. There were concerts at our annual school presentations in a building outside the school. Some books were also presented to me as prizes for my classroom achievements. We had British books and did mathematics using the strange British currency of pounds, shillings, pence and farthings. The Kenya currency was simply shilling and cents with 100 cents in a shilling. Despite having been introduced to British currency in school, I still had a problem with the change handed to me during my first visit to Britain in 1957. There we had to deal with twenty shillings in a pound, twelve pence in a shilling and four farthings in a penny. I found that one pound could be converted into 960 farthings. Some people even used guineas which converted to 21 shillings.

In Mombasa, we finished our school at lunchtime and the school buses (green and brown) took us home in shifts. My trip on the green bus was the last trip of the bus. During the wait for our bus trip, we played football on the sports ground. Near the playing field there used to be an enormous baobab tree which did not have much leaf on its branches, but it had large fruit pods. These pods were filled with many mushy seeds that were not tasty. With the boys, I ended up playing football in a non-Christian group that played against the Christians. There was no conflict between the two groups but for some strange reason, we had a gathering for a fight of Christians versus non-Christians. The Christians pushed forward their selection for the fight and to my despair someone pushed me to face him. As my opponent was bigger than me, I agreed to fight him only if there would be no holding involved. They agreed to do that, and we started the fight. It was the first time in my life that I got into a boxing fight. I can't remember the action in the fight. All I remember is that after we had been throwing punches at each other, my opponent is the one who backed out and stopped fighting. My supporters were cheering me for a victory.

Luckily there was no injury on me from the fight and it surprised the other pupils in the school who started showing me respect.

One day at school, there were two girls fighting. When I asked someone as to why they were fighting, to my surprise I was told that they were fighting over me. One of them called Juliet was older than me and in a class above me. She used to sit in the school bus opposite me in a corner by the entrance door at the back of the bus. During the bus ride, she was deliberately touching my foot with hers. Then we used to regularly touch each other with our feet. That was the only action that took place between us and it used to be a real thrill for me. During the school bus travel there also used to be a Harley Davidson motorcycle following us regularly. On it was a man who was following that girl. It thrilled me that she showed affection to me when there was a man out there showing his interest to her.

During the period when we were being looked after by my uncle, a young African had been employed as a servant. One day there was a dreadful fight inside our house. The servant was beating up my older brother, Krishan. That upset me and made me go to the rescue of my brother. I picked up a hockey stick and swung it at the servant. That stopped the fighting. The servant touched his head and found that there was blood coming out. To my surprise, he just ran away out of the house. We did not have any of our male grown-ups in the house and I had no idea of what was going to follow. That made me run out and go to the entrance of house of our Seychelles neighbours. When the African boy returned to our house with a grown-up, the boy was pointing his finger at me. To my surprise the boy's companion gave one look at me and then simply walked back with his lad. He saw that I was too small to be challenged. That was a great relief to me. I had been driven into a real fight at a young age to protect a family member.

Mabeni Primary School

After my primary school, my uncle placed me in a government school where no fees were required. Strangely, there was a problem for me to be going to a government high school because I had been in a non-government primary school. That resulted in me having to repeat class 7 in a government primary school in January 1952. There were different schools for different people and even for the Indians because of different Indian languages. My primary school was only for the Punjabis. During the first five years of that school the Hindus had studied in Hindi and the Sikhs had studied in Punjabi. Then after class 5 they were all taught in English with their own language being only one subject. There was no problem for me with the classes in English, but Hindi was something I could understand, but did not know how to read and write it. In the school exams, I had the highest marks in a lot of subjects but in Hindi I would be given a zero.

There were no sports fields at the school and during the breaks we would play some games in small spaces. I remember playing the Indian game called *kabadi*. Two teams were on opposite sides of a middle line. A player from one side would come into the other side exhaling his breath with any sound; it could be saying "*pudd, pudd*" or whatever. He had to get back into his own half before the breath expired and no sound could be produced. While in the opponents' half, the attacking player would try to touch one or more opponents and escape back into his half while still producing his sound; whoever the opponents touched would be out of their team. The intruder would be eliminated if any opponent caught him and held him in their side until his breath expired. The winning team would be the one with the last remaining player on the field. One day I remember catching a bigger opponent in my half but was being dragged towards the dividing line while he was still making his sound. At the boundary, I managed to wiggle him over a small wall and he ran out of breath. That gave me the courage to take on bigger boys in physical contests.

At one of our school gatherings in a hall I sang the English songs that had been taught to me at the Convent school. My audience was amazed by my ability to sing in English. Initially, my walk to school was with some neighbouring friends, but later my loving uncle thrilled me by giving me a bicycle which made it much easier. That was the biggest present I had ever received. At the end of the year I did very well in my exams, other than in Hindi, which I could not even sit. Enough had been done to enable me to enter the Allidina Visram High School (AVHS) the following year for my secondary school education. In 1952 we heard of the death of the British king while his daughter was in Kenya. That made Princess Elizabeth to become the Queen at an early age. The coronation did not take place until the following year when I was in my secondary school. It was then that we received some memorial of the coronation.

Animal life

In our garage, we kept chickens that would produce eggs and chicks. One day, a flying kite swooped down and picked up one of the chicks. To my surprise, the hen went flying after the kite up to the roof of the house before coming down and rushing back to the remaining chicks. Inside the house we would also see a lizard that roamed around the walls and ceiling to catch insects. It was good to have it there to get rid of the insects. One day we saw the lizard on a tree by the house opposite where we used to climb up and sit around for a chat. We threw stones at it to chase it away and found something falling to the ground and was flicking about. It turned out to be the tail of the lizard and later learnt that the lizard would deliberately shed its tail to deflect the attention of the attacker that threatens it. On the trees and bushes outside we would see lovely large lizards with orange coloured heads. They would remain in sight when someone was looking at them, but they would disappear as soon as someone looked away. There were chameleons with the colour changing capacity to sneak up to an insect and catch it with its long tongue. The chameleon had a curling tail that was used to grip the branch when it threw out its tongue. It would move very slowly and change its colours to mix in with the location to hide its presence. If we went close to it, the body of the chameleon would inflate to look dangerous. I later found out that the chameleon would not attack, even if it was picked up, but I never held one.

Beside the outside walls of our house, there were several bowl formations in the ground created by an insect living in the sand for catching ants and other insects that slid down into it. If the inside of the bowl was touched, some sand would roll down. However, if an ant was to slip down the slope it would end up struggling to crawl back up. That is when the jaws of an insect would spring out, catch its prey and disappear under the sand. I never got to have a proper view of the whole insect that was probably the one called the mole cricket. Another insect in our environment was the millipede. That was an attractive insect about six inches long. It had a black crustaceous body and two chains of numerous red legs on each side. If touched, the millipede would curl into a spiral on its side. Then it could be picked up gently and held within the hand without any repulsion from it. When placed down, it would uncurl and move forward slowly with the little legs flowing like waves. On the other hand, there was another multi-leg insect that was dangerous; that insect was the centipede which had a soft body and far fewer legs than the millipede and moved fast. We always kept away from centipedes.

At night, there would be large bats flying around for feeding. The bats that we saw were the ones that ate mangoes. They were also the suppliers of mangoes to us waiting below them. During the day, they would hang upside down at the top of the coconut trees under the hood of leaves. In the evening and at night they would fly out and try to eat mangoes. They ended up, at times, knocking down the very ripe mango even before they could take a bite. We would be sitting and waiting for the sound of falling mangoes. Then we rushed around to the direction of the sound to pick up the falling mangoes and the lucky one picked up a mango that had no bite on it. There were many birds that flew around and there were wild pigeons that came and used a box we had placed on the roof at the back of the house.

Life at home

The house in which I was born and lived in for a long time was on a small mud track. In six plots on each side of the track there were Indian families and one Seychelles family. North of us, there were another ten Indian homes on the sides of the tarmacked Makupa Road. Behind our houses there were many African mud houses. A narrow, tarmacked road west of us joined up with Makupa Road and had some mud-houses that also had a small Arab shop. To the east of us there was some open space that also included a well from which the Africans would be drawing water. On that side, there was also a house in which lived Christian Goans and a little shop run by the Khojas, which was a Muslim sect. There were also many mud houses in which the Africans lived. The mud track between the houses in our street was used by people, mainly as a footpath and occasionally by bicycles. We used that track as a play area. The presence of a car on our track was rare. We had two rainy seasons during which the mud track used to have water flowing through it after heavy rain. We would make paper boats and sail them in the little stream for more than a hundred yards. We played various games with a soft ball on the unused plot between the houses that were opposite us. There was a mango tree in that plot on which we climbed a lot and sat around in the branches.

When we played out in the open, there were occasions when a young African boy from the mud houses behind us would turn up and sometimes throw stones at us. We would chase him away by throwing stones back at him. Then that boy started putting up a pile of tin cans and hitting them with sticks to create a noise to attract our attention. He spent a lot of time doing that and started producing some sort of musical noise. On reflection, I feel that the African boy was trying to link with us Indian children, but at that time it was not easy. We had a lot of different ways of life in the European, Asian and African communities. Our social lives were separate. However, a grown-up African who came and lived together with our old African servant in the house garage had an unusual way of producing musical sound. That peaceful African came from inland Changamwe and stayed at our garage to work in Mombasa. What was most unusual was that he produced music with a small wooden box that had some metal spikes on the box. The metal spikes were only operated by the thumbs to produce music while walking. That African used the box on his long walks of several miles between his home and our house and would produce music for himself all the way.

At home, we ended up grouping together with other children in our two streets. We even played together after it got dark. As we lived practically on the Equator, it always got dark at about the same time throughout the year. I don't know how the choice of our various games would change. There were many Indian games and some English and Seychelles games. Also, we had games played together by children of varied ages and some by boys and girls. Next door to us arrived some new Gujerati neighbours who were Hindus like us. One day, a new Gujerati boy in the house beside ours would not listen to us and three of us ended up beating him up to make him fit in with our activities. Normally, Gujerati boys were not prepared to fight, but that one would have thrashed us if we had taken him on singly. However, after that he became a great friend and used to tell us about the interesting history of Indian life about which we knew nothing, as we were not taught anything about India at school.

One day there was a strange commotion behind our house. I saw the police chasing an African who must have committed some crime. They were looking for him outside the African house that was right behind us, but the culprit seemed to have run into the house. Then there was a disturbance in the thatch roof at the back of that house. The culprit pushed open the thatched roof, slid out and jumped down onto the ground. As he ran away in the lane behind the house, the police spotted him and chased him down the lanes between the houses. Finally, they caught him and thrashed him down to the ground. Then they tied him up and tugged him away to the police station. The twenty Asian houses in our two streets decided to pay some Somalis to guard our houses from any burglars coming to our houses at night. Those tall Somali night watchmen would only be carrying a stick and would be chewing some plant to remain wide awake at night to keep us free of burglaries in our houses.

When we were being brought up by my uncle, we were practically vegetarians. If any meat was to be eaten by us boys, we had to prepare it ourselves. As we didn't have a servant and my brothers did not fancy doing it, I took on the task that I had seen the African servants had been doing. Immediately after the throat of the chicken was cut, its body movements continued and made me feel sick. That resulted in me deciding never to do any killing for food, but instead to go hungry. One day I put on my canvas boots. After tying up the laces and standing up, a severe pain made me give out a yell. I rapidly took off my boot to find a scorpion roll out. That was the second time in my life that a scorpion had stung me. Another day there were bees near our bus station that were attacking people who were scattering away. It seems that the bees had been stirred by a stone entering their hole when someone was trying to knock down a mango from the tree. While we were looking at the site from a distance there was a buzz beside my ear and I felt a pain in my neck. That made me realise that it is not a good idea to try and watch bees stinging other people.

Opposite us lived the D'Silva Seychellois family in the same design house as ours. They were the only white family sharing a street with Asians. As the family of the Seychellois could be black or white, they could not share accommodation areas in the town for white people only. Their girl, Anna, was about the age of my elder brother and she was great with her companionship with the boys. In their house lived her parents as well as the family of her older sister. I played with the two boys who were younger. Anna's white brother produced three children with a white woman. Their two sons would come and stay in the house opposite us and were good company for me. However, their father had married again, but that time he was married to a black woman. There was another related family of white Seychellois living nearby in an area occupied by black Africans in their mud houses. Their lovely girl used to come to our street and although she was older, I found that we ended up being in the same class in my last year at the convent school. To my surprise she would ask me about some French homework that we had to do despite the fact that the Seychelles islands were first occupied by the French and the island people's language was based on French.

During my primary school period, we went to school only during the mornings for six days a week. After lunch I did my school homework and then went out to be with my neighbourhood friends and engaged in a variety of activities. Sometimes we would get up in the early morning and go out for a walk in our neighbourhood to pick up the unscarred mangoes that the bats had dropped during the night. During the day, we would climb up mango trees which were taller than our houses. One day I was trying to reach a lovely mango and ended up grabbing the branch and pulling it up towards me to get at the mango. That branch broke and resulted in me falling off the branch on which I was sitting. Luckily, another branch below enabled me to stop falling and avoid crashing to the ground below. Another way of getting at the mangoes was by throwing stones or sticks from the ground to knock them down. There were times when we would collect mangoes that were not ripe and they would taste sour, but we ate them. We would cut slices of the mango and dip them in a mixture of salt, pepper and red chilli before eating. That tasted great. The other fruits that we used to go around and collect were berries, cashew nuts, guavas and paw-paws. As we never had any money in our pockets, we had fun picking our free fruit.

The cashew fruit is unknown to almost all the people I have met, although they have all eaten cashew nuts. The fruit is the size and shape of a pear, but it hangs upside down compared to the pear. What is most unusual is that the seed hangs outside the fruit. That soft fruit is very juicy with a strong acidic taste that results in it not being eaten. The seed is covered in a hard, grey oily skin that has to be burnt off before one can get at the tasty seed by cracking open the shell. I remember the arduous task of collecting the seeds and burning off the skin on a fire. Then we undertook the task of opening the burnt skin to get at the single white seed in it. The seed was tasty, but it required great effort and mess to get at it. The other tasty fruit was the guava and the tree of the guava was not very big, but it was easy to climb up it because the thin branches were very strong. One day I was up the guava tree by the house of the Gujerati who were out. Because the branches were strong, I decided to walk along the branch to the shelf at the front of that house. I lost my balance and fell onto the concrete steps at the front of the house. My bottom hurt, but I had to tell my friends not to call anyone for help as I didn't want to be punished for doing something silly. Fortunately, that fall did not cause me any great pain during my youth. Beside Makupa Road near us there were trenches for a new house that had ended up not being built. We started using those trenches as a play area and had great fun playing various fighting games in it.

The paw-paw fruit comes from another strange tree. It has a thick straight stem rising to the clump of large leaves at the top covering the fruit pods hanging underneath the leaves. The tree looks like a large umbrella. The main stem is not very strong and is not worth climbing up it unless one does not weigh much. Although we had two papaya trees on our plot, one day we went there after sunset because we were going to be stealing some paw-paws of another house. In the garden of some Gujerati people at the end of our little street, there was the paw-paw tree that was right beside the outside wall at the front. I managed to twist one paw-paw off and drop it down for my friends to catch it on the other side of the wall. Due to the noise that we created, the owner came out and all my friends ran away with me still clinging to the top of the tree underneath the dome of leaves. After looking around the man then walked back to his house. Fortunately, he went past me without looking up and it was a great relief for me to slide down and run away without getting spanked.

During my youth, most of the items that we used for amusement, games and activities were constructed by ourselves. Catapults were made from a forked branch, old tube rubber and a little bit of leather. Old cycle wheel rims became our toys as we drove and manoeuvred them with a stick in the grove. We also constructed a driving toy using little used wooden spools that earlier had sewing thread on them. Two spools nailed to a wooden bar would rotate and become the wheels. The wooden bar with the wheels was hinged in the middle to another bar coming up to a wheel that the operator could manipulate with his hand. While we pushed the device forward with the one hand, a connecting string allowed us to steer the wheels on the ground by controlling the wheel at the top with the other hand. We also played with a metal device that would have been constructed by a metal mechanic. At the end of two hinged metal bars there was a cylinder on one side into which the other bent bar would fit. The hole at one end would be filled with an explosive mixture bought from the chemists and the other end would be put into the hole to cover the explosive. Then the two bars were held together to keep the explosive intact and swung down to hit a hard surface to create an explosion. The idea was to sneak up close to someone and create the bang behind them to make them jump. That was a dangerous toy and we did not use it very much.

Many traders would appear at the house doorstep for sales of various things. Asian cyclists would bring cloth for sale. Africans brought milk carried in tanks strapped to either side of a bicycle. There used to be an African fruit seller who would bring a range of fruit on a large two-wheel trolley that he pushed. African women would bring fruit while carrying children on a sling on their backs. Arab sellers would be carrying a coffee pot on a charcoal fire under it for the sale of very small cups of black *kahawa*. They sounded out their presence by rotating one cup inside another cup with their thumb in one hand while carrying the large pot with the other. Although we couldn't drink the black coffee on sale, I did enjoy the sounds from the coffee seller. An Arab shop at the west end of our track sold a variety of items. It would have a large basket with Arab *halva* in it. *Halva* is a tasty sweet jelly that I enjoyed eating. During my early life, I remember buying a single cigarette from that shop and then four of us went out of sight of people to an area behind the shop. There we lit the cigarette and then each of us had a suck at the cigarette in turn. We had decided to do something we had seen older boys doing. I found that smoking was not pleasant, but we carried on with that awful activity to catch up with the others. However, for me that was the occasion that put me off smoking for life.

At our doorstep, we used to have traders on bicycles or on foot who brought tooth cleaning sticks for sale. During my young life, I used to clean my teeth with those sticks called *dattan,* instead of toothbrushes and paste. Those were long sticks from the acacia plant that we would buy and then cut up into small sizes and used each stick only once for cleaning our teeth. First, we chewed on one end to make it into a brush shape and then use that brush to clean our teeth together with a little salt. The material in the stick was what made our teeth healthy and I never had to see a dentist in Kenya. Instead of the stick we sometimes used some bark that we would chew and then used the chewed bark to clean our teeth and neutralise the mouth to any decay. When we were at marriage gatherings near our house, we children used to be given food on a piece of banana leaf that became our plate. Those leaf plates were the early version of disposable plates.

One day a large truck had got stuck in the soft ground off the road near our home. A towing vehicle had arrived and connected a large thick chain to the truck. There were loads of people standing around and watching the truck being dragged out. Then suddenly, there was a loud bang when the towing chain had snapped. The broken end went flying out and hit an African right in the face and knocked him down. That man was picked up and we saw that his face was covered in blood. Then to my surprise I saw that he walked to the road with someone to catch a bus to get him to a hospital for treatment. Near our town centre, there was a large open area market place called *Mwembe Tyari* (ripe mango) where one could find all sorts of things as well as food and fruit. There I picked up some odd things. On Sundays, that area would be used by Africans as a pleasure area where there would be African music and dancing as well as the alcoholic drink being made from coconut, called *tembo.* I went there only once and saw the wild dancing done by African men and women, but it would have been dangerous for young me. Still it gave me a glimpse of an amazing African pleasure activity.

The sudden appearance of double-decker buses in Mombasa was a delight for me. It was a delight to go and sit at the top where there was no driver. The entrance to the bus at the back was an open entry with a pole in the corner. One day I saw the unusual exit from the moving bus by an older boy, just outside his house in our neighbourhood. He hung out sideways from the pole, placed his left foot out to the ground at the same time as releasing his grip and using his other foot to engage in running with body leaning backways to slow down. He must have trained for that unusual form of exit from a moving bus that would be going past his house.

My sex education

During my young age, I had started puzzling about sexual activity, being responsible for the creation of life. I had seen the strange activities of dogs, chickens and ducks, but was unaware of the purpose. Later I learned that was necessary for the creation of young ones amongst the animals, humans and plants. I could see the sexual activity in the animals and the humans, but I could not figure out how the plants could be having sex. They could have been performing underground activity to create the young ones that would then pop out of the ground. One day I was telling my Seychelles friends about my understanding of the creation of young ones by humans, animals and plants. I was amazed at what they told me. I was told that the humans would unite in their sexual activity many times more than was needed for producing their children. That was the time when I felt that there was a lot more to be learnt about life.

My childhood games

There were many games that used to be played by various groups of boys and girls in our neighbourhood. For many of these games we picked up or constructed the components, with only some of them requiring us to buy something. We did not seem to have any seasons for those games which occurred at random.

Bantey (marbles)

One of the games that I played required us to contribute marbles into a pile. Then we tossed up a coin to decide who would go first. One player would hold all the marbles in one or both hands and gently roll them into a ring drawn on the ground. If any marble rolled out of the circle that roll had to be repeated. Then the player had the task of knocking out a single marble by throwing another marble from about six to ten feet. The idea was to knock out only one marble from the ring without disturbing any other. Usually the aim would be for the back end or the sides of the ring and it wasn't easy. The throwing player could make up to three attempts to knock out a single marble. Then, the other player would take on the task. That would continue to be repeated until someone managed to knock a single marble out of the ring to win the lot. I often came back home with more marbles than I took out. At home, I used to hide my bunch of marbles in a basket in the food store.

Gadum gada (spike)

That was played with a metal spike that we struck into the dry ground. One player would throw the spike into the ground close in front of him. If it stayed up he would pick it out, take one more step and again strike it into the ground again. With his strikes, he would continue to move away from the starting place along any chosen route until the spike failed to stay up after the throw. The distances moved could be more than a hundred yards. From the point where the spike had fallen the other player had the job of hopping back to the start point on one leg. The spiking player would closely follow him. If the hopping player placed the other foot on the ground, he would be punched from behind by the other player with the back of his fist. The runner would then start hopping again to stop being pinched. The other option for the hopping player was to run back to the start, faster than the puncher and totally avoid getting punched.

Guli danda (wedge and stick)

A *guli* was a small piece of wood that was tapered at both ends. The *danda* is only a stick with which one of the players would scoop the *guli* from a little slot in the ground to send it as far away as possible. The opponent would be standing in front to try and catch the *guli* to put out the scooping player. If the *guli* was not caught it had to be thrown back to hit the stick that would have been laid on the ground behind the scooping slot. If the *guli* failed to hit the *danda* then the other player would use his *danda* to hit the *guli* away. First, the hitter had to tap one tapered end of the *guli* on the ground to make it jump up and then to hit it to make it fly away as far as possible. That time the opponent had two choices for catching the *guli*. One choice was to catch the *guli* as it rose from the ground during the tap; the problem with that attempt was that the hand catching the *guli* had to be moved away fast, otherwise it would catch the sweeping *danda* that would be coming down to hit it. The other option was to stand where the *guli* was likely to get to after the hit. The height to which the striker would tap the *guli* depended on whether the opponent was standing beside the *guli* or far in front of it. To swap places the opponent had either to catch the *guli* or hit the *danda* that was laid on the ground.

Kabadi

That game was even played at my Mabeni primary school. Two teams on opposite sides of a line sent one player at a time into the other half sounding out a call like "*pudd, pudd*", = trying to touch an opponent and returning to his half still with breath and sound. It would be easy to catch an opponent at the start of the game but difficult when we were down to about a couple of players in each team. The team with the last remaining player was the winner.

Khusti (wrestling)

Khusti was severe wrestling with each wrestler trying to force the opponent's back to touch the ground. We tended to do those fights just for fun, but only occasionally. I remember seeing some Pakistani wrestlers doing *khusti* at the stadium near our home.

Kidhi-kadha (Hop scotch)

That game I sometimes played with girls. A set of boxes was drawn within a large rectangle in which we hopped on one leg most of the time. A flat stone was thrown into a box on one side, starting with the closest ones. We then had to hop towards the box on one leg but could put both feet down along some connecting boxes. When we reached near the stone, we had to be on one leg to pick up the stone without touching the ground with the other arm. After picking up the stone we had to hop back to the start and then throw the stone into the next stage. If the stone failed to stay in the next box, then the opponent would take over the task of completing his or her round. The winner was the one to finish with the six boxes in which the stone had to be thrown and picked up successfully.

Hop and catch

One team would be in a marked ring and the other team would send in one player, hopping on one leg to chase around and touch as many of the opponents as possible until he lost his hop. Anyone touched in the ring had to vacate. The hoppers would continue until all of the opponents could be touched or when they had no more hoppers. Then the roles would be reversed. It was only when any of the runners in the ring remained untouched that their team would have a score; the other team then had to beat that to be the winners of that round.

Hide and seek

One player had the task of finding the others who would be hiding. The seeker would close his eyes beside some wall or tree with hands covering his face and counted to a hundred to allow the others to run away and hide behind a tree, bush or house. The seeker's job was to move around and try to find any hider. On seeing someone, the seeker had two options. One was to touch the player. The other was to shout out the name and touch the start post before that person could rush out and touch the post before the seeker. When the seeker was away from the start point, other hiders would try to run back and touch the start point before the seeker could touch them before they touched the post. Eventually it would be the task of the person who had been caught to become the new seeker.

Blind catching

A blindfolded person had the task trying to touch other people who would be making calls and running around. Generally, the blindfolded player only walked briskly. The others would be running around close to the blindfolded person, but they would dodge around to avoid being touched. One day, in my blindfolded position I remember chasing the sounds created by a girl. Suddenly I felt a big hit in my face as I had crashed into something. The girl I was trying to touch had gone behind a coconut tree while calling out. I went straight into the tree and ended up with a bleeding nose. That silly girl had not realised that hiding behind a tree and calling out was not supposed to be done in that game.

Horse jumping

All the players would be divided into two teams. One team would get together by a wall and form themselves into the shape of a horse. That was done by bending down and grabbing another player at the waist from behind and that would be followed by the others doing the same. The front player had to grab a wall or a tree. One at a time, the opponents would run from behind the horse, jump onto the back of the horse and try not to fall off. They would continue pilling up on the horse. After that the result of the competition would be that either the horse collapsed or one of the riders had fallen off the horse. If the horses stayed up until one of the riders fell off, then the roles would be reversed. If the horses collapsed first, then the riders would have another go. That used to be great fun.

Seven stones

Two boys would play this game with seven suitable stones that were placed in a pile that tapered to the top. One player constructed the pile and would be standing beside it. The attacking player would throw a tennis or rubber ball from a small distance to break the pile of stones with one of his three throws. The thrower who collapsed the pile of stones, then ran to the collapsed pile and replaced the stones before he was hit with the ball by the opponent. The defending player had to catch the ball or run to pick it up and try to hit his opponent before the thrower could reconstruct the pile.

The player piling up the stones had the task of dodging the ball thrown at him. Then their roles would be reversed and the winner would be the one who had managed to replace all the stones back into a pile.

Ghathee (knot)

All players except one would be sitting in a circle. One player would be walking outside the circle, holding and hiding a *ghathee*: that was a knot made either of rope or cloth. It had to be small enough to enable it to be hidden by the player holding it, but big enough to enable the players to swing it and hit others with it. Generally, the circling player holding it in one hand would tuck it under the other armpit or his shirt. While walking around the sitting players he would pretend to place the knot behind them. Any sitting player looking behind would place himself into two different situations. If the sitter did find the knot behind him, he would pick it up and chase the original carrier who would run to take up the vacated position without getting beaten by the knot from behind. If the person looking behind did not find the knot behind him, he had to stand up and run around without getting beaten by the player holding the knot. The knot carrying player could also be having two options. If that player was still holding the knot when he sighted someone looking behind, then he would try to catch and hit that person with the knot before he sat down again. On the other hand, the circling player may have already placed the knot behind someone else and would not be seen to be chasing the runner. That is when all the sitters could look behind themselves and the person who finds the knot would pick it up and chase the original knot holder in attempting to hit him before he could sit down in the vacated position. If the rotating player had placed the knot behind someone and managed to walk the circle without it being detected, then he could pick it up and start beating his victim all the way round the circle until the victim sat down. Both would be running as fast as they could. When chasing a little one running slowly we would then only do some gentle hitting with the knot. We played these games with boys and girls of all ages. The person who had suffered the knocking would then become the next one to go and place the knot behind someone else. That game used to be great fun.

Chapter 2

High school in Mombasa

Allidina School

Starting in January 1953 my education was in Allidina Visram High School (AVHS) for four years. That school was on the cliff at the northern side of our island. To the east of us, the old harbour for dhows was in sight. Close to us on the western side of the school there was the floating Nyali Bridge that was leading to the northern part of the mainland. The school was a nice big stone building that had been built in 1921 by the family of Allidina Visram after his death in Mombasa. He was a highly successful businessman in East Africa after having come from the Kutch area of India. The school was for Asian boys of any religious belief.

I cycled, together with a couple of neighbouring boys, to and from the high school. At the start of the school day, the assembly in front of the school was addressed by the principal of the school. We had to be dressed in white shirts and shorts, but we did not wear ties. The wearing of neck ties in our hot climate had been imposed on us at the convent school due to some strange British form of dressing. From our assembly, we went into our classes in orderly fashion. There would be prefects standing in the corridors to ensure all movement was orderly. We sat through our lessons and had a break halfway through school time. The end of the school day was at 1pm and we departed home for lunch and the rest of the day. The attendance was for six days of the week. All of our learning was done in English, but we also had one period for the study of a language which would be part of the examinations that we had to do. The languages chosen for study by the school were only the Indian languages of Hindi, Urdu and Gujerati. Once again, I was in a situation of having no idea or advice about what I could or would be doing to catch up with the Hindi lessons. Our final qualification at the end of the school education was to be for the Cambridge Overseas school certificate.

The lessons in class were enjoyable and resulted in me always putting my hand up to answer the questions that the teachers threw at us. My teachers were impressed with my answers. In one of our history lessons the teacher, Mr Patel, asked the class about the white flag that Jean of Arc in France was carrying. I gave the answer that it was the flag of France. He accepted it, but before he continued with the lesson somebody else came up and said that it was the flag of peace. The teacher then turned to say that the second answer was the correct one. It amazed me that earlier he averted telling me that my answer was wrong. Another day, that teacher surprised me by saying that he had gone and told the principal to move me up to the next class because of my excellent participation in the class, but the principal had rejected the idea.

It was during my first year at the secondary school that our attendance period was changed to have us coming back after lunch for five days of the week. Saturdays would remain as mornings only. That meant we had to go back home for lunch. It created a huge uproar from the students. Strangely, one day the students went on strike. When we came back after lunch the students remained outside of the school ground by the roadsides. The teachers and principal tried to get us to enter the classrooms but failed to do it. None of us entered the school that afternoon. Then some police cars arrived at the school. The next day we found that some pupils were going to be thrown out of the school. The afternoon classes remained in use and we settled into the new class times. Our principal was transferred to a school in another town and we had a new principal and vice-principal.

At the high school, we were all given some memorial for the crowning of the British Queen in London in 1953. She became Queen after the death of her father when she was in the Treetop hotel in Kenya in 1952. As a celebration for the coronation of Queen Elizabeth II, a Coronation safari rally was held in mainland East Africa (Kenya, Uganda and Tanganyika). It lasted for several days and we followed the actions reported on the radio and in the *Mombasa Times*. During one of the car rallies there was the death of a driver in a riverside crash. He was from an Indian family in Nairobi whose relatives we knew in Mombasa. Peugeot cars used to do well in the early days. It must have been the world's toughest rally and was later called the Safari Rally. After 1953 we had the chance of seeing the Queen and Prince Philip motoring past us on Makupa Road close to our houses. I remember waving to them from the roadside and was delighted to see them waving and smiling back at us. We had no sports field beside our school, but still did some physical training lessons by stripping off our shirts. None of the school sports were part of my activities as I was unable to participate in any of the school teams for hockey, football or volleyball. The school sports ground was a long way away from school, but it happened to be nearer my home. Then, during one of the school sports days I won a competition at our sports ground. It was during the sack race that I ran in a sack without falling while all the runners ahead of me were falling. The person that first crossed the line happened to be me. That sack race was the only one in which I was the winner.

At home, I spent my time with many friends in my neighbourhood. Sometimes we would go and play various games with our Sikh friends who lived in a nearby walled area on the north side of Makupa Road, opposite the bungalow of the hunter who had earlier shot the three wild lions in Mombasa. One day, I was surprised to see a Sikh boy who was covered in plaster over most of his body and who would be brought out and placed on a reclining chair to watch us playing around. It seems that he had broken most of his limb bones in India when he had been met by a ghost. Beside the tarmac road and houses on the north side there was ground on which we played. While trying to play hockey, a swinging stick came and hit my face, which resulted in blood coming out of my eyebrow. That put me off wanting to play hockey again. During a cricket game in a school event, I was to experience another pain in my body. After my spell of fielding, I was padded up for batting. When a ball was thrown at me, my swing out with my bat missed hitting the ball and was followed by a severe pain between my legs. That made me have no interest in ever wanting to play cricket again.

My time in class at school was enjoyable except during the Hindi periods. As I had not even managed to learn the alphabet and the writing, the teacher made me leave the classroom and amuse myself somewhere else. Neither the school nor I bothered about resolving that problem. At the end of the year there would be no marks given to me for Hindi, but in many other subjects there would be top marks for me. Strangely, a geography lesson triggered me into becoming interested in our solar system, although that is not what was being taught. It was the revelation of the earth being in existence in a field of planets in a solar system that triggered me to learn more about our solar system and the stars. There was a library not very far from our house from where I could borrow books. I learnt that the sun itself was a star and I started loving the sight of the stars in the night sky and the Milky Way that I could see around me every evening.

One day I was cycling back from the town centre and there were lots of people and policemen on the opposite roadside in the *Membe Tayari* area. After cycling back to see what was going on, a policeman came up to me and asked me for a licence for my bicycle. It surprised me to be having a licence for my small bicycle. That policeman took my bicycle away and gave me some paper that told me what had to be done to get my cycle back. Then in a court a judge spoken to me in Swahili and fined me for breaking the law. My uncle paid the fine for me. Later during my young life, there was another shock for me of being in a British colony. On entering an Indian barber shop in town to have a haircut, the barbers told me that their shop was only for white people. That is when I felt disgusted with the barbers for having taken up such a job. English education had been a great joy in my life, but there was much more for me to learn about my life on our planet. I was also not fully aware of the treatments that the Africans were receiving in their own country. Later in life I was to realise that the laws in Britain were not the same as the laws that were being imposed in the British colonies.

During one of my school holidays I went and stayed in the small town of Voi with my eldest brother who was working for East African Railways. That was the area where the construction of the original railway line had been halted due to attacks from man-eating lions. There was still plenty of wildlife around that area. Fresh elephant dumping could be seen in the mud tracks close to the houses. One day I had a frightening sight of a lizard the size of a small crocodile rapidly moving around the area close to me that made me run into the house. The large lizard had a forked tongue. My brother had a friendly Sikh family on a visit from Moshi in Tanganyika where they lived. On their return home they took me to stay with them in Moshi. At their home there was more for me to learn about the identity of the Sikh. In their home I had taken a shower and on coming out one of the young boys said to me that he had seen me naked in the shower. To my surprise the Sikhs don't even take off their underpants even when they are showering. That made me learn about the five Ks that a Sikh should do all the time. When translated the Ks stand for hair, comb, sword, metal wrist band and pants. The Sikhism requirements arose during its harsh establishment in India.

All the students in the school were channelled into one of the four groups that would gather together during some afternoons around midweek for discussions and debates. My association was with the Atlas House group and in the final year I became their chairman. During those meetings, we participated in debates that developed our capacity to talk to a group of people. There was even an inter-school debate in which we took part in at another school in Mombasa. In a great hall, a large group of girls were sitting in front of us and closely looking at us. It was great to be talking to the biggest audience I had ever faced.

At school, the time spent in class for the study of English literature was delightful for me. We were reading the book, Richard II that had been written by William Shakespeare about four hundred years ago. Taking part in Shakespeare plays was a great joy for me. Also, I enjoyed the reading of poetry by William Wordsworth, Oliver Goldsmith, Geoffrey Chaucer and many others. English literature became a delight for me for the rest of my life. We attended general science classes in another building away from the main block. The physics and chemistry classes were very interesting. However, during our biology lesson, we were going to be shown the inside of a frog. A dead frog was placed upside down on a board and the cutting started from his chin down to its bottom. The skin was then opened and cut further to reveal the body parts. Then I noticed that the eyes of the frog started opening up and the teacher sprayed something into its face to close the eyes. It really sickened me to know that it was a live frog that was being cut open. That was the most disgusting lesson during my school period, during which I learnt nothing about the body of the frogs.

After school time, I would sometimes cycle to town and meet up with some classmates. We spent a lot of time together just talking about life with each other and sometimes one of them would take me to a Hindu temple. He would go through a host of actions that were not familiar to me, but it was fun for me. In the temple, there was a statue of the holy cow. My family were in the sect of Arya Samaj which did not have temples or statues, but it was part of the peaceful Hinduism. The Aryans came to India from northern Europe several thousand years ago and who gathered together and prayed beside a fire in the open instead of at statues in temples.

Another activity that the school provided for us was boy scouting outside the school hours. The Sikh teacher was our scoutmaster and took us out on delightful camping days. The skills of making rope knots, camping, tracking and signalling had to be learnt. One day at home we were trying out the Semaphore signalling with a couple of small flags. An African who was walking by asked us what we were doing with the waving flags. When we told him that we were sending and receiving messages with the boys more than a hundred yards in front of us, he didn't believe us. We asked him to tell us what to say to them and he could walk up to them and find out if they had received the message. Then we signalled with Semaphore flags to say *Jambo Rafiki* (hello friend). The African then walked to the boys at the other end and that was followed by him turning around and waving to us with his hands before moving on.

Towards the end of my time at school we were told that a selection of scouts in Mombasa would be able to participate in a camp up-country where boy scouts from the whole of Kenya would be gathering at the start of the next year. From the mass of scouts at the camp a selection would be made for a Kenya group of scouts that would then be sent to Britain for the Jubilee Jamboree of scouting. The reason why Kenya were sending a scout troop to Britain was that the founder of scouting, Lord Baden Powell from South Africa had spent his later life in Kenya and was buried in Kenya.

In 1956, my preparation for the final school examinations and the scouting selection for a trip to England wholly engaged my life. To do some revision before the exams I ended up taking my book to a seat that had been built on a mango tree to do my reading in peace. My older cousin used to tell me not to take the risk of climbing and sitting on the mango tree to do my studying. During the last year at the school we were being prepared for the subjects in our final examinations from Cambridge. We had to sit for seven examinations consisting of English language, literature and history as well as mathematics, general science, geography and Hindi. An overall grade would be given on the complete set of results obtained. For each subject the result would be given grades that were labelled as being very good, credit or pass, instead of percentages. The overall result achieved would then be classed as certificates of first, second and third divisions. Suddenly, I realised that in order to get the best grade in the overall result I needed to get pass marks in Hindi. That made me start crash learning Hindi myself. It was in December 1956 that my final examinations were taken after four years of study in Mombasa. We then had to wait until the next month for the examination result.

1957

After my school examinations, my attention was transferred to scouting. The Mombasa group of scouts had to go to the boy-scout Rowallen up-country camp near Nairobi. There we were grouped with other Kenya scouts from which the selected ones would make up four patrols for the Jubilee Jamboree in Britain. That would be two patrols of Africans, one of Asians and one of Europeans. My Sikh teacher from Mombasa was also at the camp as one of the selectors. We were thrown into a variety of scouting activities over a week and were being monitored for selection.

One day we were told that something unusual had happened outside our camp. Two Africans, with large cutting blades called *pangas,* had been sighted and arrested by the police. These guys would have been from the *Mau Mau,* a Kikuyu group who were involved in killings that we used to hear about in Mombasa where there were no Kikuyus. During our up-country camping time, it was the first time that I was close to the political problem affecting Kenya. On another day during the scout camping there was another fright for me. When I was leaving the tent on my own one evening, it surprised me that none of the lights around us were on and it was completely dark outside. That made me get hold of my torch and just as I was rushing out, the problem was suddenly solved. That day we had an extra layer of canvas put over our tent and it had a low panel at the front of the entrance. The view ahead of me was blocked by the panel ahead of my face. We needed to dip our heads to move in or out of the tent. It was a relief that the fright was only momentary.

After the end of our scout camp, we were sent away and waited for the selection result. I was staying in Nairobi with my uncle and family when I got the stunning news that I had been selected to go to the Jamboree in Britain in August. My uncle took me round the flats and proudly presented me to the neighbours with delight. That was an astonishing achievement for me. Suddenly my whole world was opening up for me. A delightful steam train took me back to Mombasa. At home, I started getting congratulations from all my neighbours for my scouting selection. Strangely, I was the only scout from Mombasa to be selected for the Kenya group. My school teacher was also going to be on the Jamboree trip.

The results from our Cambridge examinations arrived the next week. There was another delight for me to experience in my life. Not only had I got the top grade in the school, but also strangely got a credit grade in my Hindi exam when a simple pass would have been okay for me. My existence on this planet had widely opened out. That was followed by a further advance in my life by being accepted by an Indian charity group to have further education in Nairobi at the Royal Technical College. The year of 1957 had given me the greatest uplift in my life. What surprised me was that there would be a break from education for nine months because the technical education at the college started in September instead of our usual January. British people mysteriously started their year of study in September. Despite my English education I could not comprehend the English mentality.

The unusual start of the college study in September gave me plenty of free time for some new life experiences. As well as my boy scouting activities I worked as an assistant in a Sindhi shop for some months. My brother played football for Arsenal on the AVHS ground near our home and I started playing there during their evening training games. Usually there would not be full teams for the game and I started getting involved with tackling the bigger boys, robbing the ball and started scoring goals. Before the start of the practice games there would be a selection of the teams by two captains. They would toss a coin and start picking in turn their players from the group that had turned up. To my surprise the person who had won the toss started picking me as his first choice because that would guarantee his side winning. However, I was too small to play in their competition games against teams like Liverpool, Chelsea, Coast, Lou and Faisal. Those were the games in the football grounds of the Mombasa stadium and nearby open fields.

There was love and respect for me from many people in our neighbourhood for my achievements in education and selection for a boy scouting trip to Britain. The prayers in my head seemed to have been helping me in my life. It was great to be living together in an extended family. My uncle had given me a brand-new bicycle when I was at my high school. My mother used to do various women gatherings in celebration of my achievements. The cooking that she and Auntie did was on small coal fires or on small portable oil cookers. They would sit almost on the floor on a *patada* (stool) from where they would roll out the *chapattis* and cook them on a flat pan followed by a short toss up above the charcoal to inflate them. The spiced vegetables were cooked in various ways. We also ate rice and yogurt. The yogurt that was eaten was always plain or with salt and it was always made at home by the little remaining yogurt being used to trigger the process for the next day. If we had run out of yogurt, then one of us would go and fetch a little bit from one of the neighbours in the evening. We had no fridge. Our water was cooled naturally by a large clay pot on a stand that was filled with water from the tap. The pot cooled the water by a slight evaporation through it. The water would be picked out by a scoop on a handle.

Jubilee Jamboree in Britain

In July 1957, I set off for Nairobi from where we would make our trip to Britain. It would be the first time I would be flying in an aeroplane. The flight was from the RAF (Royal Air Force) Eastleigh aerodrome in Nairobi. The aeroplane flown by BOAC (British Overseas Airways Corporation) was the Lockheed Super Constellation on which four sets of propellers were driven by piston engines. We were strapped in separate seats and on the floor there were big bamboo sticks that were being taken for our camp site. There were lovely air-hostesses in uniforms who were treating us very well.

After we took off from the ground and flew into the air. it thrilled me to be seeing the land below us. During our flight the aeroplane had to stop to refuel at Cairo and at Rome. During the flight, we could unlock our seat belts and had the chance to go to the cockpit in turn. I went to the cockpit at night and found that the view was better than from the cabin. When I asked the pilot about how he knew which way to go to London he said that he was following the pole star. It amazed me that he was using the knowledge that I had started learning in scouting about using the stars for finding one's way around. During the night, we slept in our seats. Then we flew over the Alps in daylight and could see the snow-covered mountains. The flight was a real delight for me. After landing at Heathrow airport near London we stepped out of the aeroplane in the parking area and walked to a building. From there we were taken to different homes by English families.

It was the first time in my life that I was to be staying in the home of any white people. The English custom of eating with knife and fork had been shown to me at an invitation lunch to the Rotary Club in Mombasa together with my teacher. That was my first go at using a knife and fork for eating. In London my stay was with the Page family in Southgate whose young son was a scout. For me it was a great experience to be staying with an English family. While returning to the house after a little walk around it surprised me that the time was 9 pm. For me the sun had always been setting around 6 pm and was amazed to see it was still up after 9 pm. That was when I learnt something new about my planet Earth that had never been mentioned in school. After my first few exciting days in London, we were taken to the scout camp at Sutton Coldfield near Birmingham.

The Jubilee scout camp was spread over a large area occupied by scouts from all over the world. We erected a gate with the bamboo poles that came with us on the aeroplane. In our patrol of seven Asians, my closest link was with Tony Fernandes from Kericho in western Kenya. The rest of that group included three Sikhs and two Muslim boys. Over two weeks we met scouts from around the world and participated in many gatherings. We saw scouts in various fittings from different countries. When walking around to meet other scouts, I would wrap a blanket around me on which I had sewn flags of many countries around the world. Our African scouts presented their traditional dances to the crowds. Many people from Britain would come and talk to us. One day we had the rare occasion of a special visit to our camp site by Her Majesty Queen Elizabeth and Prince Phillip. It was a delight to have had them on our location and the African dancers gave a display. Strangely, not only was the founder of scouting buried in Kenya but also Princess Elizabeth became a Queen while in Kenya in 1952. We mixed with scouts from all over the world and the local people of Britain. At the end of the Jamboree there was a big gathering of all the scouts. We sang together and bid farewell to each other. That attendance at the Jubilee Jamboree had been a great experience of a get-together with people from around the world and the local English people who were very different to the white people in Kenya.

After the Jamboree, we were taken on a journey around Britain in coaches. In Edinburgh, we were taken to their houses. Tony and I were taken by Duncan, a scoutmaster. We had a great time with him and his wife. One day they took us to a bank and asked us to take a note with the name of his wife's sister on it when they saw her at the counter. We presented the note to her and said we needed to see the person whose name was on the paper. She looked at her name and then at us and was so baffled that she left her counter to figure out the situation. When she returned to the desk, she was surprised to find that we were with her relatives and was relieved of her mysterious situation. One day I happened to say that it was a delight to be with English people when they told me that they were not English but Scottish. I had never imagined that English and Scottish people would be different people as they spoke the same language. That difference then was driven home to me when we engaged in various Scottish only activities. We wore tartan kilts, ate haggis, played a bagpipe, did Scottish dancing and went to Loch Lomond. After that we were declared to be adapted Scots and were presented neck ties of the Stuart clan. For us it was a great pleasure to have been with the Scots and for me it was a revelation of the differences in British people.

From Scotland, we moved southwards towards the east coast of England. There we stayed with the Stoke family and their son in the small town of Hebburn near Newcastle-upon-Tyne. To my surprise, the parents were as short as me. There we were taken on visits to a place of shipping construction and then down into a coal mine wearing just our vest and lamps on our heads. One evening I was taken to the club in which a crowd of young ones gathered around me. They seemed baffled at seeing someone from Africa. One asked me if I lived in a tree or in a mud house. Someone even asked me if I could speak English; that made his companions shut him up. After Newcastle, we went to Nottinghamshire, stayed in a countryside town of Retford. The son of the English family used to be a scout and after school he became a serviceman in the Royal Air Force. On a countryside trip it surprised me to see the hugeness of straw piles in the fields. He was surprised when I got him to photograph me beside the pile of straw.

At Stratford-upon-Avon, we had a look at the Shakespeare theatre and saw statues of characters that I had read about in school. After seeing university buildings in Oxford, we continued south and stopped and met Lady Baden Powell and her grandchildren. My final stay in Britain was with an English family in Hayes, Middlesex. As we did not have any further gatherings of our group, I took the opportunity to go in my scout uniform and see an Arsenal football match at the Highbury stadium against Bolton Wanderers. It surprised me that there were trains underground that took me to a very big stadium. During the match, I cheered the goal that Arsenal had scored and was surprised that there was a lack of cheering by the crowd beside me. That was because I was standing with the opposition supporters. They were puzzled by the sight of me in my scout uniform. Still, my cheering continued for my Arsenal side that secured a win.

We finally flew back to Kenya after about a month and returned to our homes. My trip to Britain was almost like a dream about a trip to another planet. Then I had to prepare myself for a move to Nairobi to start the new stage of my life. That was for the study of electrical engineering in a college for a period of five years.

Chapter 3
Engineering in Kenya

Royal Technical College, Nairobi

Amongst us Asians in Mombasa in the early 1950s it was rare to have a higher education. There was no university in Kenya and it was only the rich folk who could send their children to England for university degrees. Some people sent their children for some higher education to India where they also had relatives. The only learning option after school in Mombasa was a certificate for doing some school teaching. Then in 1956 the opening of the Royal Technical College in Nairobi had started a new option for education in Kenya. Fortunately, there was an Asian group that donated bursaries for further education and I was lucky to have been given support for the whole period of my further education. My study of electrical engineering in the college would require a period of five years because most students in Kenya would only have a school certificate, equivalent to O-levels (ordinary level) in Britain. The Cambridge advanced level courses (A-level) were later offered to Asian schools in Kenya. As the college also started running courses for architecture, art, domestic science and others, its name was later changed to Royal College. At that time Kenya was still a British colony. For me that period of study away from home was going to be an exciting new phase of existence for five years.

My college life started in September 1957 and it was the first time I would be living away from home of family or relatives. Our hostels were located less than a mile away from the study area. Most of the engineering study was in a separate building, although we attended some lessons in the main building where the cafeteria was also located. The combined engineering group of about twenty Asians and Africans was to stay together for two years and then would be split up into separate electrical, mechanical and civil engineering groups. There were no European boys with us, but there were a few of them in other college departments. Most of the girls in the college were studying Domestic Science and were mostly Asians. There were only a few European and African girls in various other departments. Many of the leading lecturers in my engineering department were from Britain and there was also some Asian staff. Having been to Britain for the scout gathering, I then understood the British notion of education years starting in September. It was because Britain experienced long warm days during July and August when holidays could be enjoyed by a whole family together. With Kenya straddling the equator there was no need for the British timing for our education. Our schools had not been affected by the British system.

In the dining hall of the hostels for the boys, there were separate tables for vegetarians, meat-eating without beef, meat-eating without pork and the rest of the tables were for those who ate everything. The Hindus were mostly vegetarians, but some would eat meat except beef, as the cow was a holy creature. The Sikh boys loved the meat table minus the beef. Although I was a non-vegetarian, I joined the vegetarian group as we received lovely spicy food. The girls in the college were in a separate hostel away from our location. They were mostly Asians together with some African and English girls. After our get-togethers with the girls for sports and social gatherings some of us would walk with them during their return to their hostel.

Our attendance in class was for only five days of the week. After the end of the class we had the opportunity of getting onto the sports grounds near the hostels before dinner time. At our location near the equator, the sun always set shortly after 6 pm and it would become night time within 30 minutes. Right from the beginning of my time at college I got involved with the football group. The altitude difference of 5,500 feet between Nairobi and my home town of Mombasa at sea level resulted in my body struggling. There was a very friendly sports coach who helped us a lot with our sport life. One day at the college it surprised me to hear that my name was in the selection for the college football team, for a match in my first year at college. The selected team was made up of mostly Africans and had only three Asians. That resulted in me having friendly associations with Africans in class and in sports. There was also another group that played friendly football games on Sundays with an outside team brought in by a white Catholic priest. Our team would be made up of a lot of Catholic Goans with whom the priest was linked. We played those football games on some Sundays. The sport of hockey was mostly indulged in by Asian students. Although hockey did not interest me, the hockey team dragged me to join them in the goal, because I could kick a ball. After a trial the college team picked me to be a goalkeeper for them. It amazed me to be selected for two sports in my first year at college when my school days had been without any sport. Maybe my body had been slow in growing up as fast as my brain.

During my first two years at the college, all the engineering students were taught together in one group. The college required us to wear a red gown with a normal shirt, trousers and tie. The necktie became a state of superiority in Europe, although its origin was for protecting the human body from a cold situation in wintertime. Next to our college in Nairobi there was the Norfolk Hotel that was mainly used by tourists. They would be dressed up for being in a wild country and were surprised at the sight of us wearing ties and university gowns. In addition to the academic studies in the classrooms, we spent time in the workshop for a range of engineering tasks. For me that was an introduction to the use of tools for construction. I enjoyed being involved with the woodwork construction, metalwork, drilling and welding. We were given overalls for wear in the workshops. One day I was using a large standing drill and ended up breaking the drill; that puzzled my instructor. That made me learn that the side of the drill is not used for cutting. On another day, a piece of hot metal came flying out from someone nearby doing metal work. It hit me like a bullet just above my left elbow and nearly resulted in me passing out.

In our hostels, there was a common room where we played table tennis and listened to music. One of those rooms was also used for learning to dance. We boys had to pair up to learn the dancing that we would look to be doing with the girls in the college dances at the end of the terms. That was the first time I would be doing the dances of foxtrot, quickstep and waltzing. We also indulged in jiving for jazzy music, but that was based on individual approaches. Getting into the tango steps was not easy. The Africans were very much into their dancing and didn't need any training.

Amongst the Asians it was mainly the Christian Goans who already danced at their clubs and I was amongst a few who were starting to learn to dance and listen to more western music. During the college functions, we started my dancing with girls. Initially my dancing was only with the Goan girls, as Indian girls would not come onto the dance floor for the European dancing. When the music was delivered by an African band, the music sounded different and the dancing changed; the Africans would be indulging in various forms of dancing. Later, during the jiving, my dancing with a girl had great coordination in our movements and we would regularly dance together during jive music. Ballroom dancing was an enjoyable activity for me that also gave me friendships with many girls. After my participation in dancing with many Christian girls, my social time was mainly with them.

It was a delight to have relatives in Nairobi, but my uncle was worried about me travelling on my own to visit them. He had been working with the police for Nairobi security and feared the Mau Mau. Their leader Jomo Kenyatta was being held in prison and I remember seeing the photograph of one of the leaders who had been shot dead in a forest. There had been a few British farming people killed by the Mau Mau, but there had been the massive number of African deaths that included the Mau Mau as well as people killed by the Mau Mau. It was only later that I began to see that the Mau Mau violence was a nasty fight against the British rule in Kenya.

Kenya hitch hiking

After the end of our first year at college we had two months' holiday. Those holidays resulted in me engaging in a new adventure altogether with a classmate. We decided to hitch-hike around East Africa. To start with we set off for Kericho and Kisumu to the west of Nairobi. An older cousin of mine lived in Kericho and we went and stayed at his house. From there we managed to get to Kisumu and stayed with my friend's relatives. It was the first time that we saw the large Lake Victoria. On our return to Nairobi we were given a lift by an African who was amazed by our adventure. He moved his wife to the back seat and had both of us with him in the front seat where we could easily chat with him during the drive. Hitch-hiking gave us pleasant contacts with other people around us.

From Nairobi, we continued our hitch-hiking to the coast for Mombasa and Tanga. The first lift for us from Nairobi was by a Sikh who could not understand that we were doing this form of travel for fun. He dropped us out on the open main road as he had to turn off to his house well off the road. From that isolated spot, we finally got a lift in a truck trailer. The African driver put us under a cover on the load on the trailer at the back. We were on our own there as the truck swayed around when the road turned to a dust track for most of the way. It got dark and rainy and we felt some severe braking and horn blowing during the trip. Then at night our truck slowed down, swerved and stopped. We found that the truck had slipped off the wet muddy track as it tried to gently go past another heavy vehicle that was also stuck in the mud. Between the two stuck vehicles there was space only for smaller vehicles to pass. We spent the rest of the night on the truck and looked at our options in the morning. When I asked the drivers why they had been horn-blowing and braking at night during our drive they said that some lions had been crossing the road.

During the day, we felt that it was safe enough to leave the truck and walk to the nearest town of Voi that was about ten miles away. We must have walked a mile when a car appeared behind us and we waved it down for a lift. The African driver was surprised that we were hitch-hiking. Halfway to the small town of Voi we were shocked when we saw a pair of cheetahs by the roadside. The driver then said that we were lucky to have been picked up by him. Voi was the town where early railway line building had slowed down due to man-eating lions of Tsavo. Also, it was where I had stayed with my brother when he was working there. We went to the house of someone I had met before. There we were given a meal and then set out to sit beside the main road for a lift to Mombasa. Later an Englishman picked us up and took us comfortably all the way to Mombasa. During that trip some animals were jumping off the road as the car approached, but they were only wild deer. The driver was impressed by our trip of adventure.

Trip to Tanganyika

To accompany my colleague to Tanga I went and found a school friend of mine who had relatives living there. The three of us set off together along a narrow road beside the coast. We managed to get a lift and then reached a point where we were forced to stop. There were cars parked on both sides of a flooded stream going across the road. Although there had been no rain in the area the water was coming from up-country where there had been heavy rain days earlier. The drivers had to wait for the water level to subside before we could continue across the concreted track over which the flood was flowing. Bigger trucks and Land Rovers crossed the stream safely while other cars had to wait for the water level to drop.

An Indian family managed to arrange a Land Rover to tow them across because they needed to get to a marriage. The car was then roped and towed into the stream. Shortly after entry into the water the towed car started to drift towards the edge of the road where there was a drop. That car braked heavily and was honking its horn to make the Land Rover stop the tow, but it continued to be pulled ahead. That made me feel that we were about to see a disaster. Fortunately, the Land Rover stopped in time and eventually they managed to retrieve the stricken car from the verge. It was a great relief to see people being rescued.

While we waited for the water to drop there was another event. A drunk African was taking a herd of cows into the stream to get across to the other side. People failed to stop him doing that and then we saw that the cows were being swept off the track by the stream flow. About four of them fell into the water at the edge of the concrete road and were swept down the stream. The other cows came back out of the water to our side. To my surprise the cows in the water were swimming with their heads out of the water and managed to get out on both sides of the stream. It was amazing to have witnessed two disasters in one day in which, fortunately, there were no casualties. We spent the night in the car and continued our journey the next morning. On our return to Mombasa we got a lift in a Volkswagen Beetle car that was being driven with its engine cover at the rear strapped in an open position, because the normal air flow did not provide enough engine-cooling in those hot conditions. At the place where the stream crossed our road there was no water to be seen on our return trip.

Hit by malaria

After my short stay in Mombasa I went up-country by train to stay with my relatives in the village of Limuru that was west of Nairobi at a higher altitude of over 7,000 feet. My uncle was an electrical contractor working around the beautiful countryside of European farms as well as the large Bata shoe factory. Then a strange illness hit me. My body felt very weak for long periods in the day, but then there would be periods when I felt okay. My uncle called in an English doctor who checked on me and found me to be suffering from malaria. He said I should be sent straight to hospital. I must have picked up the disease in Mombasa from the mosquitos, with the infection not appearing until three weeks later in Limuru where there were no mosquitos. It was the first time in my life that my body was unable to avoid malaria. I was rushed to Nairobi and taken to the house of my relatives there. An Indian doctor conducted various tests on me and presented the medicines to be given to me by the family. My relatives looked after me for several days and my body slowly started to recover. I lost about twenty pounds of my weight, which resulted in me weighing 110 pounds. The Indian doctor later told me that the red cells in my blood had fallen to a level of 50 percent. Fortunately, my body recovered and I began to feel better when it was time to head back to college, although my weight was below average and my hip bones tended to stick out. Furthermore, the red cells in my body must have taken up a new distorted state for future protection against malaria.

College, second year

In September 1958, we continued with the previous subjects at the college. My colleagues were surprised at my slimness. My usual weight started to return slowly. In hockey there were many friendly matches with local teams and the Makerere University visiting team from Kampala in Uganda. There were also friendly football matches played on Sundays in the Asian group against European teams brought in by the sportive priest. Then during one of my friendly games I had severe pain in my right knee in during a tackle. The doctors found that the cartilage in my knee had been damaged and told me to lay off playing football for several weeks. As we were in our final term at college the rest of the college year ended up with me not playing in any sport. It was a miserable time not being physically active. Beside our hostel there was a swimming pool in the grounds of the YMCA that we could use at discounted rates. That resulted in me spending my time swimming to keep up my physical activity. At the pool, we met one of our lecturers who was swimming with various unusual strokes. The lecturer was happy to give us instruction on swim strokes. The odd thing about the swim strokes was that one had to dip the head into the water and then breathe momentarily with a lift of the head out of the water, something which our lecturer was doing so easily.

Kilimanjaro 1959

After the end of the academic year I was lucky to have been offered a place for a mountain climbing expedition for a fortnight. We were sent to the Outward Bound Mountain School at Loitokitok on the Kenyan side of the highest African mountain of Kilimanjaro, standing at 19,340 feet. Kilima is the Swahili word for mountain. If the mountain had been called Mount Njaro it would not have sounded as good as the Swahili name of Kilimanjaro. The Kenya and Tanganyika boundary had a weird kink in it, which put Kilimanjaro in the Tanganyika territory. That occurred during the early days of European colonization of African countries. Initially, Kilimanjaro was planned to be in the British colony of Kenya which also had Mount Kenya in its territory, but Kilimanjaro was then handed to the German territory of Tanganyika, which is why there is the strange kink in the boundary between the two countries. During our visit both countries were under British rule and there was no boundary restriction.

At the Mountain School, we got together with twenty participants from all over Kenya. We were split into groups that were made up of combinations of Africans, Asians and Europeans. Two of my college friends were also there for that adventure. We were at the foot of the mountain that stood out in the sky. Although Kilimanjaro was nowhere near the highest mountain in the world, it stood out as a huge mountain as there were no other peaks in sight. We were nearly on the equator, but the mountain was unusually white with snow at the top. From the foot of the mountain we had a great sight of our challenging adventure. For us Nairobi students it was a benefit for having been at an altitude that was roughly the elevation of our base camp. We went through nearly two weeks of training to get fit for the climb to the top of Africa.

On the first trek, we went up and spent the nights in caves which were at an altitude higher than 10,000 feet. The strange thing was that those caves had been expanded by the Germans for accommodation during the earlier world war, for keeping an eye on British forces on the Kenya side. On the next higher outing, each one of us had to construct a separate shelter for a night using natural materials from the surrounding area. I only managed to find a few sticks and leaves to construct a small protection hut against a stone wall. It was only big enough for me to be able to slide my sleeping bag under the cover. From inside the hut parts of the sky were still in view. Then one of the Africans showed us the shelter that he had constructed. It was a fully protected hut into which one could walk in and not see any sky. Despite that, my little hut enabled me to survive the night and walk out the next day. One of the strange things in the mornings was that there the sheets of ice that had formed above water puddles during the night. The high altitude was making us struggle and we often stopped and sat down to regain our strength. The African lads would rush around, pick up some sticks, light a fire and enabled all of us to have a cup of tea.

Our climb to the top of Kilimanjaro would be done simply by walking up a steep slope. However, we also went through some mountaineering skills of rock climbing and descending. We finished off by coming down a nearly vertical cliff on a rope held by someone at the top. It frightened me to be doing that. Eventually, I had to set off down the cliff using the rope suitably wound around me. Although there was a big drop below me the rope around my body made me feel safe. Strangely, I even went through the process of pushing myself away from the rock. That was an action that had frightened me earlier. To my surprise, my push away from the rock had won me the prize for the best safety action during the descent.

The training days had prepared us for a climb to the very top of Kilimanjaro. Our first night was spent in a cave. Then we set off for the Kibo huts that were located at the base of the steep slope of the volcanic mountain. During that phase of climbing we were in the clouds and muddled up the slope to those huts that were at an altitude of about 15,000 feet. Only a little amount of time would be spent in the huts in an attempt to get some sleep before we started climbing at midnight so that we could go up and descend below the level of the huts. During the climb, we were closely in line as a group. It was a struggle for me going up a steep slope as we had no tools for helping us with the climb. Some climbers were having problems and strangely one of the fit Africans said that he was seeing red and feeling weak. To my surprise there was a Sikh lad who had a broken arm in plaster but he was continuing up the steep slope.

We got to the rim of a crater just as the sun was rising. The mountain was the remains of an earlier volcano. There was a fantastic view of the scenery around us. We then continued along the rim of the crater to the peak of Kilimanjaro. There I had the strange experience of walking on snow that was over most of the mountain peak. The sight of land all around a long way down was thrilling. At last we got to the peak of the mountain that was called Kaiser Wilhelm Spitz. We had finally got to the highest point in Africa where we took photographs. It thrilled me to have been at the peak of our huge continent.

When going up we had to climb up solid rock, but going down we could go on the loose stone and sand. Long steps could be taken, pushing through the loose stony soil and running to the hut. I got there before anyone else and rested in a hut until everyone came down. From the Kibo huts we continued down to another set of caves where we spent the night. Finally, the next day we got down to the mountain school, packed our backpacks and were getting into the coaches. That's when I stopped and looked up at the mountain. I couldn't believe that I had been up to the top of the beautiful sight that I was looking at from below. That had been a fascinating achievement in my life. Kilimanjaro is the highest point of Africa.

Nairobi work experience

Our college arranged for us to be given work experience for a month during our holiday break. After the expedition, I went to the Post Office maintenance department for work experience and ended up staying with my close relatives in Nairobi in a ground floor flat within a two-storied building. There it was delightful to be with my younger cousins who also used to come and stay with us in Mombasa during some holidays. My work experience was with a group who were servicing telephone equipment with which it was not easy for me to get involved. There was some nasty interaction with an English foreman and that period of work experience for me was not pleasant. After returning to Mombasa for the rest of the college break, I went swimming in the sea by the nearest beach. The use of swimming goggles was a great help. It was there that my swimming could be done with my head in the water for movement together with the correct breathing actions. That enabled me to start making the correct actions required for front crawl, breast-stroke and backstroke, to build up swimming speeds.

Life during college days

After the second year at college we split up into separate engineering groups for the next three years. In my electrical engineering class there were only three students. In our studies during those years we learnt many formulae and theorems. The use of complex numbers became common in our studies. A complex number has a real and an imaginary component that fitted well into the real and imaginary components in AC (alternating current) power. In the electrical laboratories, we had practical sessions with electrical machines. We did practical work for the installation of domestic wiring. On one occasion, my wiring installation resulted in the length of the cable I had cut off from a roll being a foot short of the switch that had been installed. Cutting a cable a few yards longer would have been all right.

My sporting activities recommenced when my knee recovered. My football games were for the college team, but in hockey, my activity was in the forward or the half-back positions. Although I did not become a regular first team player, the hockey team took me on a tour around to Moshi, Arusha and Tanga at the end of the college year. It was a delight to have had a very enjoyable time with the team, as well as the Indian folk that we met on that tour. After some of those matches the opposing team did not believe that I was not in the college first team.

During the next college year, we students had the opportunity of going with some lecturers for a walk around Ngong Hills near Nairobi. It was lovely to be walking in wild countryside. When we were going downhill, we could see a herd of wild buffalo at the bottom of the hill. Then we heard shouts from the group behind telling us that they had seen a single buffalo heading up in our direction. That is when we had to track back up the hill and return to our transport. Going out to the beautiful countryside in Kenya required courage and due respect for the wildlife. Towards the end of the academic years we had rag-days at the college for which we constructed displays for parading through the town. Our construction changed a vehicle into the shape of a boot. However, it was extremely difficult for the driver to see what was ahead of him. It was great fun to be part of the fancy dressed students parading and singing through the town. One year we had an unfortunate accident with one of the parade displays. A student had tripped up beside a heavy trailer display and got run over; then we heard the devastating news that the lad had lost his life.

A new sport was set up on our sports grounds. Beside the hockey pitch we could start playing basketball. It was an American sport and required tall players, but due to the lack of interest I ended up being selected for the college team. We enjoyed friendly matches with some European teams that played the sport. At the swimming pool our lecturer then gave us some tips on diving from the diving boards and my time at the pool became regular and enjoyable. Then, after a suggestion from the lecturer, we started a college swimming group. I was selected as captain and arranged an annual event for swimming and diving. We started getting many girls coming in for swimming. Out of nothing, swimming became another active sport for me at the college.

From not having represented my school in any game I ended up, in my later college years, representing the college against Makerere University of Uganda in the sports of football, hockey, basketball and swimming. During a presentation of our sports achievements at the college, Tom Mboya, who was then a leading politician of the Lou tribe, presented the trophies. It was a delight for me to have received three cups from Tom Mboya. Unfortunately, he was assassinated before Kenyan independence. Another day we had the leading politician, Julius Nyrere from Tanganyika who gave us a talk about the approaching independence. He was later to become the first president of Tanganyika. The leading man in Kenya was Jomo Kenyatta who had been in prison and was released in 1961. I had finished at the college in 1962 and it was in 1963 that Jomo Kenyatta became the Kenyan president.

In the college, another sport was introduced by our sports coach. He was also involved with boxing and had been using us as ushers during boxing events in town. It was not until I had seen live boxing, that I realized how violent it could be. Eventually, he got boxing started in the college and got me involved in the training. When the first college boxing contest was to be held, there was no option but for me to take part in it. The boxing ring was set up between our hostels and my fight was to be with an African. We two met up and decided to be gentle with our behaviour in the ring. We had been circling round each other and heard the crowd saying "box". We had no choice but to start pounding each other. By the end of the second round, I felt knackered. In the final third round, a punch from me resulted in him being partly out of the ropes. The referee stopped the fight and made me the winner. The next morning, there was a black eye on my face and people in the college were asking me who had attacked me. After that fight, boxing was never going to be a sport for me. Just watching a boxing fight was going to be more than enough for me.

In 1960 the Olympics were being held in Rome. I had decided to join a colleague to go hitch-hiking to Rome for the events and started the process of getting a passport. To my horror it turned out that my birth was not even registered. The process of registering my own birth had to be done with help from my relatives and we finally managed to do it, but it was too late for me to get my passport for the Olympics.

During the college holidays I had some work experience with the East African Electricity Board in Nairobi. I was transported in the back of a van with the African technicians involved with replacing electricity supply cables. The Asian foreman in the front seat would be directing the others for the jobs. One day the foreman placed me beside a technician who was on a ladder up a pole working on the cable. Suddenly, the electricity cable came off the pole and fell on a car underneath. To my surprise on our return to the company centre, a supervisor asked me why I had not supervised the technician to prevent the accident. Once again, my work experience was awful. We were there to learn about working.

In Nairobi, there were some football grounds belonging to the East African Railways (EAR) beside the house of my relatives, where a group of Indians were playing football on the ground. Football with the Indians was good fun for me. My fitness and skills had developed sufficiently to enable me to keep good control of the ball and to score goals. They would pick me up from college to play with them at the weekends. Later, during college holidays, there were times when I would be staying with my relatives in Limuru and the Asian football team would even drive 21 miles to pick me up for a football game in Nairobi.

Many of college Goan friends for football were also involved in social activities in the city. The Goans were Christians with many Portuguese names as Portugal held the state of Goa in India and continued to do so even after the rest of India had become independent in 1947. Social life in Kenya tended to be grouped into various racial groups, but for me there had been wider contact with various Asian and Seychelles groups. European and African families generally lived in different locations from the Asians.

In 1960, our college name was changed to Royal College, Nairobi which was affiliated with the University of London. My studies continued as planned for a college diploma and a graduate membership of the IEE (Institution of Electrical Engineers) in London. There was plenty of effort required for the technical learning during the last three years of study. My final work experience was with the Kenya Broadcasting Corporation (KBC) in Mombasa in 1961. Both my brothers worked for EAR (East African Railways) in Mombasa. Baldev was doing clerical work and Krishan worked on the electrical railway engines. I stayed with my family in a flat on Makupa Road that was near our original residence. My final work experience was in the town studio in Mombasa. That was enjoyable for me because of my participation in various activities during the radio recordings and broadcasts.

In my final year of study there was great tension in preparation for our final examinations. In 1962 we took two sets of examinations, one from the college and another from the Institution of Electrical Engineers (IEE) of London. The results of our college examinations for a diploma were given to us at college and I was greatly thrilled with the result of achieving that diploma. Then we returned home and waited for the results of our IEE exams. Once again, it was a thrill for me having passed in all the subjects which meant I would become a Grad IEE (graduate member of IEE). My intense period of education was to be over and I had to concentrate on a life of employment and earning. I was lucky to have been fully supported for gaining my education.

Family life

During my last year at college my eldest brother was the first one in our family to get married and was having his marriage arranged. That is when it amazed me that we Hindus were associating our marriage with our caste system. To me, the religion of people I associated with was not important, let alone their caste. Whilst travelling on a train to Mombasa I had been talking with another Indian student who told me his name and followed that with saying that he too was a Brahmin. It amazed me that he knew that I was from a Brahmin family although that had not been mentioned. That is when it surprised me that the caste of an Indian can be identified by their surname. Indian marriages were normally arranged within the same castes or with girls only moving up to higher caste. For me it was necessary to get settled in my employment and career before embarking on having a family of my own.

My first paid job

The Kenya Broadcasting Corporation (KBC) was the company with whom I started working as an engineer at a radio transmitting station on the north side of Mombasa. Every day at work we went across the floating Nyali Bridge near my old school. There was little for me to do at work. The radio station only transmitted Swahili programs during the early morning and later during the evening for every day of the week. After the introduction to the transmitters, the task of running the station was given to me with an African assistant on a shift that had two sessions. The first session was in the afternoon and evening and that was followed by an early morning session the next day. Then after midday we would have a day off when another pair would run the station. The work required was for us to monitor the new transmitters and to call the manager if there was any problem. My assistant, Idi, was a big jovial chap and it was nice to have his company. The other person present would be the driver who transported us to and from work.

One day they were extracting some petrol from a big drum to use for a stove by dipping a rubber hose into the drum, sucking the fuel out and quickly transferring the hose into a can. Naturally some fuel ended up in their mouths. I showed them a simple method of drawing the fuel from the tank. The transfer hose was dipped into the tank, the open end was closed by one's thumb and then the hose was drawn out and down to the can before the thumb was removed. The fuel automatically flowed out with gravity. The flowing stopped when the open end was lifted above the level in the tank. They were amazed at what they had been shown. That's when I felt that my engineering knowledge could be useful, even in my ordinary life.

At work, the Africans were using an unusual system of clock timing. My African assistant wore a watch that indicated that the time was six hours different to the normal clocks and watches. He explained to me that the African day begins at sunrise when the watch would be showing zero hours. By mid-day his watch would show 6 o'clock and at sunset it would show 12 o'clock. The next 12 hours would be for the night from sunset to sunrise. To make his watch look more like that of other people for the timing of the day, Idi used to wear his watch upside down. That way he would use his other method of setting his watch, but by wearing it upside down made it look like the watches on other peoples' wrists. Therefore, he was able to fit in perfectly well with other peoples' totally different concept of time keeping.

At work there was plenty of time to look around the vast isolated area of two large transmitting aerials. There I started noticing some wildlife. It was not elephants and lions, but birds and insects that were providing me with delight. A long-tailed bird on our wire fence became a regular source of entertainment. The patch of grass between the fence and our building was his territory. That was the bird known as the pin-tailed whydah. He had a long black tail, white neck and chest, red beak and dark brown wings with white patches. He would be hopping off the fence, flipping around and singing to attract females. I called him the dancer. Whenever a less colourful female arrived, he would get excited by flipping around and singing. One day another male arrived at the scene, confronted our bird and to our dismay forced our bird off the area. We were disappointed to see a less interesting bird sitting around, doing nothing. Thankfully the other bird became bored and decided to fly away somewhere else. During my next work-time the old friendly bird was back on his fence and ruling his territory. That whydah entertainment had captured my lifelong interest in bird watching.

On the paths to our antenna, there were clusters of ants and it fascinated me to see their strange behaviour. There would be lines of ants going in opposite directions, carrying things. Sometimes they would be carrying blades of grass and other times it could be white eggs. Carrying the white eggs across the path was done through a tunnel. Strangely, the tunnel was made up by ants linking together with each other. There were some larger ants that were not moving around. They had large pincers in front of their heads for providing protection to the workers against any threat. By making a small movement with a thin stick in front of those guards I could see the rapid biting action from them. It was fascinating to see the behaviour of other life forms on our unique planet.

Sometimes we had heavy rain at night and afterwards we would have a mass of insects flying around our floodlights. They would continue hovering around the lights until they collapsed in a heap on the floor. My African friends would collect these finger-thick insects and cook them for their meals, but that did not interest me. Those insects were called mayflies and it puzzled me why the insects were attracted to a human light at night. It was only later that I was able to figure out the reason for the flying insects to be circulating the lights in the open. For millions of years they had been using the stars for flying in a straight line by maintaining a constant angle with the star. Only since human lights started had begun appearing recently, the poor creatures were directed by human lights to their life terminations.

During my employment days, there was a lot of free time during the day. That enabled me to continue engaging in many sporting activities. An English team that played basketball matches against Royal Navy teams from visiting ships invited me to play with them. With the Arsenal football team, the Asians played in matches in the stadium and some other grounds and it was a delight for me to engage in those activities. We were in the lower league of the football teams. In the top league in Mombasa the football teams included Liverpool and Chelsea. My brother in Mombasa had bought his first car, a green Morris saloon in which he would take us around on drives to the beaches and other places. He even took us to the drive-in cinema at Changamwe located after the causeway to the mainland. Then I began driving lessons and managed to get my driving licence after my first test. It was a great treat to be allowed to drive the family car and enjoy it. One day on a narrow dirt road, I was overtaking an African driver when his car turned across me without looking or giving any signal and bumped into my side. That accident was a bad start to my driving days.

Search for a job in Britain

After having been educated as an engineer and having had a delightful visit to Britain, it made me feel like getting an engineering job in Britain. That made me contact many engineering firms for a job. Most engineering firms said that they would be happy to see and to let them know when I would be coming to Britain. However, there was one that said that they would be sending their staff to Kenya and asked me to come for an interview. Although my job application was for the Engineer Branch of the Royal Air Force, their reply to me was from the Flying Branch that were recruiting engineers for flying duties. Although the job offered was puzzling to me, it would be easy for me to go and meet them in Nairobi and have a look at the offer.

In Nairobi it was revealed that the meeting was not just for an interview, but also for a mental aptitude test for flying. After a written test with some English lads, there was an interview; they then told me that the RAF would be prepared to offer me a flying job after their medical test. However, for my medical test they needed me to fly to Aden, for which several days off work needed to be arranged with my employer. The armed services lives or their rankings were a mystery to me. After the last world war, I could not imagine there ever being a world war and was attracted by the prospect of an adventurous flying job. The RAF took me from Nairobi to Aden on an enjoyable flight. That flight made me feel excited for a new life. Aden was an Arab country that was another British colony. There was accommodation for me in the Officers Mess during my stay for the medical test, the result of which would be given to me later. While waiting for a flight back to Kenya there was an opportunity for me to see the delightful officers' beach club. After my return to Kenya the RAF sent me a letter stating that they were offering me a job and for me to let them know of my decision in the next six months. That is when my final decision was made to join them for my new adventurous life starting in August 1963.

My sister Krishna got married in July just before my departure for Britain. Her husband was of another Sharma family from Nairobi. It was great to have met our new relatives before my departure to a place where there were no relatives or close friends. The only British families who I knew were the ones who had met me during my scouting trip in 1957. My enrolment into the RAF occurred in Kenya in August 1963 and my flight to Britain was from RAF Eastleigh in Nairobi. The first flight was to Bahrain where I spent a night in some RAF accommodation. When I was going to the bathrooms for a shower with a towel wrapped around me, an English lad rushed up to me and asked me to wash his towels. He was surprised at my reply. Later that evening he was even more surprised to see me coming out dressed from the officer's section of that accommodation.

A flight from Bahrain took me to London. The next day a train took me through some beautiful countryside for the initial training centre of RAF South Cerney near Cirencester in Gloucester. When I got onto a bus a group of Iraqis rushed to me and spoke in Arabic. They were surprised to find someone who looked like them was unable to speak in Arabic. When I arrived at the base accommodation it felt nice to be meeting up with my new RAF companions. However, when I went to pick up my new uniform at the store, the attendants gave me an Iraqi uniform and were surprised when I asked for an RAF uniform. A completely new phase of existence was starting to open up to me.

Chapter 4

RAF life start in Britain

Initial military training

It was in September 1963 that my initial training was started at RAF South Cerney in Wiltshire for a period of four months. During the first month, we were put together in dormitory accommodation where we had to be prepared for bedside inspections. After that, we had separate bedrooms in another accommodation where there were no inspections. Finally, bigger rooms in the Officers' Mess became our accommodation, where our rooms were tidied by some staff. That gave me a taste of military life and started making me learn about the personnel and ranking structure in the armed services that was made up of the commissioned officer category and the other categories would be non-commissioned officers and other ranks. The commission is given by the monarch to selected people who would be serving the country. We were given sessions in a classroom as well as in training fields. Parading was enjoyable, but not likely to be part of my flying job.

It was the first time in my life that I held a real fire-arm. On a firing range I could not believe the trouble it would be to fire live weapons. The rifle was fired from a lying down position. To my dismay, all my shots completely missed the target. The instructor told me that the target range setting had been clicked to reset position by the previous operator and had not been set up by me for firing. Then a revolver had to be fired using only one hand. It was like the firing method seen in cowboy films. However, my revolver would flick around during the firing with a single hand and my shots were spraying around rather than hitting the target. Finally, with the continuous firing machine gun my shots were hitting not only my own target but also the one beside my location by the time I finished firing. That's when the gunnery coach came and told me that in the event of a war, I was to charge my enemy with a bayonet fixed to my rifle and not to waste my time with the bullets.

On the obstacle course I had been doing well and was crawling through a barbed wire tunnel on the ground when my elbow suffered a cut and ended up with severe bleeding. That resulted in me having to abstain from parading drills with rifles but I continued with all the other activities. Later, during the rifle handling drill, the staff told me off for not keeping up with the others. Inside airport hangers, various sports were being played. It was a delight for me to be playing some football games against the Iraqi teams. However, during a hockey game I felt scared due to the wild hitting of the hard ball by players with little skill. Many of my companions were not active sportsmen and their late tackles ended in tripping me onto the concrete floor. They were surprised at my ability to break my fall and get up uninjured. One day the station team selected me to play hockey with them in a match against another RAF station. One of my instructors was playing and at the end of the game he apologised to me for not making suitable passes to me during the game.

A long weekend holiday in August enabled me to go by train to London and visit the English family that had accommodated me during the 1957 Jubilee Jamboree of boy scouting. It was nice to be with the Page family after six years and I ended up visiting them again a few times. During some weekends on duty at South Cerney, we had religious gatherings which were only Christian gatherings. There was a split between the Roman Catholic and the Protestant. As my friends in Kenya had been Roman Catholics I decided to go to the Protestant group and could not notice any difference. During our normal classes, we were required to give a talk. That resulted in me giving a talk about Hinduism and intrigued my companions who knew little about other religious beliefs.

During the last month of our training we had been in the Officers' Mess accommodation. We had uniforms and civil suits made by tailors from London. When not in uniform, we had to dress only in suits and could only wear sports jackets on Saturdays. We also had to wear hats with our civil clothes when we went out. In the officers' accommodation, some civilian workers would be cleaning up our rooms and polishing our shoes. During my childhood days my shoes had been polished by an African servant in the house. Having my shoes polished by white people had been unimaginable to me. The company of my new bunch of colleagues in the RAF was a delight. They were surprised that I had been born and educated in Africa.

In the evenings at the Officers' Mess, we gathered at the bar where my friends enjoyed drinking the bitter beer and my drinks were not alcoholic. There used to be a lot of smoking in the bar and in the common room which made it uncomfortable for me. During my final period at South Cerney in November, we heard the devastating news that President Kennedy of the USA had been shot dead. He was the man who had managed to stop the Russians from establishing missile sites in Cuba. I wondered if my new life was going to be affected by global problems. The enjoyment of hearing some classical music in Mombasa on the BBC overseas broadcasts had been a delight for me, but I knew very little about it. However, one of my colleagues on my course had previously been in the RAF music band and he gave me some good guidance into classical music. He recommended that I start listening to Tchaikovsky music. That was my introduction to classical music that was to become a great pleasure in my life.

After our training, a farewell parade took place and we were commissioned to the rank of Acting Pilot Officers with a thin blue line on our jacket sleeves beside the wrist. One day, at our base, I was walking with a friend when we saw a couple of airmen crossing in front us and saluting. We turned around to see who they were saluting and then realised that they were saluting us in our new uniforms. We gladly saluted back in response to the respect shown to us. Then from South Cerney we set off to different training stations for our different aircrew categories, namely pilot, navigator and air electronics. Being an electrical engineer, I had been offered the air electronics category during recruitment and decided to remain with that field, although I could have asked for a different category. My next location for training was RAF Topcliffe near Thirsk in North Yorkshire. When we were departing, some of my companions tossed their civil hats into the river as we would not be required to be wearing them outside our working period.

Warfare air electronics

The training for my job as an air electronics officer (AEO) took place at RAF Topcliffe during the whole of 1964. There were seven of us in a group, made up mostly with people who had already been serving in lower ranks. My room attendant was delighted when I handed him a pair of boots that would not be required for my Topcliffe training. Amongst the various lessons in our flying training we also had the task of learning the use of the Morse code in radio communications, both for flight safety as well as for secretly coded messages that were being used in flying activities. Morse signalling was a new challenge for me after the Semaphore hand signalling that I had been doing with flags as a boy scout. We learnt to produce the sounds that represented letters and numbers by pressing a key in sequences and to be listening to the sounds to identify the letters and numbers. I ended up being able to record 25 words per minute. Our final test required us to be able to use only 18 words per minute. Then we were shown the use of the same code when using a lamp. That turned out to be incredibly difficult for all of us and we were presented with the system at only 8 words per minute using light signals. The use of a different part our brain caused us to struggle with that form of communication. As we didn't expect to ever be using that form of signalling during our flights, we were not tested for them. People who are not sailors will not be aware that lighthouses on our coasts are flashing their identity using the Morse signalling at a very slow rate.

During a two week break in the summer most of my colleagues went to their homes, but I decided to go on a mountaineering expedition course in Scotland together with Dave Kennedy for our holiday break. At a hostel in Coylumbridge, we joined up with various other groups of climbers and enjoyed the social activities in the mixed company. Our group training was for developing some climbing skills. One day we were doing a roped-together walk across an iced slope and did some training for fall protection. Each climber would slip down, slam the axe into the ice to stop the slip and then would crawl back to his roped mates. During my fall, my axe must have been slammed into some soft ice and allowed me to slide down. So, I slammed hard the next time and stopped sliding. Then, there was a pain in my chin and blood was coming out. My face had hit the other end of the ice axe during the re-slam. My chin was cleaned and taped by the others. Fortunately, there was no need for me to be taken to a hospital and we continued with the other activities.

When we were scrambling along a rocky slope, we were suddenly diverted into helping someone who had fallen down that slope. We saw a man at that location lying on his side on a stretcher with his face down and his eyes shut. It made me feel very sorry for that man as he must have experienced some terrible fall. We then carried that stretcher down the rocky slope. At one point during our descent we stopped and the man on the stretcher then got up and turned out to be another instructor. That's when I realised that the rescue had only been a training exercise for us, I was relieved. After a week of lovely activities on the mountain and with the mixed group of people we returned to Topcliffe. To my surprise my colleagues who had gone home during our break told me that they had seen us on television and were disappointed that they had not come with me. Unknown to me my mountain trip had been an opening for mountain safety training and the BBC had been filming us from a distance. I have never seen that programme.

Our flying training started in June in the Varsity training aircraft. We flew around the coast and inland in those twin piston engine aircraft going through a range of training exercises in communications, electrics and safety. We went through more than 100 hours of flying for our training in aircraft electronics during the next six months. We sometimes had strangers talking to us on our radio communications. I was told that those were Russians on a false fishing boat in the North Sea trying to keep tabs on what we were doing. Those strangers sounded friendly, but we were told not talk to them. During the ground training there was a totally new examination system that used multiple choice answers. It was the first time that I had to answer each question by a single selection from four given answers. We didn't have to do any writing and it surprised me to use that system for most examinations during our training.

Aircraft crashes

One evening we heard some terrible news. A Varsity aircraft had crashed on our runway. Two of our training staff pilots had been doing their own regular flying requirements and had shut down one of the two engines for doing a landing with a single engine. Just before their final landing they noticed that they had failed to lower the undercarriage and pushed on the engine power to go around again. Sadly, the single engine power on one wing had lifted the wing on that side and caused the other wing to dip down. Due to the closeness of the ground, that wing touched the ground and resulted in a sudden fatal crash on the runway. That was my first experience of a disaster created in a flash during my RAF training period. It made me feel sorry for them, but I couldn't imagine myself ever being in such a situation.

During the end of our training at Topcliffe, we were programmed to visit another RAF station for a look at the Valiant bomber aircraft. The week before the visit we were told that the aircraft had been grounded and would not be flying again, but we still went there for the visit. There we heard about the incident that was grounding the aircraft. The AEO on that Valiant flight was someone I had met at Topcliffe and he told me what had happened. An incident occurred during their flight at low level. They heard a big bang and the crew of five checked all their systems and looked out as well to locate the cause of the bang. Nobody could find anything wrong with any system or structure and the crew did not have to jump out of the aircraft. The aircraft then climbed out of low altitude and was flown back to their base to land safely. After their landing, a disaster occurred to the aircraft. As the aircraft slowed down both wings dropped down but were still attached to the aircraft. The main spar that was holding the wings together had broken in the middle, but in the air the lift on the wings was keeping the wings and the aircraft up. After landing and slowing down, the lift forces dropped and so did the wing tips. The crew luckily stepped out of the collapsed aircraft in complete safety.

The reason that the V bombers had started low level flying was due to anti-aircraft developments in the Soviet Union. In 1960 the Soviet Union had shot down with a missile a high very altitude reconnaissance aircraft that was flown by American, Gary Powers, over their territory. After that, all British high-level bombers had to be diverted to low level flying for penetration into enemy territory. That's when the heavy bombers designed for flying at 45,000 feet were practising low level flying at only 200 feet and dodging over the terrain. The V bombers were designed to fly at high altitude and high subsonic speed for attacks with ordinary bombs of dynamite. However, the stress received from the severe ground shocks during low flying caused cracks in the aircraft structure and nearly resulted in a loss of the Valiant aircraft and crew in 1964. After that, all of the four-engine V-bombers were grounded and checked for hidden cracks. The Vickers Valiant was grounded for good and the Handley Page Victor was converted to a high-level tanker aircraft for refuelling other aircraft in flight. Only the V shaped Avro Vulcan B2 could cope with the stress of low-level flying. However, for added safety, the bombers had to be flying at lower speeds during the regular practice flights and with suitable stress metering installed on the aircraft to detect any cracks in the structure.

Sports

Sports activities were readily available for participation by the personnel on Wednesday afternoons and weekends. My interest in football resulted in me immediately joining that group and I was selected for the station team for a match against another RAF station. After having scored two goals in that game I was looking forward to more football matches with other RAF stations. However, after the football match, someone who had seen me playing hockey at South Cerney came and asked me to join the station hockey team. He felt that there would be no problem finding football players for the station team, but for the hockey team desperately needed a hockey player and persuaded me to join them. I agreed to join them. When we met up for a hockey match, it surprised me that the players in the hockey team had no idea of how to be playing in the sport. Instead of making controlled passes, the hard ball was hit blindly towards the opponents, which was dangerous even for their own team-mates. I regretted having allowed someone to drag me into playing hockey for RAF Topcliffe.

In front of our accommodation there were some tennis courts and one day, the friend who had dragged me into hockey asked me to join him for a game although I had never played tennis before. He had to tell me the rules of the game and we got started. I managed to play with him until the time when he had to go as he had some other commitment. However, someone else turned up and was looking for a game. That resulted in continuing to play tennis and started making me to get familiar with the sport. After our game, that player asked me where I had been playing before and was astonished to hear that I had started playing tennis that very day.

One day we went for an indoor hockey competition in six-man teams from several RAF stations. We played five matches in an aircraft hangar in which the goalposts were at a low level. During my second game a ball had gone into our goal. To retrieve it I had to duck down below the goal post to bring it out of the net. However, on my way out I had straightened out too early and banged the back of my head on the goalpost. I must have passed out. Strangely my next memory was hearing a referee's final whistle. I found that I was on a hockey pitch in a hangar and couldn't even remember who I was playing for. A companion came up to me and said that was our last game. I couldn't remember anything about any of the games I had played after the second game. My friend said that I had passed out temporarily but had recovered and was back in the play. He said that he had seen me doing well in all the games and had even scored goals. Although there was no bump on my head it was the most puzzling experience in my life. I had been active even when I was not awake!

Social life

Many of my Asian college friends from Kenya had come to Britain for engineering work and experience and we met up in London. Two of those friends even visited me at RAF Topcliffe and it was nice to be together with old friends from Kenya in a new environment in Britain. At the weekends, there would be social meetings and dancing at nearby teacher training colleges of Ripon and Darlington. After a nice dance with one of the girls, I was surprised to be kept on the dance floor with her for many more dances. However, I could not manage to revisit Darlington again. Later, it was one of my companions at Topcliffe who had teamed up with that lovely girl and they even ended up getting married. During some weekends, we were taken out in our uniforms to visit a home for disabled children in the Hambleton Hills to the west of Topcliffe. For me it was fascinating to be with those kids; I even spent a lot of time with one lad in a wheelchair who showed great delight and affection. He even ended up wetting himself in the excitement during our visits.

It was a real delight for me to receive an invitation to the wedding of Paddy Stronge who I had met at South Cerney. For me that was not only my first invitation to a wedding in Britain, but also my first invitation to a Christian wedding. Until then, I had only been to Hindu weddings. At the wedding in Gloucester it was nice to be meeting up with other companions during our initial training. It was a great social gathering for me. At our RAF station there was a music group that would play classical music and talk about it during some evenings. On the radio in my room it was a delight to be listening to classical music on a BBC channel, which was later called Radio 3. In the Officers Mess, we had a piano room where a colleague would play classic tunes on that piano. The ability to play a piano was totally out of my reach. The music of Tchaikovsky was my first delight. That resulted in me going to the Royal Albert Hall in London to listen to the Tchaikovsky music of Swan Lake. That turned out to be not only the music but also the ballet dancing associated with the music. Since then, classical music and dance have produced a real delight for me in my life. During my London visits, it was possible for me to stay in the RAF Officers' Club and was thrilled with the free access to very interesting displays in London, all of which were expanding my view of life. The open art galleries and the museums in London were very interesting and enjoyable.

Since coming to Britain and being in the RAF, my mode of life and clothing had changed. There would be regular formal dinners where we would dress up in our uniform dress suits. The female officers originally had a room in a separate corridor where men were not allowed, but later it ended up being anywhere in the accommodation rooms. One day I was talking to another officer who had been newly promoted from the lower ranks. To my surprise he told me to see him if any of the other officers were not treating me fairly. My actual feeling was precisely the opposite because of the friendship that I was having with all the others.

Sea survival training

Towards the end of our time at Topcliffe in December 1964 we were given a practical experience of being rescued from the sea in the event of having jumped out of our aircraft in flight. From the east coast, we were taken in an RAF rescue boat and dumped into the cold sea wearing nothing other than our overalls and carrying a raft pack. I was so shocked by the cold sea that my friends later told me that they had seen me looking white. A pull on a cord resulted in the raft inflating and enabled me to crawl into it, pumping out the water and pulling the cover over my body. Later, a helicopter arrived, a rescuer revealed himself to me. We got linked and the helicopter winched me up and went around to pick up some more survivors from the sea. Then we were flown to the shore and dumped out. The only extra item we had brought on the long trip from Topcliffe, was a towel to try and dry out our wet overalls. That training was a real shock for me. It seems that in a later sea rescue training, someone had died during the training. That resulted in some better kit being used in future sea rescue trainings in cold water.

My next sea survival training session was carried out during the summer when I was doing the maritime operations training. That time we went to RAF Mount Batten on the south coast from where we were thrown into the warmer sea of the English Channel where we wore a proper immersion suit. That sea rescue training was for me an enjoyable experience. In January 1965, we had completed our training and were given a passing out parade during which we were presented with a flying symbol for our uniforms. That was the AE symbol with a single wing for the new aircrew status of Air Electronics. From there we all went to different RAF stations for different aircraft and different tasks. Air electronics jobs were usually on aircraft that were being used for bombing and maritime patrolling.

RAF Coastal Command

My first posting was on the Shackleton maritime patrol aircraft controlled by Coastal Command. The training centre was at RAF Kinloss in northern Scotland but was moved south to St Mawgan in Cornwall halfway through our conversion training. Six months of ground and flying training for our maritime patrolling in the Shackleton aircraft was mainly meant to keep tags on Soviet ships and submarines during the Cold War phase of our existence. That was the state in which humans displayed their aggressive stance to others to maintain peace in the world. To me the actual use of nuclear weapons in anger was unimaginable. The Shackleton aircraft was a development of the Lancaster bombers of the previous war, with some versions still having a tail wheel. The four sets of propellers on the wings were driven by new Griffon piston engines and because of the low positions of the engines the propellers had to be split into two sets of contra-rotating propellers on each engine. Each of the four engines drove three propellers one way and another three the other way to produce enough thrust for the heavy aircraft. The pride of the aircraft handling on the ground always positioned the two sets of propellers together for each engine after the aircraft had parked.

Inside the Shackleton aircraft there were various seating and operating positions. Right in the front of the Mark 1 aircraft there was bench seating behind the domed windscreen, but the Mark 2 aircraft, with the squadrons, would have a pair of guns. On the floor at the front was the visual bombing sight that the navigators would use in a lying down position. Behind that position, the two pilots sat abeam with a space between them for passage between the front and rear of the aircraft. Facing forwards, the wireless operator sat behind the captain on the left and the flight engineer sat behind the co-pilot on the right. Then two navigators sat facing sideways to the port side and split their tasks between route navigation and target tracking. Beside the navigators there was the sonar operator position used during submarine tracking. After those seats, the radar operator sat facing forward with black curtains around him to enable him to concentrate on the radar display for detecting submarines, as well as providing navigation fixes. After that we had the galley on one side and a bunker on the other side.

At the rear of the aircraft there was a rotatable seat beside each lookout position on each side that enabled us to lean out to get a wider view through a dome window that could be opened inwards to enable photography with an electric camera. Beside one seat there was the operating panel for the firing of display flares upwards and another arrangement for the physical dropping of smoke flares onto the sea surface. Between those two seats there was access to the radar antenna below the floor. During the flight the pilots would extend the radar antenna downwards away from the aircraft to enable good, all-round coverage. Before landing the antenna had to be retracted. The main entrance into the aircraft was via a small set of steps on the starboard side which would be close to the ground after landing as the aircraft had a small tail wheel. Behind the entrance door there was a small toilet with a screen around it. At the tail end of the aircraft there was a small clear portion through which one could look out, mainly by lying down. For me, it was big enough to put myself into a sitting position and enjoy the sights behind us as well as the falling weapons and devices.

The operating task on the Shackleton aircraft required good teamwork by the crew of ten. My job as AEO required the coordinated handling of the electronics team of five within the total team of ten. Different tasks were required during our operating periods and during our transition periods between our base and the operation area. In our areas of operation, we flew at one thousand feet above the sea and manipulated the aircraft for the drop of sonar buoys into the sea for tracking submarines. The electronics operators also had to shift around during certain tasks when we were submarine hunting or attacking. My task would be to set and control the varied operations by my team that also included galley operations. Before our flight we picked up food and drink for the flight. During our training flights, we also had instructors on board. The handling of my task in flight turned out to be immensely intensive and energetic. We went through various stages of training during twenty flights which totalled more than 110 hours of flying time. Some flights during operations were for 12 hours, but on others we flew for less hours. At one stage of our training we went on a flight from Cornwall to Gibraltar. We spent the weekend there before the return flight. Some of the flying during our training was done at night. The final check flight turned out for me to be the most intensive period in my life. I don't know how I managed to go through that flight and be given my rating for Shackleton operations. I was also delighted by the congratulations from my instructor after that flight.

Dental operation

In Yorkshire, I had been given a later dental appointment for the removal of my wisdom teeth because there was not enough room in my mouth for them. There was no dental problem with any of my teeth at that time. As I happened to be in Scotland for that appointment in Lincolnshire, I had to make my own way south to Lincoln. Luckily, an RAF transport aircraft just happened to be at Kinloss for a flight to RAF Waddington in Lincolnshire that was near the hospital base where my dental operation would be carried out. During that flight, I noticed that there was a trailing aerial that was just like the very long trailing aerial for HF communication on our Shackleton. After landing, I happened to comment to the pilot that it surprised me that his aircraft also used a trailing aerial like our Shackleton. However, that surprised him, because he was not supposed to have a trailing aerial. He had to have it fixed before his next flight. At the dental location, I had my first anaesthetised operation to remove my four wisdom teeth plus an extra tooth on the inside of my lower front teeth. After a stay in the hospital for a day of recovery, I then returned to Scotland by train.

Life in Cornwall

After completing the aircraft training, I was delighted to be notified of a posting to Singapore. As my flight to Singapore would be via Aden, I asked for a break at Aden to allow me to visit my family in Kenya. To my disgust my posting was changed to Aden where a Shackleton squadron was also based. Despite my objections, I was posted to Aden and had to stay put in Cornwall for about three months with the 42 Squadron using the Shackleton Mark 2. That squadron did some display flying around Britain. We flew on air displays at Bally Kelly in Northern Ireland and at Finningley in Yorkshire. We didn't have a full crew on those flights and that enabled me to look at the operations carried out by the other crew.

It was on my last flight in Cornwall that the captain asked me to do the firing of the double barrel Hispanic canons at the front of the aircraft. As there were no firing canons on the training aircraft, we had only been shown them on the ground and had not done any firing, I agreed to give it a go; I lined the barrels towards the target of floating skids in a firing range and pressed the firing button. The shock of the guns must have reduced the 160 knots aircraft speed by ten knots. The speed at which the barrels would move was faster than expected and it was a job for me to line them up to the target. It was taking time for the bullets to hit the sea. The co-pilot told me that he had never seen the gun barrels appearing in front of him during the firing. My bullets went out wildly into the Atlantic Ocean. For me it seemed that the experience of firing a gun from a Shackleton was a taste of the fighting life of World War II airmen in the Lancaster bombers from which the Shackleton was developed.

During my time in Cornwall, I had the opportunity to attend the weddings of two more of my close friends from my Topcliffe days. Alastair Steadman used to drive a Minivan and during our breaks in Topcliffe I had been with him to his home in Wales. He was marrying a girl in Wales and it was a delight to be at his wedding in Swansea. My trip by road was with David Kennedy who drove through immense traffic in Exeter and Bristol, where we arrived late at their house for a change of clothes, only to find that they had already left the house. There we found a note telling us how to get in. We managed to get changed and arrived at the wedding in time. We were thrilled with the wedding and meeting many delightful people.

The following month David told me that he was getting married on 25 September and asked me to be the best man at his wedding. That was a great privilege for me. He was going to marry the girl with whom he had spent a lot of time with when we were at Topcliffe in Yorkshire. During our training period we had been together during our training and also in our leisure life.

A break period between my postings enabled me to go to London by train and stay in the RAF Officer club. I visited the art gallery at Paddington Square where beautiful paintings could be seen for free. My walk around London took me to Buckingham Palace where I met an American couple outside. They were amazed to learn that I was serving the RAF. They told me to be fighting the British rather than serving the old colonialists. It's a pity that I did not ask them what they could be saying to the Red Indians in America. My life had been opened up by a country that had not only offered me an education, but also a lot more for my working life.

On my return to Cornwall on a train, there was a young woman with two little girls in the compartment. One of the girls came and sat on me and talked to me as if I was one of her relatives. It was a delight to be experiencing friendliness with people I had never seen before. In Cornwall there was time for me to get involved with the station hockey team at St Mawgan: at a local tournament where someone came and asked me to come for selection in the Cornwall county team. It was disappointing for me to tell him that I would shortly be leaving Cornwall for Aden.

Chapter 5
Shackleton flying in Middle East

Flight to the Far East

It was in November 1965 that the RAF transport aircraft flew me to RAF Khormaksar in Aden located at the south of the Yemen. That was part of the Middle East Air Force division that included Bahrain and Sharjah in the Persian Gulf. On arrival at the 37 Squadron base I was told that my new crew would be flying off to the Far East before the end of the month and would be away from Aden for three weeks. To my surprise, the squadron was happy to let me go to Kenya to see my family and assured me that all the preparations for the long trip would be completed by others in the crew of ten. My new captain was Ivor Gibbs. The flying squadron was small compared to other Shackleton squadrons, but the servicing ground crew were also part of the squadron located in one airport building. Because of the hot climate, our khaki working uniform had open neck shirts with short sleeves. On our legs we wore either trousers and socks or shorts and stockings together with khaki boots. The squadron and crew were introduced to me before I set off for my trip to Kenya.

It was a Hercules aircraft in the transport division of the RAF that flew me to Nairobi. That was a turbo-prop transport plane with four engines built by the USA and I was the sole passenger in a small space beside a wide area for cargo transport, with no access to the cockpit. Although a headset had been given to me it was difficult for me to natter with the pilots about the flying or to see the cockpit display. In Nairobi, it was a delight to be with my sister Krishna and her new family. Then in Mombasa it too was a delight to meet up with my oldest brother, his wife and a little girl who was the first descendent of our generation. They were living in a block of flats near the football stadium. My mother was staying with my brother and used to hold religious gatherings with other women every time she heard about me doing something new in my career. After a delightful time with my family in Kenya I returned to my new RAF life in Aden.

My new crew in Aden set off eastwards across the Indian Ocean at an altitude of 9,000 feet in the tail-wheel Shackleton aircraft. Along the way we encountered a string of thunderstorm clouds ahead of us. As we were not a pressurised aircraft, we normally did not fly at altitudes above ten thousand feet and started dodging between the clouds. Eventually, we were caught by one of the big clouds and were swept up, although the pilots had the control column pushed fully down. On passing up through 10,000 feet we all had to sit in positions where we could do some oxygen breathing. The turbulence continued to push us up to about 12,000 feet. It was a relief when we eventually vacated the storm cloud and then descended to our lower altitude. Our landing was at an RAF Gan on one of a chain of tiny islands south of India and Ceylon. There I happened to join the crew for a drink of lager and found that my head started spinning. From then on, I always drank water first whenever I needed a drink for a thirst. Some of my colleagues also started seeing that it was a good idea in hot weather, whenever we became dehydrated. From the island of Gan, in the Indian Ocean, we flew to the Butterworth base in Malaysia.

After a couple of days of rest, we continued to RAF Changi in Singapore. Together with a Changi-based pilot, we went on a patrol flight in the Strait of Malacca to detect and deter Borneo ships due to Borneo/Malaysia conflict in those days. On my radar screen, I detected an object in the sea that was moving and directed the aircraft straight towards it. The visual sighting turned out to be a small island and not a ship, which baffled the crew. The radar in the affected heat and turbulence had ended up showing me a movement in a stationary target and taught me to be aware of equipment capability in the hot environment. Later in a ground-based trainer, we also carried out some flying exercises for tracking submerged submarines. We would drop sonar-buoys from the aircraft to track underwater submarines and then drop tracking torpedoes to sink the submarines. Those were exercises that had been part of my conversion training, but my crew did not have that training facility in Aden. It surprised me to be posted to Aden where there were no Soviet submarines. It turned out that my activity in a squadron could be different to what I had been trained for.

From our RAF base in Singapore, we flew off northwards over the sea to Hong Kong. Suddenly on the way, we had a strange encounter. Two American jet fighters were flying on either side of us but struggling to fly at our slow speed of only 160 knots. Eventually we established radio communication on an emergency frequency and found that an American aircraft carrier was right ahead of us and was requesting that we did not overfly it. The American fighter pilots were thrilled at having seen our 'Lancaster' bomber and we gave them friendly waves of goodbye. That happened to us offshore of Vietnam in December 1965 when trouble was brewing up in that region.

Our approach for a landing at Kai Tak airport of Hong Kong was extraordinary. Fortunately, the weather was fine. In our descent for the runway we were heading towards a very large chequered board on a hillside with buildings around us and no sight of the runway. About a mile from the chequered hillside we turned right and then the pilots could see the runway ahead extending into the sea. We flew low over the buildings to ensure that we landed close to the near end of the runway and stopped well short of the other end which was terminated by the sea. Hong Kong was cramped with buildings and people. We had a lovely few days there with a taste of Chinese foods and views of many sites. During our exit flight from Hong Kong we flew round the airport again to enable our co-pilot to obtain his approach clearance for the airport for future use. With a lovely view of the surrounding area we did a flyover and flew back to Changi in Singapore. A couple of days later we set off for a refuelling stop in Butterworth in the Malaysian mainland and then continued to Gan Island in the Indian Ocean. Finally, we were back in Aden a week before Christmas. That excursion on an operational aircraft over three weeks, over a vast area of our planet was for me, a thrilling introduction to my active service life.

Aden Protectorate

During the Christmas break it was a pleasure to be spending time with my new companions and their families. The social contact would mainly be with the officers' families. I had social days with the family of Ivor Gibbs

94

and had a Christmas dinner with navigator Bob Lydall and his family. Another AEO on the squadron, Russ Todd, was a good friend and it was a delight to spend time with him and his wife Mary at their flat. Based at Aden there were transport aircraft, Hunter fighter jets and helicopters. In addition to the aircrew there were many other friendly officers in the engineering, administrative and aircraft movement departments. Although people from the same section tended to group together there was plenty of comradeship with others. My room in the Officers Mess was located upstairs and had two beds in it. Occasionally, the room had to be shared with some other officer. As it was not air conditioned, my bed was placed by me to be under the fan that was kept running all the time at night. The bathroom was shared with an adjoining room. I ended up having several showers and changing my clothes during the day.

Aden happened to be in a state of emergency due to the uprisings from two different local Arab groups. Despite Britain having planned to hand over the territory to the locals four years later in 1969, the two different Arab groups were trying to be the first to kick us out and take over the place. Armed British soldiers were around in many places and we were told not to enter the old town in the crater. Although local people were being held and checked by the army, I didn't notice any violence. It was a delight for me to go freely for shopping in town, swimming at the Officers' club by the beach and even went walking up to the top of the crater with a squadron mixed group. There were large crowds in the town when a passing tourist ship was around. Later, our crew was joined by a Nairobi college friend of mine, Ralph Fonseca. We spent a lot of time together and one day we decided to go into the old crater town as, being of Asian origin, we were not going to be seen to be British servicemen. We had no problem and looked around at articles not priced for tourist trade. One day I was on the telephone for the armed services and talking to the operator for some connection. While he was connecting me up, he asked me what part of Yorkshire I came from. He was amazed to hear where I came from. I couldn't believe that I sounded like a Yorkshireman.

1966 Middle East flying

The following year we flew on various bombing and other training flights around Aden in January. At the end of that month we set off on a search flight that was to be the longest flight in my life. We were airborne for 14 hours and 45 minutes. The target for that flight was to find a tanker ship in the Indian Ocean that was suspected of sailing from West Pakistan to Mozambique to deliver fuel destined for Rhodesia. The reason for locating the ship was to stop the fuel delivery to Rhodesia where Ian Smith had declared independence from Britain. He had done that to maintain the white minority control of the country to prevent the Africans becoming independent. We flew up and down over a vast section of the route area of the Indian Ocean between Pakistan and Africa. At our low altitude of flight, we could scan the ocean with our radar. We flew up and down the Indian Ocean and scanned 40 miles either side of our track. We picked up every ship in the connecting area and then we flew down to identify them along each track. We were only looking for a ship called *Anzouletta* going for Africa. We didn't see that ship. Finally, we had to go for a landing at a diversion aerodrome due to the meagre amount of fuel remaining in our tanks. Instead of Aden we headed for Masirah Island that was nearer to our location.

We had started work two hours before take-off for preparation and briefing. All of us were tired by the time we had to fly back. Captain Ivor went and laid down on the floor in the nose of the aircraft to have a little sleep before landing. The co-pilot moved into the captain's seat and I sat in the co-pilot's seat. It got dark and we were slowly tracking to the airport at an altitude of 4,000 feet with the auto-pilot engaged. I was looking out in front of the aircraft and the pilot was leaning forward from his seat to illuminate the approach chart for the Masirah runway using the light under the front panel. Then we heard the navigator saying, "Why are we climbing?" That is when both of us in the cockpit looked at the aircraft attitude display and noticed that it was in a climb position although it had been set for the auto-pilot to fly at a constant level. Adrian tripped out the autopilot and pushed the control column forward to level the aircraft. I noticed that our airspeed had dropped from 160 down to less than 120 knots because we had been climbing without an increase in power. We had been climbing slowly up and the speed had been dropping. If it had dropped below 110 knots, the stall warning would have sounded to alert us to take control manually. Without immediate pilot action the auto-pilot would have tripped off, the aircraft would have stalled, dropped altitude and possibly start spinning. Luckily, we were in the safe recovery state due to the call from the navigator. Then we looked at what had gone wrong.

The co-pilot had been leaning forward to light up his approach chart. That is when his right elbow must have pushed back the additional small auto-pilot control knob on his right-hand arm rest. That little knob could be used to control the auto-pilot to turn left or right and it could be pushed forward or back to adjust its flying attitude. It was that control knob that made the aircraft start climbing without any increase in power and therefore the airspeed was continually dropping. The navigator had noticed the climb because he was trying to shoot the stars with his astro-navigation gear which required level flying. That's what prompted him to query our climbing attitude and thankfully saved not only embarrassment but also our skin. After that long, tiring flight we landed safely at the island of Masirah that was just off the Oman coast, rested the night and flew back to Aden the next afternoon.

Radar mystery

During that trip over the Indian Ocean my radar screen had displayed contacts that were much further than the 40 miles that we should have been detecting at our flight altitude of only one thousand feet. That resulted in me selecting increasing ranges for the radar displays to see how far the radar could display the targets in that area. To my astonishment there were massive radar returns from ships that were four times further away than our radar was supposed to detect at that altitude. Normally the radar wave travels in a straight line like light and should not have been going along the curvature of the earth. Then I realised that those waves do bend when they go through different mediums. Any object that we see with our eyes will look smaller the further away it is located, whereas the radar screen produces bigger radar displays of objects that are further from us, because the radar waves expand as they go further. Later in my life I was to be told about another strange incident that had occurred during a Shackleton flight in the Mediterranean when I was based in Malta. Just like the radar display at long range we could even be sighting with our eyes objects that were beyond the horizon. That incident will be related later.

Shackleton flying days

At the end of January 1966, we flew south to my home town of Mombasa in Kenya. Before reaching Mombasa airport the navigator told us that we were crossing the Equator, but no one managed to see any line below us. Instead, we found that we were flying over a beautiful carpet of small white cumulus clouds laid out in long strings. It was a beautiful garden of white flowers in rows over a massive area. Later, I realized that we do see those sights from the ground, but we don't get the stunning view of them as we do from the top of the clouds. The sight of cloud formations around and below me continued to delight me during my flights. In Mombasa, it was a delight for me to be staying in the magnificent seaside hotel, called the Oceanic on the east side. We were given a lovely break of three days. That enabled me to see my family members in Mombasa again. That break for us appears to have been done in preparation for some forthcoming operations. The month of January 1966 had been a delightful period of dramatic flying experiences in my new life.

Our Shackleton flights also required us to get used to the noise level of the aircraft. Four piston engines with contra-rotating propellers were producing a lot of noise in the unpressurised aircraft. To reduce the noise, the engine speeds could be finely adjusted to synchronise the rotations for least noise generation. This would be done only on a level flight. There were four little rotating dials on display for the engines in front of the pilots. The speed of engine No. 1 was used as the reference and the dial would be stationary. The dials for the other three engines would be spinning at the speed difference with engine No. 1. The throttle of each engine was adjusted in turn to stop the movement in the spinning dials. With all engines running at the same speed, the dial rotations would be stopped and the noise generation was reduced to the minimum, but not nil. The high frequency and noise levels in the Shackleton aircraft must have certainly reduced hearing levels for some aircrew. Any time that the aircraft power was touched, the noise returned to its high level. Somehow, my hearing seems to have survived the many years of noisy flying in the Shackletons.

A nice slack time at the squadron gave me time to settle into the various activities in the office. On a couple of flights around Aden, we did some practice bombing and gun firing on a range. In the earlier days the actual gun firing had been used to deter the local revolts and had only been done the day after leaflets had been dropped at that site. The use of bombs or bullets in anger would only be done by us after a special operation ordered by our authority. Another bombing was done on a target towed by an RAF boat at night. That was an adventurous sport activity for me. In the evenings, I met up with some pilots of jet Hunter fighter aircraft and arranged to go flying with them in that fighter. Although I had been taken to the aircraft on the ground, I failed to find any free time for a flight in it.

South of the Equator

Our squadron commander had been away from Aden at meetings related to the forthcoming task of maritime blockage in the Indian Ocean due to the Rhodesia crisis. The blockage was going to be against shipping carrying cargo to Mozambique in East Africa for the inland Rhodesia colony where the white leader had declared independence from Britain. To carry out surveillance flights in the Mozambique Channel we would have to operate from a location nearer that area. In mid-March 1966, we were the first crew to fly out from Aden and initially stayed at the delightful Oceanic hotel in Mombasa. Until we got clearance for a move further south, we had to operate from Mombasa that was just south of the Equator. We flew south, surveyed the Indian Ocean for about 12 hours and found nothing of interest. For our flight on the next day, we were instructed to land at Majunga in Madagascar after our survey. Majunga is on the northwest coast of Madagascar island that had been a French colony. At the airport, we were met by some of our ground technicians who were the only other RAF people at the location. A crew from another squadron in the Mediterranean were to come there later. Our aircrew was split up into different small hotels for accommodation. There were language problems as it was the first time that we had gone to a French colony. Even our co-pilot could not make his A-level French be understood by the locals. Still, we settled in and went through the French style of eating.

At Majunga we received a signal to tell us that we should be doing a surveillance flight in the Mozambique Channel, but there was no indication of the target ship that we were supposed to be looking for. I had been listening to the BBC world channel on my portable radio and happened to hear the name of the ship that was suspected of supplying Rhodesia. The ship was called the *Manuella*. That was our only briefing for the task on the flight. The next morning, when the transport arrived to collect us there were crew members from one location who could not go flying because their stomachs had been upset by the tap water they had been drinking. We could only assemble a bare crew for the flight and decided to go flying. We gently patrolled the channel with no sighting of that ship or any other suspicious one. After a fruitless flight for six hours we landed and waited for suitable ground support and flight information before taking off again for a search. Also, there was a need to sort out our accommodation and better food supply. I met up with a woman associated with a Frenchman and with whom I could speak in Hindustani as she was an Indian Gujerati girl. That Indian enabled me to have better contact with the locals.

During March and April 1966, we flew ten flights from our base in Majunga on the Madagascar northwest coast for durations of up to 11 hours and surveyed the Mozambique Channel. Our flights might have been the cause of the fuel ships avoiding sailing that channel. The accommodation in the town for our crew was in two separate bungalow flats. In the free time that we had, life was calm and peaceful. There was no sport life for me. It was a joy for me to be listening to music on the radio and my tape recorder. There was little contact with local people, but later we had contact with some young French girls who spoke English. One day we showed them our aircraft on the ground and they were delighted. After we had returned to the UK some of those girls had gone to France and contacted us on the telephone. There was one girl who even got married to a colleague of mine in Scotland.

In the Madagascar Channel of the Indian Ocean we continued with our surveillance flights. On our trip in April 1966 we did sight the suspected ship, the Greek tanker, *Manuella,* heading south and then tried to establish radio communications with a British frigate on the VHF frequency (very high frequency) given to us but failed to do so. Then we flew around to locate the frigate and eventually we sighted *HMS Berwick*. As we were circling around the ship to engage in some communication, a bright light started flashing at us, trying to communicate. We had a flash lamp in our aircraft, but I could not get any of my four experienced signallers on board to perform the task of visual communications. There was no option but for me to perform the task myself. Sitting in the nose compartment I flashed my light at the navy to indicate that we were ready. After every word transmitted there would be a pause until a single return flash had been made by the receiver. It was only when their flashing light had slowed down enough for me to be able to read it that I flashed back to them. Then we engaged into an information exchange. Eventually I communicated with the flashing light the radio frequency on which we could talk to each other. It appeared that they had a problem with their VHF radio and we eventually arranged to communicate on the HF radio that was normally used for long range communications. On the radio we gave them the location of the target ship and flew in that direction. After we had guided the frigate, it was the task of the Navy to check and block the ship if required. We understand that the *Manuella* was made to divert its track away from the Mozambique port.

We had been away from Aden for a month before flying back to our base with a night stop in Mombasa. After a week's break in Aden we ferried an aircraft to Britain for servicing and did not need the full crew. That time we flew from Aden up the Red Sea, across the Suez Canal and landed at El Adem in Libya for refuelling; that was followed by a flight to RAF Luqa in Malta for a night stop. The next day the aircraft was flown and deposited at Bally Kelly in Northern Ireland. All of our flights in our unpressurised aircraft were flown below ten thousand feet and we had to avoid the high Alps. Then we returned to Aden in the RAF jet transport aircraft on a single flight.

Flying operations across the equator

During 1966 we flew on various operations strung out on both sides of the equator between the Persian Gulf in the north and the Mozambique Channel in the south. In the Persian Gulf, we stayed the night at our RAF stations that included Muharraq in Bahrain, Sharjah at the western coast of the peninsula and Masirah Island and Salalah on the Indian Ocean side of the peninsula. From our airport, we were flown on transport flights to Bally Kelly in Northern Ireland to pick up the aircraft we had dropped off about two months earlier for its major servicing. We flew back to Aden via St Mawgan in Cornwall, Luqa in Malta, the Suez Canal and the Red Sea.

Our office hours in Aden started at 7 a.m. and finished at 1 p.m. We had plenty of free time after lunch. I bought a small motorcycle and rode through town to the Officers beach club for swimming and sun-bathing. Aden was in a state of emergency as there was an uprising from the Arabs. There was a group of Arabs being detained by armed British soldiers beside a power station near our Officers Mess. For some strange reason the large electric power station had mistakenly been constructed on the wrong side of the runway. Aden airport had an east-west orientated runway on the flat land between the peninsula and the mainland. The constructors had been misguided by the map markings at the two ends of the runway which were only there for use by pilots during take-offs and landings. The numbers at each end of a runway were an indication of the magnetic direction for the approaching aircraft to be flying for landing and not a magnetic direction out from the centre of the runway. The constructors mistakenly took those to be compass bearings from the centre and constructed the power station on the wrong side of the runway. That is why we had a huge power station close to our accommodation and the sports grounds where hockey was played. The bare ground in Aden was what I had been using in Kenya for hockey.

During July and August 1966, we went to Majunga a couple of times. One of those trips was with direct flight to and from Aden and the other one was with stops in Mombasa each way. On our flight across the Indian Ocean from Madagascar to Mombasa, there was an unusual sighting when I was sitting in the co-pilots seat at night. We were flying over the sea and the navigator was in the process of shooting the stars for navigation. At the end of his calculation the navigator called for a heading change and made the aircraft turn several degrees to the right. Shortly afterwards I noticed that there was a bright light below the horizon on our left side. It looked like the moon below the horizon, but the moon was elsewhere. It puzzled me to see the light below the horizon and wondered if it could have been a ship on fire. Suddenly it occurred to me that it might be the gas flame from the oil refinery in Mombasa and requested the navigator to check his astro-navigation fix. He jumped up for another position fix and then called for a sharp left turn straight towards the horizon light. The navigator had made a mistake in his earlier astronomical scan. He had ended up shooting a wandering planet instead of the fixed star he had chosen for one of the three points he had to use for working out our position. On the heading that he had worked out earlier we had been steering to Somalia. It seems to me that some people cannot tell the difference between a planet and a star. One flickers, but the other does not. A star is like a big flickering flame a great distance away from us in comparison to a planet that is a small steady light at arm's length.

In July 1966, we were on a flight from Aden directly to Madagascar at night. During our flight, we heard a distress call from another Shackleton aircraft that had taken off from Mombasa for Aden. They were in northern Kenya when they had an engine fire that they could not put out. The Air Traffic control directed them for landing at a small nearby airport that was having their runway illuminated by fires on either side of that runway. On their way to that airport the engine fire had safely been put out and the Shackleton crew then decided to continue ahead for Nairobi with the better runway and facilities. We later heard that they had landed safely in Nairobi and there were no casualties or injuries.

Mount Kenya

Back at base in Aden, there was a period when we had very little to do and were contemplating what activity to undertake. That triggered me into convincing the crew that we should go up Mount Kenya. The squadron agreed to let us do it and we set off to Kenya in RAF transport flights. The expenses for a car and accommodation were paid for by the squadron. At the Embakasi airport in Nairobi we had a chance to see the fire damage to our Shackleton aircraft that had been there for a month. There was a massive damage to the engine on the left wing. Fortunately, that did not result in a catastrophe for the crew. When we got to the hotel in Nanyuki near Mount Kenya, two of the crew said that they would not be going any further. The rest of us walked up the mountain and could only get to the highest point for walkers. The highest peak of 17,000 feet required mountaineers to be suitably equipped. We went up to the iced peak of about 15,000 feet. The sight of the mountain, the lovely scenery and amazing plants was great. The experience of that mountain climb in Africa was a delight to us. We had been near the area where a certain young woman had visited and had stayed in a treetop hotel in 1952. She had climbed up the tree as a princess and had come down as a queen.

Persian Gulf operations

In October 1966, we flew on anti-smuggling patrols around the Persian Gulf and took some army officers with us. We spotted a collection of boats on the Indian Ocean side that were most likely to be smuggling in some men from Pakistan. There was a boat loaded with personnel off an island beside which there were stationary boats including a trawler, a tugboat and dhows. The British army was trying to help the Gulf States in preventing illegal immigration and the officers were delighted with their trip with us. Later, we were surprised when the army officers offered to take us on a desert trip.

From Sharjah in the Persian Gulf we were taken in four Land Rover trucks out eastwards into the desert for two nights. That trip turned out to be a very enjoyable experience for me. We motored over the desert area and reached a spot where some tents had been erected. The army personnel set up a dinner for us. Without any form of lighting around us the clear night sky was a fantastic sight. The Milky Way was brighter than I had ever seen it before. One of the army officers told me that he became addicted to life in the desert and planned to transfer to the Trucial States army later. The next day they took us further into the desert towards the eastern area of the Gulf peninsula through a rocky valley which could be heavily flooded during some rainy period. At the end of the valley was another beautiful, quiet and peaceful sight of a green plantation including palm trees with hardly anyone around. Then we motored back and spent another night in the desert. The lovely shapes of sand dunes around us and the clear sky above were beautiful sights and a wonderful experience in my life. It would have been a brilliant holiday outing for many people. That bonus experience for me was a result of an unexpected teaming up with the British Army in the Gulf.

On one free day at Sharjah we planned go to Dubai for a look around and do some shopping. That day we met the RAF crew of a VIP aircraft that was going to Dubai to pick up some VIP guests for a flight to Britain. To our delight, they offered to fly us to Dubai just ten miles away providing we took off our shoes before entry into the aircraft which had a lovely clean carpet. That day we had the delight of our shortest ever flight between two different countries, added to the fact that we went one way in a VIP aircraft.

I had a surprising experience in my flying time when we were in a maritime exercise with the Royal Navy in the Persian Gulf together with ships and one submarine. We were protecting our ships against the *enemy* submarine which was submerged. Our radar would try to detect the submarine when it would extend its periscope out of the water to look around and launch its torpedoes at the ships. If the submarine detected an aircraft, it would dive down and away for another attempt. During the exercise the radar operator was directing the aircraft towards the small spot he had detected. We started to drop some sonar-buoys to track the submarine that had dived down before we had chance to spot it. As we continued after the first drop the pilots spotted a shoal of dolphins creating a visible splash and called for the sonar-drops to stop. After we had flown over the dolphins, I later picked up a signal from the only passive sonar-buoy that had been dropped. That gave us a submarine bearing from the sonar-buoy in the direction of the dolphins and we concluded that the submarine must not have dived deep down and was creating a surface wave on which the dolphins were riding. Although we could not see the submarine, we only needed to follow the dolphins to attack the submarine. We dropped a little depth bomb and back came the reply from the submarine by a flare from the sea, admitting that it had been hit. The submarine must have been puzzled by not hearing anything from us as we had not dropped any active sonar-buoy that produces sound waves in the sea for detection. It was the dolphins that had helped us to attack the enemy submarine. I felt that the forces could do well with enrolling dolphins for our maritime service.

In November 1966, we took some additional personnel on a reconnaissance flight for locating and photographing some trigger points for the protection of the army base. The rebellion of the locals was beginning to affect our inland army base at Habilayn, which needed to set up an airstrip for evacuation. For their own protection, they needed to set up oil lamps on the hillsides to help them locate and fire back at night attacks by the locals. The following year that area was under siege, even though the British forces were withdrawing from the country. Later, we also ended up being involved in active night flights above that area.

My brother's wedding in Dar-es-salaam

It was in December 1966 that I took some days off work to get to Kenya to be with my family. That time it was for a special occasion when my eldest brother, in Mombasa, was going to drive to Dar-es-salaam in Tanganyika to be at the wedding of my brother Krishan who was getting married to an Indian girl. Just short of Dar-es-salaam we were going up a slope on the edge of a hill. Suddenly there was a bang and the car swerved right across the road and was heading towards a downhill drop. My brother swung the drive back and we ended up gently slamming into the left hillside and stopping. As our car had no seat belts in those days, I ended up banging my head on the windscreen. Luckily the windscreen had not smashed and we were able to get out without having any major injury. The crash was caused by a puncture in the front right tyre. Eventually we recovered and got to the wedding location in Dar-es-salaam. My brother Krishan had been working there for East African Railways since 1964 and had decided to get married to the daughter of an Indian family with whom he got on well.

1967 adventures

Between December 1966 and my departure from Aden in July 1967 we had a lot of mixing of the aircrew on flights. We flew from RAF Sharjah in the Persian Gulf, delivering and collecting aircraft for major servicing in the UK and some flights to Mombasa and Madagascar. Overall, I must have spent more days away from Aden than those in Aden. It was in February 1967 that we carried out many reconnaissance operations from Sharjah and Masirah around the Persian Gulf and the Gulf of Oman. The air traffic control at Masirah would only give us a clearance for landing after the runway had been cleared of donkeys that used to stray in to feed on some grass. In the bar at the base there was a door that was labelled as Masirah Scenery. On opening that door, we found that all we saw was bare flat sandy ground and had to shut the door to retain the air conditioning in the bar. During our stop there we were asked by a station hockey player for us to play against his RAF station team who were preparing for some armed services competition in Muscat. Ralph and I decided to give them a game with our crew of ten, provided we were supplied another player. They gave us a Pakistani worker to make up our hockey team. Because our co-pilot did not fancy running around, he got padded up as our goalkeeper. The rest of the crew were spread out in some formation. We took on the opposition and gave them a fierce fight. Strangely, we even ended up in beating the Masirah team. They were shocked that a flying team could beat a hockey team on their home ground. The Shackleton crew were delighted to be able to become a hockey team as well.

In March 1967, we then went to the UK in a transport flight to collect our Shackleton from Bally Kelly. However, that was the period when a war had started between Egypt and Israel and we could not fly back via the Suez Canal. As we could not fly over high ground we were programmed to fly via Africa. We then had to plan a four-day route via Libya, Nigeria and Kenya to return to Aden. It had been a problem in Malta that made us route our first flight from Britain to Tripoli in Libya where we landed at the American base called Wheelus AFB. When having drinks in the evening with some other aircrew out in the open, we were shown a small circle of sticks they had piled up and had set fire to. In the middle of the circle there was a scorpion. As the creature was surrounded by flames and could feel the heat from all directions it curled its tail into its own body and stung itself to death. I felt really disgusted to see the lack of respect that humans had for other forms of life on our planet.

The next day, we took off from Tripoli and flew south over the Sahara Desert for Kano in northern Nigeria. Flying for six hours above the desert did not have anything like the delightful view that I had experienced when we were motoring on it. After booking in at a hotel in Kano, we were taken out to the tourist attraction of Kano which was an old walled city. As we wandered around, we were swamped by a crowd of children. They were beautifully dressed and to my surprise the little girls even had red lipstick. All of the kids were extremely friendly and spoke English. I was delighted to have seen and contacted the most unusual collection of kids. We then went up the stairs to the top of a tower. From the top I could see lovely views all around. To my surprise all of the children below us started to wave to us at the top. It was a great delight for me to wave back to the mass of cheerful kids below us.

There was also a nearly distasteful experience for me in Kano. I must have been turning in my bed in the morning when I was woken up by a hotel waiter telling me that he had poured me a tea and then he quickly rushed out of the room. After having the tea and getting changed I noticed that the top pocket of my uniform jacket had been undone. That was the pocket in which my wallet had been placed. Fortunately, my wallet and all the money in it were still there. Luckily, it was my body turning in my sleep that had saved me my wallet contents. From Tripoli, we flew over the delightful countryside to Nairobi. There my captain allowed me to drop off from the flight back to Aden. That enabled me to spend some time with my family and friends in Kenya and would make my own way back to Aden after a break.

During April and May 1967, we flew in two exercises with the Royal Navy *HMS Onslought*. One exercise was around Aden and the other was around Mombasa. On one of those exercise flights over the Indian Ocean off Mombasa I experienced a wondrous sight from the gunnery position at the front of the aircraft. As we flew around low clouds, a full circle rainbow appeared and would be moving around with us before suddenly disappearing. Not many people are aware that a rainbow can be a full circle. The circular rainbows appeared several times during that flight. My flying period also presented me with a new vision of our beautiful natural sights.

During our flights from Aden we escorted a navy fighter aircraft on two trips around the inland hills and valleys. I sat in the tiny space at the back of our aircraft and the single pilot in the Gannet aircraft and I waved to each other. He then made some strange waves with his hand and made me notice that one set of his propellers had stopped rotating, but another set continued rotating. The Gannet had a set of contra-rotating propellers like ours, but each set was being driven by a separate engine. By shutting down one engine only half of the propellers stopped rotating, but the other half continued providing the thrust with extra power from the operating engine. That pilot must have enjoyed seeing the puzzle in my face. I tried to get my captain to stop both sets of contra-rotating propellers on one of our engines, but he didn't want to play the game. Escorting the Gannets around the hills that day was good fun for me.

Close encounters in flight

We were flying through lovely scenic valleys and I was lying in the front bomb-aimer's position to look at the beautiful scenery below. The navigator called for a turn into the valley on our left when the other navigator said that we had not reached the valley that had been planned. The senior navigator continued to take us through his selected valley that got narrower and suddenly it was blocked ahead. As there was not enough space for us to turn inside the valley, we had no option but to slam on the full power of all four engines and the pilots shouted to the flight engineer to inject the engines with protection fluid necessary at full power. From my bomb-aimer's position I could not see the sky ahead, even though we were in a maximum climb attitude. I even felt the urge to vacate my position from the front. Instead of going past me the ground below continued to zoom up towards me. There was a moment when my heart was in my mouth. Then, suddenly, the ground disappeared, and the sky appeared. That was a great relief for me after a short intense fright during a flight.

On another day, we flew out into the north-western desert to locate the rebels bringing in explosives into Aden and the army would do the rest. Our navigators found that we had no maps of the area for the search. Our headquarters in Steamer Point sent us the maps of that area. With the vast area of the desert there were hardly any features to be seen. Still the navigators needed the maps for drawing their route and the height markings for safety. When flying over the desert we saw a dust storm ahead of us and climbed up to our safety height before entering the storm. I was sitting at one of the two lookout seats at the back of the aircraft as we entered the dust storm. Suddenly, both of us at the back saw sand dunes passing us at our level on both sides and shouted out to the crew. The pilots immediately piled on the power and continued climbing until we were out of the sand storm. Only then could we look at what had happened. The navigator then admitted that he had failed to see that the numbers for heights shown on the map we had been given were in metres and not in feet, which our aviation maps always have. We were lucky to have seen sand dunes passing us from the sides and not encountered one directly from the front. Strangely, during my flying days I had been in situations where lives could have been terminated instantly and yet that never made me quit flying.

It was in my later life that I became aware of a similar situation that had been experienced by civilian people flying in 1947 in the Avro Lancastrian aeroplane with a tail wheel. My Shackleton Mark 2 also had a tail wheel. The Lancastrian Mark 2 for passengers was flying to Santiago from Buenos Aires over the Andes Mountains that were under the clouds. On believing that they had crossed over the mountains the crew contacted the airport by radio using the Morse code to state that they were descending for their approach for landing. After that, the airport failed to make any contact with them, nor find any crashed aeroplane. Strangely, that mystery was solved in the 1990s when the wreckage of the 1947 air crash was found. It had crashed on the eastern side of the mountains because the crew had started descending far too early. The Lancastrian crew had no idea of their speed over the ground because they were unaware of the jet-stream of more than 100 knots that was against them. The simple mistake that the crew had made was similar to what we had made in our Shackleton flying when we were very close to ploughing into the sand dunes in the Middle East. Our mistake was caused by us not noticing that the heights on the map presented to us were marked in metres and not in feet, as used in all our flying maps. I have no idea when our bodies would have been discovered if we had been buried in a sand dune.

Real action flights

During May 1967, we flew on some flights that required real action from us. The first one was on 15 May when we flew on a very special mission where the bombing ban of more than two years had been lifted just for that flight. Several twenty-pound fragmentation bombs were to be used against some terrorists who were smuggling in bombs that were being used against the forces in Aden. We took off at night and patrolled out at sea, waiting for a call from the inland army. Our target group were sleeping in a cave and our army men were waiting for them to come out. Finally, we had the call to start the attack and flew inland. As we started getting closer to the target, we had a call from the army to abandon the attack. The enemy had heard the aircraft and fled. The reason for the attack to be abandoned was that they had joined up with a group of wandering Arab people.

The RAF and Navy encountered nothing like the regular fighting that the Army dealt with. I felt great respect for our soldiers in their duties. With the massing of nuclear weapons there was little chance of world warfare, but we didn't expect to be involved using ordinary bombs for real. That was the first time when we came closest to be involved in doing a killing in our job. It would not have given me delight, but it also did not give me a fright. It was going to be for the protection of other people's lives.

The other flights on which we were involved with fighting actions was in the inland army base area at Habilyan. I flew on three sorties that were used mainly for illuminating the mountain area to help our army to fight back night attacks to the base that was in the process of evacuation. We did not use any weapons, but we flew around the area at a high level and fired out illumination flares to help the army. Below us there would be flashes from the attackers and the army. To me it looked like a spectacular firework display. We were not involved in any fighting action. In the morning after flight at night, we were shocked to hear what the ground-crew told us. Our aircraft had been hit by a single bullet that they found lodged in a post by the radar operator position. We thought that we had been flying high enough for safety, but it must have come from someone sitting on a hill with a rifle and we must have been close to in a turning. We were lucky that the bullet had not hit any person in the aircraft.

In the Officers' Mess we used to hear explosions and saw tracer bullets flying up the nearby hillside. Just before I left Aden there was a violent attack by the British army against the rebels in the old town of Aden where Colonel Mitchell (Mad Mitch) had killed some rebels, even before he had been properly authorised for the attack. My last flight on the tail wheel Shackleton Mark 2 aircraft was when we dropped a thousand-pound bomb into the ocean. That was not done in anger, but for dumping it into the sea in an inert state. My next posting took me to northern Scotland for flying in the Shackleton Mark 3 aircraft that had a nose-wheel.

Biggest shock in my life

It was during my last year at Aden that I was ready for a family life of my own. Despite my immense satisfaction with life in Britain, my Indian origin persuaded me to have my lifetime bondage with an Indian girl. My search for a wife was during my visits to Kenya. Finally, I found a young girl from a family who had known my family for a long time. After the end of my tour of duty in Aden in 1967 we got married in Kenya to enable us to start a new life. Inconceivable to me, that marriage was later to become the biggest failure in my life. For my relief, I have had to totally erase the memory of that relationship from my mind.

Chapter 6

Maritime aviation from Scotland

RAF Kinloss

Scotland was the land that I had first visited in 1957 as a Kenyan boy scout. In 1965 a few months of my RAF training period had been at RAF Kinloss in the Moray Firth. Then in 1967 my posting on the Shackleton Mark 3 aircraft with 201 Squadron made me return to Kinloss in Scotland. My first car was bought by post from Aden. It was presented to me at RAF Brize Norton in Oxfordshire. That Morris Minor estate car enabled me to drive to London to be with my sister and family for a few days. Then from London it took me ages to drive up to Forres near Kinloss in Scotland. The Mark 3 Shackleton aircraft of my new squadron felt very different to the Mark 2 which was a formation of loose rivets flying in close formation. Despite that, flying in the Mark 2 Shackleton had been great fun for me. The improved Mark 3 aircraft had a nose wheel and two additional jet engines added to its four piston-prop engines. The jet engines were only used for take-offs because of the increased aircraft weight. Those engines were not visible as they had been tucked in behind the two outer prop engines and used the same fuel. The interior of the aircraft looked and felt much better, but most of the operational equipment was the same as before.

My new crew of eleven on the Mark 3 Shackleton was captained by an Australian and the navigator was my companion from Aden. We flew from Scotland on long range operational flying exercises (LROFE) and practice bombing sorties over the small militarised island of Theddlethorpe. One day we had to abandon our bombing as there were fishermen who had intruded into the military zone to pick up some of the fish that had floated up to the surface after one of our bombs had splashed into the sea. I felt sorry for the fish, but it would have sickened me if we had killed any human during our practice bombing. Our low-level flying gave us the lovely scenic views of the northern coast of Scotland. On a flight in the Pentland Firth we flew close to a beautiful Spanish sailing ship and the photograph I had taken with the camera in the aircraft was selected as one of the prize winners for that year by the RAF Coastal Command.

Persian Gulf again

Most of the squadron departed from Scotland for operations in the Persian Gulf in December 1967. That detachment was for three months, where we would be assisting the Gulf States in tackling their illegal immigration problems. Four of our Shackleton's were flown to Sharjah and some of us were taken there by our transport aircraft. Even our squadron commander was out there with us. That detachment was going to be a big break for a lot of the staff who would be away from their families. We started our surveillance flights for detection of dhows in the Indian Ocean, east of the Trucial States peninsula. In 1968 there were many flights from Sharjah and we sighted many of these small sailing ships. We also got chance to see them on the ground under construction in Dubai. That reminded me of my sailing across the Indian Ocean from Africa to India on a similar dhow in 1945. Despite the fact the dhow we had boarded had sunk near the coast of India, it was a delight for me to be looking at them.

After some bombing and gunnery practice sessions on a firing range in the desert at the Jebajib location I also carried out a duty as a firing officer on the ground for controlling the aircraft on their bombing runs. The drive to the bombing site was also an adventure for me. First, we drove from Sharjah along the open sand track of about ten miles to Dubai. From there we found ourselves on a lovely tarmac road in the desert. Then we came to a big roundabout that only took people back to where they had come from. It seemed to be a desert pleasure drive for the locals with plush cars. However, we continued driving on sand in the direction for our bombing range. Occasionally there would be a track left by some vehicle. At the bombing range, I would communicate with the aircraft for clearances for their bombings. One day a pair of Arabs appeared at the bombing site. They were trying to continue through it, we stopped them but could not communicate with them in Arabic. Then an aircraft called me on the radio for a bombing for which I gave a clearance. As they approached and dropped some bombs on a target, the Arabs ended up disappearing back to where they had come from.

During our stay in Sharjah we had many aircraft problems and ended up having a lot of free time. There was also a Canberra squadron at that location and I went flying with them on a practice bombing run. They took me flying in a spare seat, but it was a seat without an ejection fitting. They briefed me that in the event of flight problem they would tell me to jump out with the parachute strapped to me. They told me not to query their instruction as I would only be talking to the two bangs that I would be hearing next. We took off and flew to the bombing range. Instead of dropping their bombs from a level flight, the Canberra dived down from a good height, pitched down to the target in view from the cockpit, released the bomb and pulled up with a great g-force. My stomach failed to keep up with the severe forces and I managed to grab my sick bag and bomb it with food from my stomach. We continued with several bombing runs and there was nothing more to throw up out of my stomach. In my Shackleton flights my stomach had adapted, but it could not cope with the greater g-forces in the dive bombing. One experience of dive bombing was more than enough for me.

We also went on unusual drives into the desert to various locations around the area, but not as deep as we had previously been taken by the British Army. One day in a desert drive we stopped for a coffee drink at a small local place. There I found that the lad serving us could talk in Punjabi. He might have come from Pakistan on one of the boats that we were monitoring. Although we wore our uniforms, we ended up wearing the Arab headscarf instead of hats. One day I was beside a beautiful plantation and was waiting for the others to return from some excursion. In that vastly isolated position there was a man sitting sideways on a donkey and going past me. Although he was more than fifty yards away from me, he stopped, got off his donkey and walked all the way to me, bowed to me and said *'Salaam Alaykum'* to which I replied *'Alaykum Salaam'*. We shook hands and he went back to his donkey and continued with his transit. It really touched me to have a respectful contact with another human in a remote place. Later, beside a pumpkin field, a local person turned up. When I said that the fruit looked very good in the desert field, he cut one pumpkin out and gave it to me. I was greatly impressed by the goodwill of the people living in the desert.

Because of all the problems that we were having with our aircraft there used to be jokey comments about our operations. Our squadron commander decided to hit back with a plan to fly our four aircraft in a formation. After intensive servicing work we went flying in a diamond shape formation. That achievement surprised the RAF staff in Sharjah. The four-aircraft formation flying was an enjoyable event not just for us, but also for the local people in the area around Sharjah. After having been away for three months we then packed our bags and went back home to Scotland in March 1968. My flying days around the Middle East turned out to be far more than expected.

Northern Ireland

In May and June 1968, we carried out some training exercises from Bally Kelly in the Londonderry province of Northern Ireland. As the Shackleton could do without me on transit flights, I decided to drive there in my car in order to do some touring of Ireland. A scenic drive took me through Scotland and then a ferry took me to Belfast. From Bally Kelly in the north channel of the Irish Sea between Ireland and the Mull of Kintyre in Scotland we flew on various maritime exercises. There were times when we would be flying low over the sea in cloudy conditions in the channel and had to be very alert about flight safety. There had been an earlier incident in such conditions when a Shackleton had flown so low that it had bounced off the sea and lost its extended radar antenna. That particular crew was lucky to have landed safely. My car enabled me to do some touring around the beautiful countryside and meeting friendly country folk. A remarkable display of natural rock creations on our planet is the Giants Causeway on the north coast. Luckily, my tour of Northern Ireland was done at a time just before the start of the terrible Christian religious conflicts that were later to be pathetically affecting that beautiful region.

Norway

In July 1968, I had the delight of my first flight into the Arctic Circle. We flew to Bodo in Norway where the sun was up for the whole day. It never got dark and we had to draw curtains to darken a room to sleep. On our transit flights, we normally took at least one ground crew assistant with us. The flight in and out of Bodo was very scenic, especially as we had lovely weather. We flew northwards over the ocean for our anti-submarine operations. We patrolled the Norwegian Sea for detection and tracking of Soviet conventional submarines that had to come up nearly to the surface for battery charging. The new nuclear submarines could remain underwater all the time and detecting them would be carried out by replacement aircraft being developed.

That year I also flew with another crew for a trip to Norway when the day had become very short. The nights had become a lot longer and the street lights in town were on almost all the time. However, the sight of the night sky in Norway was a new experience for me. We were inside the Arctic Circle and I found myself standing underneath the brilliant wavy sky waves called Aurora Borealis that were swaying about. Strangely the green lights rose above the horizon when further away from me, unlike normal clouds that appear to be getting lower when they are further from us. During our flights we did see those spectacular waves around us. Those displays are created by electrons ejected from the sun at very high speed and become trapped by our strong magnetic fields near the magnetic poles. On another trip to Norway in winter for sea surveillance we spent some time in the sauna rooms. What amazed me was that the location had hot saunas and cold showers. I couldn't see the point of taking a cold shower after a hot sauna, but I decided to do it and felt a real shock. After that my body did not feel the cold even when we came out. My entrance into the building had been in a thick cold weather coat, but during my exit it felt that one didn't need much clothing. It seems that the Norwegians would even jump naked into cold lakes. That was something that didn't appeal to me.

On one of our transit flights back home from Bodo we had unexpectedly sighted a snorkelling submarine in the sea and the captain called for a sonar tracking operation. The Soviet submarine had not detected us as we had not been using our radar during our transit flight. The submarine must have only sighted us after we had descended. It dived down out of our sight and we dropped our sonar buoys for tracking it. From all the sonar buoys that we had dropped we got no return signals and wondered what had gone wrong with our system. After landing we snagged the system and some days later, we heard the reason for the failure. The batteries in the sonar buoys had been removed by someone during our return transit flight to hide cigarette packages from the customs man at home. In those days, each sonar buoy was manufactured at a cost as much as that of a mini car. I had not been a smoker and it puzzled me why humans like to put smoke into their lungs for pleasure. Also, I don't know why I was bringing in cigarettes for other people.

Scotland

At Kinloss we played hockey during the winter months when it could be very cold in Scotland. I played for the Coastal Command team against other RAF teams. Our team only got together for the first time to play as a team and came from Kinloss and Edinburgh in Scotland, St Mawgan in Cornwall and Bally Kelly in Northern Ireland. Those sporting activities were a delight, but my flying duties did limit my participation in some sport events around the country.

A holiday break in the summer enabled me to go touring in my car around the scenic northern part of Scotland. There were numerous islands in Britain along the hilly west coast. The roads got narrower on the hills and there were numerous passing places for the very few cars travelling in opposite directions. On a narrow road taking me to Lochinver, my brakes failed to operate and stopping could only be done with the handbrake. I continued to drive slowly for about ten miles to Lochinver with one hand on my handbrake and managed to get there without meeting another car. At a Lochinver garage they told me that it would take more than three days for my car to be fixed because they did not have the spare parts. The unplanned stay in that lovely location turned out to be delightful.

In Lochinver, an English couple from London knew about my car problem and offered to take me on their day's drive up the west coast. The man used to be a military driver during the war. Somewhere in that area there was a strange sighting of a sub-tropical garden with palm trees. The hot Gulf Stream in the Atlantic passed close by Scotland and had enabled tropical plantations. After my car repair I drove southwards and took a ferry from Ullapool to Stornoway in the Hebrides Isles. The drive around that island for a couple of days was a real delight. The local people at a small café were chatting away in their Scottish language. After I spoke to them in English, they said to me that they could not stand English people. However, they welcomed me to the Hebrides. My regret is that I had not visited the Hebrides caves at the coast. The lovely music overture of Mendelssohn about the Hebrides called *Fingal's Cave* has been a great delight for me for decades.

Home gardening had never been in my life before living in a rented cottage in the very small village of Moy on the western side of the Findhorn Bay in Scotland. It amazed me to see an elderly man digging in my front garden one day. He turned out to be one of my neighbours who had decided to sort out my garden for me. He dug out part of the front garden for a potato plantation. That is when my interest in gardening was triggered. In the cottage in Scotland there were many domestic gardening tools provided by the landlords. I even cleared the bigger area on the other side of the entrance and finished seeding it with grass to make a new lawn. Also, during the coming of the New Year my Scottish neighbours gave me a real treat for their celebrations, which are very passionate in Scotland. With them I drank some lovely Scotch whisky. My neighbours recited the Scottish poem of Robert Burns called *Auld Lang Syne* (old long since) which I had come across before, but there was a real passion for it in Scotland. That poem can be seen in Addendum 1.

While in Scotland I had started looking to purchase a house, something that had never entered my mind before. It was a magazine that had implanted in me the thought that a house purchase would be the best form of saving that a person could make in Britain. A cottage in Findhorn could be bought with a mortgage of about £2,000 and at a new bungalow in Forres was on sale for a massive £5,000. The guide who was showing me the house was looking for the gold bricks that must have been used for the construction of an expensive house. As my next RAF posting was to Malta for a maritime controller post I had to wait until my return to Britain to buy a house. All my possessions were packed in suitcases which were collected by RAF transport from the house and transported to Malta. They were delivered to me when I settled into a house there. In the military services, shifting one's job between locations in different countries was no problem at all.

Chapter 7

Three years in Malta

RAF Luqa

During my time in the flying branch of the RAF there was one period that involved a tour of ground duties starting in March 1969. That posting was for the control from the ground of various maritime flying operations in the Mediterranean. The operations were from Luqa aerodrome in Malta, which was used by both the civilians as well as the military. The new job required me to carry out the ground briefing of flying crews, receiving messages during their flight, collecting information after the flight and transmitting it to headquarters in Rome. Initially, the flying operations were carried out by the Shackleton Mark 3 aircraft. Later the four jet-engine Nimrod, developed from the Comet, came into maritime service. Our maritime operations room was beside the RAF transport flight operations, but unlike them we operated only during the weekdays, most of the time. Weekends and full day operations were only activated for some exercises or emergencies. We had three operations controllers sharing the duties and that gave me a lot of free time. My duty times could also be rearranged to enable me to start some new sport activities.

In Malta, the RAF personnel could buy a new car with complete tax exemption. A new Renault 4 cost me £450. That was paid by me in cash. Some of my friends bought expensive Mercedes cars for about a thousand sterling pounds. Additional overseas allowances were given to us and that enabled me to start saving money for buying a house in Britain on my return. In those days, ownership of a house was not common, as RAF people lived in the staff Mess, service quarters or rented houses. One of the delightful sights in Malta was the Lockheed Super Constellation aeroplane parked outside the Luqa airport. The early airliner that had four piston-engine propellers, a triple rudder tail and a beautifully curved body. That was the aeroplane type on which I had experienced the first flight of my life in 1957 from Mombasa to Britain over the Alps. It was a delight to be seeing the aeroplane that had initiated my interest in flying.

Shortly after I had gone to Malta there was a fatal crash of a Shackleton aircraft in Britain. An aircraft that was flying from Kinloss to Bally Kelly in Ireland had crashed on the Mull of Kintyre in Scotland. It had crashed due to a severe icing occurrence on the tail. Unfortunately, everyone on board that plane lost their lives. On board that aircraft was someone who had been a friend to me even before I joined the RAF. That was Ralph Fonseca who had been with me in college in Nairobi. Later, we had flown together in Aden for two years. In my RAF days, there had been various air crashes before, but the loss of my old friend made it difficult for me to come to terms with an early loss of a life. That is what all the people of the armed services on our globe needed to start accepting.

Maritime operations in the Med

The maritime flying tasks in the whole of the Mediterranean were requested by NATO headquarters in Rome for keeping an eye on Soviet maritime activities. My task in the operations centre was for collecting the information and briefing the flight crews for their reconnaissance mission around the sea area. Two hours before their flight, the crew of eleven would be briefed in a hall surrounded by massive map displays of the Med. They would then go to their aircraft on the other side of the runway. During their flight, their transmitted messages would be received by a communications setup located in our building and delivered to me. After their flight, the captain would come to our control centre and provide the information for a report on the flight. I would then transmit their significant messages and the debriefing information to our controllers in Rome.

My working day in Malta covered a 24-hour period. It would commence around midday and finish after the final tasks some time during that evening. At least half an hour before the briefing of the next morning flight I had to be back in the control centre. The task would be handed over to another controller at midday and we had 24 hours off work. Occasionally, there would be three controllers on duty and we could be having 48 hours off work during the week. At the weekends, we all had time off unless there was some operational or search and rescue flying requirement. My maritime operations job was linked with an intelligence team with which I had close contact as our jobs were also closely related. My time at work could be very intensive and prolonged, but after work there would be a lot of free time and resulted in me having many physical activities. At my annual medical check for aircrew, a young doctor was surprised to see that my blood pressure readings were the same as the normal figures of 120/80 that were stated in his textbook.

During their surveillance flights, the RAF aircraft sighted many Soviet warships and occasionally submarines. Although the guns and the radars of the Soviet warships would be tracking our surveillance aircraft there was no likelihood of any firing action. It was a practice of aggressive posturing done almost in a friendly manner. One day our aircraft had sighted a Russian submarine near the surface which then dived down after sighting the aircraft. The Shackleton dropped some sonar buoys for tracking the submarine. Then surprisingly, the submarine popped out of the water, moved close to a sonar buoy and roped it in. The Shackleton aircrew could only shake their fists at the Russian submarine for not playing the game. There was no referee for penalising them for their rule breaking.

One day there was a frightening occurrence on a Shackleton in flight over the sea. One of the outer engines of the Shackleton seized up in flight and the contra-rotating propellers broke off and went flying out in all directions. Most of the propellers fell into the sea, but bits went through the top of the cockpit and some went through the fuselage. Fortunately, no one was severely injured by the debris and the aircraft returned safely to base.

During a debriefing of the crew after their flight in the Mediterranean on another day I was told about a very unusual experience during their flight. On their flight the pilots reported to the navigator that they could see an island when they were supposed to be further out over the sea. The navigator jumped off his seat and had a look at the island that was visibly closer than planned. He jumped back onto his seat and did another navigation calculation. He worked out the same position as before, threw away his pencil and wandered off his seat to the back of the aircraft in disgust. The other navigator then took over the navigation and the crew continued their flight with the mystery of the island sighting. Although they were looking at a small sight of a massive island, it looked exactly like the small drawing on their maps that should have been out of their normal sight. That reminded me of the distance radar sightings I had in the Indian Ocean in 1966 that was caused by radio waves bending over the horizon because of the temperature changes in the atmosphere. Light waves are also electromagnetic waves that enable us to send some radio messages to long distances.

Greece

Among the various NATO exercises in which we participated there was one that was going to be run for the first time by the Greeks in Athens. To help the Greeks three of us RAF people were sent to Greece. I went to Cyprus and then flew to Greece together with the others to help the Greeks control that exercise for two weeks. Visiting a beautiful country and meeting friendly Greek people in town was a great delight for me. The castles and monuments that I had read about and seen on television were to be seen for real. The only thing that bothered me was the passage through customs in both directions. They gave me extra attention as they thought I might have been a Palestinian. In those days, young Palestinians used to hijack civil aeroplanes that would then be landed in Palestine, the passengers off loaded and the aeroplanes would be blown up.

Malta life

My stay in Malta was in a flat in Masirah that was also occupied by other RAF and Army personnel. My earlier friends in Aden were in the same block of flats as me. I also met and got on well with an Army couple living beside me and a Maltese family living opposite me. The houses of all the local Maltese were kept in an immaculate state. There were many friendly service personnel in that area, including someone who played in the hockey team that had turned out to be my major sporting activity in Malta. We played on the type of bare ground I had played on in Kenya. We played friendly matches against hockey teams from the Services as well as the civilians. We even went to Cyprus for hockey competitions for various RAF groups in Malta and Cyprus. There were many Anglo-Indians in the forces in that location. On one trip to Cyprus there was a match between my Near

East area team against the RAF hockey team on a tour of hockey. Surprisingly, we managed to beat the RAF team. After the match, one of the RAF team players asked me when I had played for the RAF and was surprised to know that I had never played for the RAF. My flying duties had prevented me from getting too involved with sporting activities.

Deep sea diving

Deep sea diving was something that I started doing by using a compressed air tank strapped to my back. We also had blocks of lead in a belt to try and maintain our depth during diving. As we used up the air in the bottle our weight would become reduced and we would need less lead weight for balance, but we could not dump off lead weights, nor do anything to maintain our balance. We ended up with being too heavy to start with and too light at the end. Still the experience of remaining in the sea like a fish was a wonderful state to be in. I managed to get through the training exercises to obtain a diving certificate to be able to able to dive on my own. The initial dives were down to sea levels that were still warm, but the deeper ones required the use of diving suits that fitted the body well. At first, we dived down to thirty feet where the pressure on our bodies would be double that on land. For deeper dives the air was drawn out at a higher pressure and reduced the time for the dive.

Being down in the sea and looking at life and scenery was to me a rare experience. The sights of fish, small octopus and many other creatures and life forms were a real eye opener for me. In a small cave, we saw lovely colours and shapes. What surprised me in the ceiling of the cave was what almost looked like a puddle of water above our heads. It was the bubble of air trapped in the ceiling created by the air we had exhaled into the sea. Diving deep into the sea opened up a delightful new experience in my life. At the end of the dive we had to come up in stages to prevent the body suffering from trapped higher pressure air. There was a lot of skill training required to enable one to dive safely. I managed to get down to a hundred feet, although I was not supposed to be doing that during the training.

Horse riding

My experience of horse riding started in Malta with an armed services club that looked after the horses and provided training to the service families. That experience had been prompted to me by one of the ground crew who was working with me and who was one of the instructors at the horse stables. They introduced to me all of the fittings on the horse and the process of getting into the saddle on a variety of horses. There was a horse that would move anywhere no matter how much its rein was pulled. One day that horse had decided to climb on the back of a female horse and all I could do was to slide off that horse. On the other hand, there was a racehorse that would react instantly against even the slightest touch on the rein. It amazed me to see how much a horse could sense.

We initially sat on horses and made them walk around and change directions. Then we started trotting around and balancing our body. Learning to ride a horse properly was a delight for me. However, when we got to the stage of galloping it really scared me. I found it hard to maintain my balance on the horse. One day I was on a small horse that felt totally comfortable, even with the galloping. That made me realise that the length of my legs determined the best size of horse for me. It was like riding a bicycle on which the legs could reach the pedals. I preferred to be on little ones. It was also nice to be meeting many friendly people in that group.

Cyprus

In Malta it was the RAF transport flights that took me to Cyprus a few times. That enabled me to have a holiday period in Cyprus. That is when I sensed the split between the Greeks and the Turks on the island. The shopkeepers would speak to me in either Greek or Turkish because they assumed that I was one of them. My tour of Cyprus also turned out to be an unusual experience. At the northern part of the island there was an armed barrier. The Turk at the barrier discovered that I was not one of them and made me dig out my passport from my bag to ensure that I was not a Greek. Only then would the barrier be lifted for me to drive through their zone. There would be another check on leaving their zone to make sure that there was no extra passenger. In addition to the political difference in human lives, there was a completely different type of countryside in Cyprus. The island provided people totally different climate regions on the same day between the sea and the mountain region.

Other flights in Malta

There were a few occasions when we had NATO crews in Europe who came to Malta during their Mediterranean patrolling. French maritime crews in American-built Orion aircraft happened to turn up in our briefing room and were amazed at the information they could gather from us in relation to their flying tasks. I had to give them a briefing for their flight that NATO in Rome had sent to us. Some Italian fighter pilots would come to Malta and even came to our room, although their flights were not related to maritime operations. On the day that the fighters were returning to Italy, a fighter jet crashed at the end of the runway during take-off. Just as the aircraft had started to rotate for take-off, a fuselage panel at the front of the aircraft popped open and blanked the pilot's vision ahead. He abandoned the take-off and braked heavily on the long runway. However, the aircraft could not be stopped by the end of the runway and neither could the pilot eject out at that stage. The fighter aircraft continued through the fence and the road and came to a halt in a field. Fortunately, it remained in one piece and the pilot was extracted without any serious injury. Then we learnt that the front panel had popped up because the pilot had stuffed too many duty-free cigarette packages under the panel. If that panel had popped out in flight the pilot would have been ejecting from the aircraft. It astounded me to see the steps that some people took to try and sneak in cigarettes past the customs man. During my returns to Britain from abroad I had been bringing in cigarettes for my relatives or friends. I completely stopped transporting unhealthy items through customs for other people, much to the disappointment of some of my flying companions.

There was also another RAF squadron in Malta that was flying the twin jet engine Canberra aircraft. Those aircraft used to be bombers and were then converted for land surveillance flights. During a final turn on its approach for landing, one engine of a Canberra failed. The aircraft started to roll over and the pilot and navigator had no option but to eject due to the loss of control. Unfortunately, the aircraft failed to continue rolling and both the crew ended up ejecting into the ground. One of the crew used to live close to me in Malta. That crash was another shock in my life.

In addition to the military operations, the Shackletons were also used for search and rescue (SAR) flights. We communicated with the aircraft on SAR flights from our control room. In December 1969, the SAR flight was for two lost Maltese fishermen who were finally located. The Shackletons dropped life rafts for the rescue and looked to guide other ships or rescue boats to the location. That day an American helicopter from Wheelus AFB in Libya happened to be near the location and was used to lift the fishermen from the sea and bring them in to Malta. That rescue was very much appreciated by the Maltese people. They even held religious presentations for the rescue of their seamen by the forces.

Another day there was a rescue operation for a tanker ship that had lost its engine and was drifting into the Maltese coast in strong winds. That day I was on duty and was given the message for initiating the operation for rescuing the crew. The launched rescue boat and the helicopter were with the ship just as it struck into the rocks. All of the crew were rescued. After duty that day, I went to the location where the abandoned ship was stuck in the rocks. There were some Maltese folk talking and saying that the RAF had done nothing to save the ship. I felt like telling them that they should have been relieved that none of the ship crew had lost their lives.

At Luqa airport there was a British European Airways (BEA) twin jet-engined Vanguard aeroplane that was used for training professional pilots. It amazed me that the aeroplane with two engines on its tail was able to reverse on the runways and taxiways at the airport. Stopping the reverse movement could be done only with the use of engine power. The slightest touch of the brakes to stop reverse movement would have resulted in the aeroplane sitting on its tail. During another NATO exercise there was an opportunity for me to go on a day return flight in the cockpit of an RAF Hercules transport aircraft between Malta and Sicily. After landing in Sicily, the aircraft did some taxying in reverse from the cockpit and I saw how it was being done. Later, during our walk around the aircraft with the pilot I remarked that our Shackletons could not taxi in reverse like his Hercules could. He then told me something about an earlier experience he had had with an Army officer who had asked him how the aircraft could taxi in reverse. After the pilot explained that it was done by reversing the propeller blade angles, the baffled army officer stared at the pilot and said, "You RAF guys are always pulling our legs."

In Malta, 203 Squadron started replacing Shackleton aircraft with new Nimrods which were developed from the Comet jet airliner. As those aircraft would be operating from Malta, I had to attend an initial course on the Nimrod at St Mawgan in Cornwall. Inside the large aircraft it thrilled me to be able to walk around on a level floor and there was plenty of space for the operation of new equipment to be installed for submarine tracking from high altitudes. For prolonged maritime flights the aircraft could be operated on only two of its four jet engines. The aircraft was pressurised with air and the crew could use light headphones and be dressed comfortably. It made me feel as though I were stepping into a new world. The Nimrod was capable of detecting nuclear submarines that did not need to surface to charge their batteries, something which conventional submarines had to do. Those aircraft started arriving in Malta shortly before the period when the RAF had to depart from independent Malta due to political developments. That also resulted in a slightly early exit for me in 1972 for my next RAF posting.

Maltese people

Malta had beautiful churches and numerous religious festivals in all the little towns on the island. At the numerous religious festivals, there would also be some big fireworks. Only when those fireworks were near my flat in Masirah did I find it uncomfortable to be so close to the noise that they created. The Maltese people had highly religious dedications. Occasionally, I went on the very pleasant and colourful Maltese buses. There was one set-up in the bus that puzzled me. The driver did not sit directly behind the steering wheel. Instead, he would sit beside the wheel and controlled it with his hands to his side. The explanation for that driving position was even more puzzling. The people believed that the steering was being controlled by God and the driver was only there for assistance. The Maltese life patterns were incredibly linked with their religious beliefs. The very active conversations in the Maltese language between passengers sitting together used to delight me. On the small island of Gozo beside the mainland it was amazing to see a very sparse area that had a big church that was beautifully constructed inside.

My three year stay in Malta was a delightful experience for me. However, near the end of my posting the Maltese people had selected a new government who had decided to clear their country of NATO forces. We started vacating Malta in 1972 when my posting was going to end anyway. Servicemen sent their families home and vacated their rented properties to be accommodated in the service accommodations. All of the furniture and domestic appliances supplied by the armed services were left abandoned in the accommodations that belonged to the Maltese landlords. The advantage to me was that my car was transported to Britain for me instead of me having to make those arrangements myself. My time in Malta was a delightful experience in my life.

Chapter 8

Vulcan bomber

Start of my Vulcan flying

When studying engineering in Nairobi, I went to see the opening of the Embakasi airport in 1959. Less than half an hour after an announcement had stated that a Vulcan was passing Kilimanjaro on its way to us at Embakasi, the bomber arrived and landed. The white aircraft slowed down with a braking parachute trailing at the rear. Later, we even had the opportunity to walk close to that fantastic aircraft. That was my first sight of a Vulcan bomber aircraft. I could never have even imagined that one day I would be flying in a Vulcan. That aircraft was one of three V-bombers that were flown by the RAF at very high altitude during that period when the Soviet Union had shot down an American high-altitude reconnaissance aircraft with a missile in 1960. After that incident the V-bombers high level attacking plans were revised to perform very low-level flying near and inside enemy territory. Shortly after that the Vulcan became the only long-range bomber in the RAF.

My flying duties were in a completely different environment. From the earlier piston engine propeller-driven Shackleton aircraft with a crew of at least ten, I was transferred to the jet engine Avro Vulcan bomber with a crew of five officers. The crew was made up of two pilots, two navigators and one air electronics officer (AEO). On their missions the Vulcans were flown not only at very high altitudes, but also at extremely low altitudes for which the aircraft had originally not been designed. Flying in the Vulcans became my main duty for the rest of my time in the RAF. The mission for the Vulcan aircraft was to retaliate the Soviet Union if they ever dreamt of a nuclear attack on any NATO country. In more than seven years of flying in Vulcans we never felt that a nuclear retaliation situation was ever likely to occur, as a nuclear war could not produce a winner on either side. The Vulcans would be operated as a back-up to our submarines and we were mainly engaged with various training operations for stopping that war. During my nine years of flying in the Vulcan aircraft we flew at both high levels and at low levels. Our high-level flights were in empty airspace above the airliners and our low-level flights required us to avoid ground obstacles. The enemy never frightened me, but there were the odd occasions when we had some scares from some aircraft problems during our training flights. However, there also were accidents when there were losses of lives.

No. 50 Squadron at Waddington

My first posting for Vulcan flying was to 50 Squadron, based at RAF Waddington, just south of the ancient city of Lincoln. During our initial training period, we had to commute to RAF Scampton, located just north of Lincoln. Surprisingly, my old friend, Alastair Steadman, was now my captain after he had converted his flying duties to that of a pilot. The Vulcan crew of five would fly as a team because each crew were required to train together for a specific target in the event of a nuclear war. Due to the intense coordination required in the task, the Vulcan crew became closely attached. The training lasted for three months and included an intense ground school and 70 hours of flying in the strangely V-shaped aircraft. It had triangular shaped wings, at the back of which there was only the vertical rudder. At the back of the horizontal triangular structure there were a set of controls in a single line, both for pitching up and down as well as for rolling left and right. The four Olympus engines had been advanced earlier for the carriage of some missiles, but the missiles were replaced later by a small single nuclear bomb in the bomb-bay and the aircraft did not need the full power, even for a take-off when only 90% power was selected. The Vulcan, on the ground and in flight, continues to remain a spectacular sight since its creation.

The crew of five were tightly packed in a very small compartment at the front. Our entry and exit from the ground into that compartment was via a twofold ladder underneath the nose, just in front of the nose wheel and came up into the cabin. Directly above the only entrance there were three backward facing seats with the plotter navigator's seat in the middle. The two outer seats were for the AEO and the radar navigator and both of those seats could be rotated to assist entry and exit. The two pilots went further up another small ladder and crawled into tight spaces at the top of which was the cockpit. The central control panel between the pilots in the cockpit had to be folded away to enable the pilots to crawl into their seats. After our entry, the main ladder would be raised up, folded and laid on the horizontal door that had been shut by hydraulic pressure. As it had been difficult for the pilots to even get into their seats it would have even more difficult for them to vacate the aircraft in an emergency. To help the pilots in vacating the aircraft, two ejection seats had been installed just for the two of them. Before our take-off, one of us rear crew would retract the safety pins in the ejection seats of the pilots and store them. After landing those pins would be restored to enable the pilots to crawl out safely. In a flight emergency the people at the lower location could jump out through the horizontal entrance opening into the air. Underneath the pilots in the nose of the aircraft there was a lying-down visual bombing position designed for the original high-level conventional bombs. That was still used for some training, although the dropping of ordinary bombs had practically disappeared. I used to lie there at high levels to look at the beautiful scenery below. The main task for the Vulcan was to deliver a single nuclear bomb. There was plenty of unused space in the bomb-bay that we sometimes used for transporting various other things.

From the outside, the aircraft was amazingly big, but the space for the crew inside was very cramped. Our seat cushions were packed dinghies which we would click onto our parachute harness if we were going to be jumping out over the sea. We also had a handle for operating a small inflator at the bottom of the seat to push us out of our seats with the dinghies in case of severe gravity situations. When jumping out in an emergency we would open the horizontal door and let the loose ladder fall out and we would slide down the chute to escape from the aircraft. Whether the parachute would pop out shortly after our exit or require us to pull a handle to open it, depended upon the aircraft altitude at the time of our parachute jump out of the aircraft. We wouldn't want the parachute to automatically open if we had to jump out at 45,000 feet. Parachute jump training was given to us, but I am content never having used it in flight. Between the pilots and the rear crew there were two awkward spaces to carry other people in flight. During most of our transits to overseas places we carried two ground crew.

The Vulcan bombers had initially been built to drop many ordinary conventional bombs from high altitudes, but that had been changed to the carriage of a single nuclear bomb for dropping from a low level. One nuclear bomb in a Vulcan could produce an explosion equivalent to a thousand Vulcans each carrying twenty bombs with each bomb weighing one thousand pounds. At the training school, we were given conventional bomb training as well. In our discussion at the end of the course we were asked for comments about the training for conventional bombing. I remember saying that it had been a waste of time. After my retirement from the RAF I found that I was wrong. In 1972 the Falkland Islands war had occurred and resulted in the only time when the Vulcan had dropped conventional bombs to make some holes in a runway.

Operational flying preparation

After three months of high-level conversion training at Scampton we had further training at our base at Waddington, which related to the amazing low-level flying that was going to be the main attacking procedure for us. The aircraft having been designed for high level flying did not have suitable lookout positions for low level flying. The limited viewpoints from the cockpit resulted in the Vulcans flying low level only on a one-way terrain track around Britain during booked times. The route began in the south Dorset coast and went clockwise around the whole of Britain over open countryside to avoid disturbing inhabitants. Then it finished well before it got to the south east populated areas. The idea was to prepare ourselves for flying low level into enemy territory to avoid detection and escape from any intercepting aircraft for our delivery to our target. There were targets on our practice routes where we did encounter enemy ground interceptions and we went through our avoidance and jamming procedures. One of our targets in Britain used to be the Wellington monument in Devon that we used to bomb with our camera.

The aircraft would be bouncing around in our manoeuvres over low ground and initially I had to perform my operations even when my stomach was throwing out. To assist the radar operator, we were completely blacked out with curtains. We maintained a low level with severe manoeuvring over rising and falling terrains, as well as countering any enemy interference. For me those flights at low level felt like being strapped in a tank that was being violently shaken from outside for a few hours. At the end of the flights of less than five hours my body was really shattered. It took me months to get my body to cope with severely turbulent low-level flying in the Vulcans. Despite that, the flights in Vulcans were some very unusual and enjoyable experiences.

After the occurrence of some accidents with Vulcans, we trained for further escape drills. We had to start practising our ability to slide down the door hatch, and grab the hydraulic jack on the way to deflect our fall to the side instead of sliding straight down. The reason for that drill was that the nose wheel might be stuck in its position right in front of us. That had happened during a landing accident in Teheran during the days of CENTO when the Shah of Persia was in power. During my Vulcan flying days, I happened to be on the same squadron as one of the crewmen who had been on that accident with the nose wheel problem. He told me that the nose wheel of the aircraft had been lowered, but it had not locked into its position. That was the first time a Vulcan had landed with a nose wheel problem. After the landing, the nose wheel had collapsed and slid along the ground. That resulted in a lot of rubble coming in through the shattered bomb-aimer position in the nose and slammed into the back of the seats for the rear crew who found themselves trapped in their seats. Fortunately, there was no casualty and, thereafter, all Vulcan crews behind the pilots were required to train for the additional jumping out drill in case a nose wheel had not locked down. We practiced sliding down the hatch, grabbing a hydraulic jack on one side of the opening and swinging ourselves sideways in order to avoid slamming into the nose wheel. During my first attempt, I got tangled up with my own oxygen hose and would have been slamming into the nose wheel if we were flying. Only the pilots would then try to save the aircraft.

Another drill was created after I had started flying on the Vulcans. An accident happened in Malta when a Vulcan on the final approach had bounced on the ground before the runway. The pilots could still control it and decided to abandon that approach and to go round for another one.

However, the severe bump had damaged an engine, a fire had started in the wing and there was a loss of control of the aircraft. The decision to abandon the plane was made, but the loose ladder had jammed across the rear door gap and unfortunately, all the crew at the back failed to escape. The two pilots stayed with the aircraft until the last moment when they finally ejected out. After that the loose ladder on the door had to be moved and strapped in the nose position before every flight.

My creation of life

It was in July 1972 that I was to experience the greatest delight in my life. A child had arrived for me at a nearby RAF hospital. At the hospital I bumped into a nurse and to my surprise she just held out her left arm on which she was carrying my little wonder. She let me have the great delight of taking my child in my arms. It astonished me that the child had his eyes open and was looking at me. I was so struck by that wonder that I placed him on a bed and moved to his right. To my surprise his eyes followed my movement. Then I gently moved to his left and once again his eyes followed me. The nurse commented that I was obviously thrilled with my first child. The sight of a creation of my own had been the most exciting day in my life. Unlike a lot of babies in that hospital, my son had black hair on his head. In my life I had experienced many delightful successes, but my creation of a child put me into a completely new status of existence. There is nothing in life that can exceed the prime purpose for our existence, namely the creation of a succession to our own life.

My son, Chetan Deep was a great delight to me, no matter what I would be doing. The physical contact with that affectionate creature was thrilling. All of the tasks associated with looking after the lovely little creature were delightful experiences for me. One day my friend Alastair had come to my quarters and was amazed at the ease with which I handled my son. He had been having problems with putting his daughter to sleep. One day in the garden I saw Chetan do something I had never seen a child ever do. He had got to the stage of crawling, but when he came to the grass on the lawn he converted to a totally different form of movement. He raised himself on all fours and moved forward like a little dog. I had never ever seen that form of movement by any crawling baby before. My little puppy, Chetan, was a tremendously delightful creature in my life.

Goose Bay in Canada

It was in February 1973 that I had the first opportunity to fly across the Atlantic to Goose Bay in north-eastern Canada. From there we could do our low-level flying over vast unpopulated terrain. Although the navigator beside me had large scale maps, I started taking my little world atlas with me to follow our tracking on our globe with views on route. Surprisingly, the latitude that we flew to in Canada was almost the same as our departure latitude in Britain. Although navigation was not part of my job it interested me to fathom in our routing. Instead of flying directly west to our destination I found that we routed in three segments to the north. I realised then that the straight line on our flat map would be a curved route on our globe. We ended up drawing three straight segments on our flat maps which were three curved flights over the ground on the same headings. We flew at very high altitude and passed close to Iceland and over Greenland. On our transit flights I used the long-range HF radio communications during transit and the pilots would take control nearer the airport on short range VHF radio.

During our flights over the cold ocean we had to wear special immersion flying suits. That was to help us for our survival in case we had to jump into the cold Atlantic Ocean. Between that suit and warm clothing, we wore another layer that allowed warm air to be pumped into the suit via a flexible pipe coming out through a water tight rubber opening. We would plug that pipe into a warm air supply to keep ourselves warm during flight. Initially, our flying suit would blow up like a balloon and we had to create a small opening to allow the air to flow out. Just placing a pencil in the wrist seal was adequate. Only at my table there was a hinged panel that could be lifted open and a periscope pulled out to enable me to look out, above and below the wings as well as left and right as far forward as the leading edges of the wings. Although it had been installed to enable sighting of any damage to the aircraft, for me it provided delightful views all around the aircraft during my eight years of Vulcan flying. As there was plenty of free time for me to vacate my seat I would go and lie down at the bomb-aimer position and look at the scenery below. Standing on the ladder to the pilot seats was another activity for me. That enabled me to look through the windscreen for the pilots, but we had to be careful with the live ejection seats. At our high-altitude flights, the clouds were always below us.

During our flights over the oceans we could not obtain any radar fixes of our position and the navigator would plug in his astronomy kit into the roof and shoot the stars for obtaining some fix on our position. In those days, the corridors of our flight path clearance would be sixty miles wide. We had the added advantage that airliners did not fly as high as us. When we got nearer to land, we could update our position with the radar. At the higher flight levels, we always had enormous rotating vapour trails from our wing tips. A further lookout position from the aircraft for me was the little round window on my side, but to get the views I wanted I had to either stand up or sit on my desk, facing forwards. The only waste option in the aircraft was for passing our water into individual rubber balloons clipped beside each seat. For our flights of about five hours we would carry in a large aluminium box with various food packages that we had selected. There would even be packs of jelly sweets that some crew had selected to take home for their kids.

Our first approach to Goose Bay was on a beautiful clear day and we even saw the white countryside and the airport from about twenty miles away. As we were expecting temperatures to be way below ours at the same latitude in Britain, we had taken with us extra cold weather clothing. The airfield was well prepared for using their runways in winter. After stepping out of our aircraft, breathing in the cold air was a new experience for me. The hair in my nose had stiffened. The aircraft would be towed into the hanger, otherwise it would have resulted in unusual hydraulic failures. Temperatures of minus 10°C were mild at that location where they even dropped well below minus 20°C, which would feel even worse in windy conditions. The accommodation rooms were in well heated buildings, but stepping out between buildings was a real challenge. That made me feel like I was stepping onto another planet.

Our low-level flying over the white countryside was another unusual experience. We flew on a few low-level routes that had no flying restrictions. As we did not have interference from any opposition forces, I could spend time looking out. Three days of low-level flying over unusual terrain in arctic conditions to locate various targets was very exciting for me. It was a real delight to have had such free space for low flying on the western continent unlike the severe restrictions we had over crowded Britain. After a week in cold Canada we flew back to warm Britain at the same latitude. Back home I could be in my shorts for hockey games. The Canadians with whom I had a chat couldn't believe that the people in Britain played hockey on grass instead of on ice.

Far East flying

The Vulcan had originally been designed to carry conventional weapons to any part of the globe during the 1950s and had a refuelling probe in the nose which was not used during my flying time. That was because the aircraft had transferred to low-level flying mainly for targets in the Soviet Union. After shelving air refuelling, long flights in Vulcans needed to land for ground refuelling stops. That month four aircraft flew on a world trip on westerly flights via North America, the Pacific Ocean and Australia. An additional Vulcan was placed in Singapore to join in the touring in Australia should there be a grounding of an aircraft in the world touring team. We were sent to Singapore in March to take over the Vulcan that had been placed there by another crew. While we waited for a hopeful call for a flight to Australia, we flew a couple of low-level sorties over Malaysia from RAF Tengah in Singapore. During our free time, the pilots decided to play squash and dragged me to join them, even though I had never played squash before. While we were playing, they told me to play the ball away from the opponent for winning a point and not to be hitting the other player with the ball. We continued with our rough games and surprisingly, I was the overall winner. Towards the end of our stay, our hopes of going to Australia faded away and we returned to Britain in an RAF transport aircraft via Ceylon (Sri Lanka) where we had a night stop. That has been my only visit to that country.

Bomber flying from home

Although the Vulcans were built to carry many conventional bombs the main task was going to be the carriage of a single nuclear bomb. Most of our training was for low-level bombing. On some of our firing ranges we would drop some bombs while looking at our accuracy. A lot of the time we dropped small practice bombs, but occasionally we dropped some one thousand-pound bombs. My periscope enabled me to see spectacular splashes in the sea. Although training experiences were amazing, I could never imagine using them in anger for real.

Sometimes at high levels we practised the evasion of attacking fighter aircraft. That was mainly to give some fighter aircraft some training to shoot down a high-level bomber. Different fighter aircraft produced different results in our engagements. Aircraft that needed to get behind us to fire their missiles at us just could not match the manoeuvres that we could perform, let alone other capabilities we had for jamming their radars. Although we did not have any weapons for firing at the attackers, I remember one day my pilot calling out "Bang Bang," on the radio when we had the fighter in front of our nose. The fighter pilot was very impressed by our manoeuvring. However, there were other fighters who could fire a missile at us from the front and we would use the counter measures that we had, but we only used those at our training location in Scotland. At low-levels, we would carry out various actions for getting away from the fighters to continue bombing our target, but we had to be prepared to use other countermeasures against ground forces.

During our landing at Waddington after a normal flight we had a strange experience. After the landing our aircraft suddenly swayed to the left. My body was swung sideways. The pilot reacted very well to prevent the aircraft from rolling onto the grass, but we felt several bumps as our left wheel knocked down several runway lights. It was only after regaining control that we realised what had happened. Normally the aircraft speed was reduced after landing by the deployment of a brake parachute at the rear that would pop out and open as an airbrake. Our airbrake had deployed out, but it had not opened as a brake until it had been deflected by the crosswind. On opening after the deflection, the brake parachute also pulled the tail of the aircraft to the right which resulted in the nose swinging to the left and nearly taking us off the runway. After that incident, I regularly extended out my periscope during our landings to ensure that our braking parachute had inflated after landing, otherwise I would have to alert the pilots to release the brake parachute. Fortunately, that never happened again.

Warfare preparations

There were times when we engaged in exercises culminating in launching the Vulcans on their main purpose missions. First, the Vulcans would fly from their bases to remote bases in groups of four to six aircraft. There the aircraft would be located beside the runway and we would be in cabinets close to the aircraft for a few days, waiting for a launch to separate targets. We exercised the security situation of being with a fully armed aircraft. We also went through launch procedures when alarms were sounded to make us wake up and go to the aircraft, but not to do the take-off. We were only required to take-off during a suitable period when we would jump in, rapid start the engines and take-off within minutes. The RAF guards had to get out of the way during that period. One day, behind our aircraft a new guard had failed to move away far enough and was blown away into the barbed wire fence, fortunately he did not suffer any serious injury. The aircraft would then launch in turn with the next aircraft rolling while the one ahead was still on the runway. After our launch from the airport we all went on separate tracks to different targets in the European countries of NATO (North Atlantic Treaty Organisation). Also, we ended up attacking targets in Britain during our returns. Most of our flying on these exercises would be at a low level, as we needed to remain low in enemy territory.

During those flights, it was sometimes possible for me to look at the scenery as we flew low-level on attacking missions over Europe. One day we detected a fighter above us, but we didn't need to perform any escape manoeuvres as it flew on without detecting us. We would then fly back at a low level over the North Sea and attack Britain. That was when I had to tell the pilots not to fly too low because, when looking out of my periscope I sighted a long sea track behind us. We had to avoid giving the fighters at high level a visual sighting of our track in the sea. Although we wouldn't fight the attackers, we needed to go through various actions to deter them from detecting us and to detach them if they had sighted us to enable us to continue with the main mission. The crew concentrated as a team with the navigators maintaining our routing, the pilots handling the aircraft at low level while I was required to take a multitude of actions to deter enemy ground and airborne forces.

The training for various operations that would be activated in real enemy territory were practised in some remote training areas. There I could jam the radars of any chasing aircraft and ground stations, eject out small aluminium flakes to blot out the enemy radar displays and fire out flares to attract enemy missiles away from us. I could even detect enemy aircraft with a rear looking radar display. We only operated some of our defensive systems in those remote training areas. Those exercise flights required intense concentration from us, even when we encountered no attackers. One day I had failed to shut down our radar jamming when we had finished our training session and when we were flying out. I was shocked to be told by air traffic control to stop jamming their radar service. All I could do was apologise.

My home in Lincoln

Before going to Malta, I had started considering a house purchase in Britain. My search was for a house located suitably by the only two RAF bases for the Vulcan aircraft in Lincolnshire. A house that was going to be built in Lincoln was selected. That house was at twice the price that I had envisaged. Instead of a mortgage of less than £5,000 I ended paying for a mortgage of over £9,000. At that time the interest rate for mortgage loans had shot up and I ended up paying out half my earnings for the loan from a building society. My first house was a four-bedroom detached house in a small cul-de-sac in the city. That was something that had been unimaginable for me. Buying that house had resulted in me not having any money to buy new furniture and I ended up picking second hand furniture. I also started laying concrete patios and steps down to the rear garden.

Having a loving child and becoming a house owner had been a delightful new state of existence for me. After my movement into my new house it a was delight for me to have my mother come and stay with us. Not only had she raised me as a child, but she was also a great help with looking after my child. That enabled me to go out shopping or on an evening. My little son, Chetan, was always with me in all my activities. He would be beside me in the garden. When he saw me digging, he would pick up a hand fork to do some digging. One day, he gave me a real scare when I had gotten near the top of the roof of our two-storied house. My little Chetan was behind me. It was a great relief to bring him down safely. From then on, I had to be very careful with my movements when Chetan was beside me. He would even jump into the bath with me. Then on another day little Chetan gave me another shock. After my wash and shave, I had come down for breakfast and then Chetan came down with blood on his face. Chetan had seen me shaving and after I had gone downstairs, he tried to copy what I had been doing with my shaving razor. Having that child was a delight for me, but it also made me more aware of the various dangers around for a child. Chetan would come and sit in my lap in the dining room at the end of his meal or when we were sitting in the lounge. The loving physical contact with my little Chetan was a great delight in my life. My neighbours in Nursery Grove became my good friends. They were Brian and Barbara Cattermole, they had two young kids and we had a close friendship during the seven years that I spent in that house. In our small cul-de-sac we had a nice social neighbourhood with people of various professions.

Bomber flying in America

In August 1973, we flew via Goose Bay in Canada to Offutt AFB (Air Force Base) near Omaha in Nebraska. From there we flew for a couple of days on various low-level routes for which we had some booked times. There was plenty of free space for low-level flying without people on the ground. We did not need to keep in any radio contact. Flying in the US territory was not as stressful to me as my UK flying, as it gave me an opportunity to look out as well as indulge in our training. We were accommodated in a roadside hotel close to Offutt. There was an amazing sight of open countryside where we saw a huge thundercloud with great bolts of lightning flashing down as it was passing us.

During the weekend, we decided to hire a car and go into Omaha. As there were six of us, including our technician for the trip, we asked for a suitable car. Somehow, I ended up being selected as the driver for our trip. The car that arrived had three rows of seats and for me it felt like jumping into a bus. The driver delivering the car was puzzled about me asking him where everything was in the car. It was the first time that I was going to be driving a car from the seat on the left side. Also, the car did not have a gear foot pedal, but I couldn't stop my left foot moving for that and ended up touching the big footbrake. All my passengers found themselves being thrown forward. Eventually, we managed to drive on the opposite side of the road that I was not used to and got to the city of Omaha. The layout of the American city had been planned before its existence and the roads were laid out in boxes on a map. People were seen only in their cars and when we were walking beside the road somewhere, the passing drivers were giving puzzled looks at us walking on the street. A week later we flew home via Goose Bay in Canada. Back home it was a delight to be in my city of Lincoln in England, in my small car and with my delightful child.

During 1973 we ended up operating from other RAF stations for more than two months because runway resurfacing had started at Waddington. Some flights for me were from nearby Scampton, but there were several operations from increasing distances to Finningley near Doncaster, Cottesmore near Stanford and Fairford near Swindon. That meant our weekdays were to be away from home. At the Fairford runway we used to see the Concorde airliner doing various ground tests before it could be flown as an airliner. The design of the Concorde was related to our Vulcan in shape as well as some of the equipment. In fact, Britain also had designs for a supersonic Vulcan bomber, but that had to be abandoned because of enemy missiles.

Farewell to No. 50 Squadron at Waddington

At the end of 1973 our tour of duty came to an end and we were posted to others posts in the RAF. The three of us from the rear crew remained together and moved to another Vulcan squadron on the north side of Lincoln. My flying time with the 50 Squadron had been delightful. Our two pilots had moved away from us to other postings. Alastair and I had been together as friends for a long time since our initial meeting in 1963. We had spent time together at Topcliffe in Yorkshire and I had even been taken by him in his little minivan to his family home in Wales where it was a delight to meet his parents. Ever since our time at Topcliffe in Yorkshire in 1964 we had nominated each other as referees for our regular security checks.

We had talked with security staff about our life experiences related to our service and social lives. It was nice to have been at his marriage in Wales and in close social contact again when we were both posted to Waddington for bomber flying. I also had the pleasure of spending some time together with Al, partaking in horse riding, at which he was very good. During my time in the RAF, it had been a delight to have had a close relationship and spent some quality time with Alastair for ten years. After that tour of duty on a Vulcan bomber, I was to be engaged in some very different Vulcan flying on my next tour of duty.

Excursion to India

There had been very little communication with my relatives in India because they did not have a telephone and even writing was difficult because it had been very difficult for me to read their letters scribbled in Hindi. That made me decide to go and see my grandmother who was in her final stage of life. I had been helping my very aged grandmother, widowed auntie and five children in a village in the Punjab for a long time. In December 1973, there was a break during my transfer of RAF duties. A flight from Heathrow took me to Bombay in India in a Boeing 747 airliner. There, another flight took me to Delhi where my relatives from my father's side lived. After spending a day with them, I set off for Chandigarh by coach. In the new city of Chandigarh, it was a delight to be with my cousin from my mother's side who had been in Kenya in 1949 after the death of my father. He had returned to India after retirement in Kenya and was living in a big new two-storied house with a garden. The accommodation was luxurious compared to the houses in which a lot of my other relatives were living. He had plenty of free time to take me around the Punjab.

My cousin took me to the village of Shamespur in which my grandmother and auntie (my *Dadiji* and my *Chachiji*) were still living in the two accommodations that I remember having stayed in as a child in 1945-46. Strangely, I could also remember some of the layout that I had seen. It was great to meet my *Dadiji* who walked around with a stick in her hand and her body at a forward right angle. She wanted me to come and meet her at her last stage of life. During the next two weeks we went and saw her as well as many other relatives in the villages of the Punjab area.

In Shamespur, I arranged and paid for the fitting of water hand pumps for drawing water from the ground within the front yard of the house and for fitting electric lights. Because my cousin was from my mother's side, we also went cycling around the Indian countryside to visit other relatives living in various villages.

From Chandigarh a bus took me to the village of Tapa where it was a delight to be spending time with my cousin from my father's side. He was the doctor of the area and even took me into an operations room where many blinded people were being given eye operations. All he did was to remove the blanked eye lenses that easily gave people some view instead of not being able to see anything. We had good fun playing volley ball with the villagers beside the house. After more than two weeks in the Punjab I returned to Delhi to catch my return flight. However, before my departure from India, my doctor cousin joined me on a trip to Agra city to see the Taj Mahal. That was the first time I had the experience of seeing the global heritage sight and felt thrilled with having been there. That trip to India was only the second time in my life that I had been there and yet it felt so much like being at home because there were so many close relatives in India. Finally, on New Year's Day, 1975, a return flight brought me back to my new home in England.

Chapter 9

Reconnaissance flying

No. 27 Squadron at Scampton

My new posting in 1974 did not require any movement from my home as the new squadron at Scampton was located on the north side of Lincoln. At the entrance to the station there was a display of a Lancaster bomber, which was fascinating to see from the outside as well as from the inside. My flying task in the Vulcan aircraft was going to be totally different from the earlier one. Instead of bombing, our main task was going to be reconnaissance flying over the sea, mainly at very high altitudes. We even had to wear modified flying kit to enable us to risk flying up to 50,000 feet. An air pressurisation failure at that altitude would require us to breathe some oxygen at a very high pressure that could have resulted in damage to our lungs. As a precaution, the system also used the high-pressure oxygen to go into a new life jacket that would inflate another layer in the jacket to prevent our lungs bursting with expansion. During our training in a ground simulator we did try out that breathing process. In addition to my lungs, my neck also got inflated and it was not easy to talk to others. My breathing cycle had reversed. Instead of breathing in I had to force the oxygen out of my lungs and found it returning into my lungs when my breathing out had stopped. That situation was not going to last for long as the aircraft would be descending rapidly to return to a flight level below 45,000 feet when the oxygen supply would revert to its normal pressures.

At the start of my tour of duty on 27 Squadron, the rear crew were the same as before and we had a new captain and a new co-pilot. I also had good social contact with them. During the early period of 1974 our flying was reduced due to a national strike by miners in Britain. Later, we were engaged in various exercises with the Royal Navy as our main task was going to be over the sea. During reconnaissance flying we had separate activities that did not require the intense coordination that we needed during our bombing runs. On some of those flights I was intensely engaged in radio broadcasts. The maritime radar reconnaissance (MRR) high altitude flights enabled us to monitor vast areas of the ocean for shipping activity. The radar navigator would code up the locations of all radar detections and present them to me to broadcast the messages that would be picked up by our sea forces while remaining silent to prevent their detection. Our bomb-bay was fitted with an additional fuel tank to enable us to fly for an extra hour. My throat would feel sore after my long transmissions. The plotter navigator maintained our flight pattern and even controlled the aircraft turns from his position. The pilots found themselves with very little to do. I used to alert them for the regular flight safety checks that needed to be carried out. On our return to base the pilots enjoyed doing some runway approaches while the rear crew would have been happy to land first time.

In the summer of 1974 we also started flying at public air shows at numerous locations in Britain. We flew on air displays at Halfpenny Green, Weston-Super-Mare and Church Fenton. Those flights enabled me to stand on the steps behind the pilots and hold tight while the aircraft was thrown into various manoeuvres. During our display manoeuvres at airports, we flew at the same heights above the ground level of those airports, but during transits between airports we flew at height levels related to sea level. As we flew to many different aerodromes for our displays, there were times when the pilots had to be alerted to set the correct altimeter pressure setting for that aerodrome for our own safety. Our display was carried out around a thousand feet above the ground of the airport. Entertaining the public below us used to be great fun for me.

Global flying to Midway Island

In the autumn of 1974, I had the experience of flying to the most western aerodrome on our planet. We flew out westwards to get familiar with the routing to Midway Island. It had that name because it is in the middle of the Pacific Ocean. Our clocks had a time difference of eleven hours. The Pacific Ocean gaps between Midway and the side continents were longer than our flights across the Atlantic Ocean from Britain to Canada. The runway covered almost the entire length of the main island. There was a small island beside the main island forming part of a big circle of shallow water. During World War II, Midway Island had been a strategic location for the Americans.

Our trip was mainly an introduction to the future operational task for the Vulcans. My flights with 27 Squadron enabled me to have a glimpse of the northern half of a vast Pacific Ocean. With our new captain Duncan Ross, we set off for Midway with stage stops at Goose Bay in Labrador, McClellan AFB in California and Hawaii. Inside the aircraft we also crammed in an engineering officer and a ground technician. After landing in California, we suffered a little problem during our exit from the aircraft. The ground engineer had pulled the door opening handle through its emergency position and the horizontal door had opened with a bang. Fortunately, there was no ground crew standing beneath the door that normally opens very slowly on the ground. We then lowered our ladder over the sloping door and stepped out to the ground. Although there was no apparent damage to the door it had to be checked properly on the ground before our next flight. That resulted in us stopping in California for two days that had not been planned.

During our stop in California, we hired a car and drove to San Francisco. Once again, I found myself to be the driver. On the multilane road into the city there were differing instructions to me for our next turn-off from the road. That resulted in me just taking a turn off those busy lanes into the city. Somehow it turned out to be okay and we drove around and finally went across the famous Golden Gate Bridge that took us from the peninsula of San Francisco to the mainland across the sea that enters in the bay. On the other side of the bay we drove around the locations of big beautiful buildings that were housing films stars. Later, we crossed back to San Francisco over the scenic bridge and toured the city. Despite the intensity of the drive, our only trip to San Francisco was a great delight. After a couple of days in California we took off for Honolulu for refuelling on our way to Midway Island to the northwest. That was necessary in case there was an aerodrome problem in Midway and we did not have enough fuel to go anywhere for a landing.

Early during our climb, the pressurisation system once again started sounding a warning and the aircraft was levelled to stay below ten thousand feet. The cabin was not pressurising because the air leak in the damaged entrance door had not been rectified properly. We could not produce the required air pressure for higher altitudes. That was the first time that I radioed a 'May Day' emergency message and air traffic allowed us to use whatever low-level altitude that we needed. As we had no other problem, we continued our flight at low level to Honolulu for that trip. After landing we had to wait for the exit door problem to be resolved. Instead of refuelling and continuing our flight to Midway, we were stuck in Honolulu for five days. That struck me like a bolt of lightning. The hotel room given to me could have housed a family. My first flight over the Pacific Ocean turned out to be a holiday in Honolulu which had never been imagined or expected. We had to wait for technicians from Britain to arrive to properly fix our pressurisation problem.

In Honolulu we hired two smaller cars so that we could have different trips around the island. To my surprise we were not on the island of Hawaii but on the island called Oahu. Although Honolulu was the capital of the state of Hawaii, the island of Hawaii was at the eastern end of the chain and was less populated due to its high volcanic activity. Hawaii is currently being created from the same volcano that had previously created all the line of islands to the north-east of Hawaii. Midway Island was the earliest one because it is the last one in sight. It was a single volcanic point that had created a string of islands in the Pacific Ocean. That's because the ground below the entire ocean is splitting open and is being pushed out sideways and northwards. On one side the sea floor is rising above Asia and on the other side it is flowing under the Americas.

One day in Honolulu we went to a zoo where I saw a dolphin doing some high jumps out of the water. Then, for the first time I saw a gorilla that was sitting in a cage. The gorilla and I looked closely at each other and both of us were puzzled at the sight of the other. One day we were lying on the beach and talking to some young people beside us who were puzzled about where we came from. We asked them to guess and they said it could be either Australia or Canada. They had no idea that English was spoken by people in England. Another day I decided to go surfing and was given some instructions and taken out to the sea. The instructor then waited in the water to have me surf back to him, but my wave took me away from him. Other surfers seemed to have been annoyed by me, because they were trying to go sideways along the wave. That resulted in me returning to the beach away from the starting point. While dragging along my big surf board on my way back, some young women on the beach stopped me and asked if they could have a photograph with me. They were delighted to have met a Hawaiian surfer. That had been my first go at surfing.

After our take-off from Honolulu for Midway we were climbing very rapidly as we were lightly loaded with fuel to avoid a heavy weight landing. When I called the air traffic control for our turn, the controller said that the turn could only be done at a certain height and was surprised to hear that we had already crossed that altitude. The controller had not expected a bomber to be climbing so fast and asked me the name of our aircraft. After I told him, he repeated the name 'Vulcan' in awe on the radio. From Honolulu we flew over the ocean to finally arrive at our destination of Midway Island that is at about 28° north. Because of our delay in Hawaii, we only had a brief stay on the island before setting off for our return journey to our home base. Strangely on the tiny island, the American servicemen also had their families with them. During World War II, Midway Island had been the turning point for the Americans after they had fended off a Japanese naval attack. Our trip to Midway was a check of the routing in preparation for later returns when Chinese nuclear test explosions would be carried out and we would be collecting some radiation air samples at a high level over the Pacific.

Home flying

After our return from the Pacific Ocean we flew our aircraft from Scampton to St. Athan in Wales for major servicing. From there we brought another serviced Vulcan back to Waddington. Those flights were short trips, solely for the purpose of aircraft transits between two locations and did not require all the checks listed for operational sorties. One day there was a strange incident when another crew flew out a Vulcan from St. Athan. That crew had rushed through their checks, took-off and in their climb found that the DC electrical system had failed completely. To their horror they found that it could not be restored at all. Fortunately, the aircraft still retained its basic flying control with AC electrical power and was above the clouds at that time. The crew had no flight instrument indications, no radio communications and had to openly talk to each other. The pilots steered westwards using the magnetic compass. Then they found a gap in the clouds, descended rapidly and flew along the coast back to St. Athens without any air traffic control. Fortunately, the air traffic control could follow their flight on radar although there was no radio contact. At the St. Athens airport there was a green flashing light from ground air traffic control that was clearing them for a safe landing. During the rushed take-off checks a certain essential switch selection for DC power had been missed. That resulted in a flat battery and an inability to recover from that situation. Luckily, the pilots could maintain basic flight control and returned to St. Athan safely instead of having to jump out of the aircraft. The ground maintenance team were greatly relieved that the Vulcan flight problem had not been caused by some servicing error.

During our maritime flying we provided information from our radar reconnaissance from a high level to the Royal Navy and the NATO naval forces. As we were not involved in any attacking activities our pilots had less to do during those flights than they did on low level bombing runs. We only flew at low level when we were on flights beside various oil rigs around Britain. One day we flew together with a Nimrod maritime aircraft to photograph each other around an oil rig north of Scotland. We had very little interaction with our forces on the sea and I found the high-level maritime flying to be tedious.

Chetan Deep moonan in 1974

At home I went through a special Hindu engagement with my son, Chetan Deep, after he had passed the age of two in July 1974. That is when Chetan could be given a *moonan* which required the removal of all the hair on his head for the start of his conversion to become a good Brahmin. The cut hair then had to be deposited in a river or the sea. During my childhood in Mombasa my hair had been shaved off with a razor and must have been deposited in the Indian Ocean near the Equator. Chetan's hair was taken off by a barber with an electric shaver. At the end of the religious event Chetan looked like a new creature. He looked lovely in his new kit and his new head. A plan for depositing Chetan's *moonan* hair into the sea then had to be worked out. As we were going to be flying to Singapore in October 1974 it enabled me to work out a plan to drop my son's hair in the Indian Ocean over the Equator.

From the pressurised cockpit we could not throw out anything from there. My suggestion of creating a small bomb to be dropped from the unpressurised bomb-bay was rejected as the crew did not fancy doing that. Eventually, we worked out a suitable process for dropping the hair out of the aircraft. The airbrakes at the top and the bottom of the wings would normally be flush with the wings and would only be extended when we needed to slow down during our landing approach. All we needed to do was to tape the small bag at the back of a lower airbrake which would be restored to its normal flush position for our take-off on a flight across the equator. On our way to Singapore we had to go through Cyprus, Masirah and Gan in the Indian Ocean. It was between Gan and Singapore that we would be crossing the equator. Before take-off from Gan, the hair packet with my son's hair was taped to the inner surface of a lower airbrake. My captain agreed to extend out the airbrakes over the equator and my navigator would call out when we were crossing the equator. My periscope enabled me to look at the airbrake holding the packet of Chetan's hair. As soon as the brake started to extend, the hair packet was seen flying out from 45,000 feet up. The airbrake was then retracted back to its reset position. It exhilarated me to have accomplished an amazing delivery on my son's hair into the Indian Ocean over the equator. That event did puzzle the airmen on the ground as well as the flight crew, but to me it was a delight related to my love for my child.

Another creation in my life in 1975

It was in March 1975 that there was another delight in my life. That was the arrival of another child for me at a hospital in Lincoln. My charming daughter was another precious linkage in my life. I decided to call my little wonder Meera Bala. To me, that lovely Indian name sounded delightful, just like the French word *Mirabelle*, a small tasty plum. She was another little creature who existed in my heart and mind all day. She must have detected that I would not make her do anything that she did not want. If she did not feel like going to sleep, I had her by my side all evening while my son Chetan Deep would be asleep. One day it shocked me to see my little Meera crawling up the stairs. I rushed up to her. She sat back and gave me a stern look for stopping her doing something that she fancied. The next day proper gates were fitted at the bottom and top of the steps. On another day my lovely daughter was displeased with me. She had been in the bath with me and after I had come out and dried myself, she did not want to come out. To my surprise she was playing with toys that she had created in her head and speaking to them in a language of her own. It was amazing to see a little child with creations in her head. As she could not be left on her own in the bath, I pulled the plug to allow the water to flow out. My little Meera started crying because her invisible creatures were draining out with the water. That made me feel terrible at having drained the creations of my little darling. In the lounge Meera would come and sit in my lap most of the time. Another affectionate child coming into my life had been another great delight in my life.

Home delight

In my back garden, I started growing various vegetables and setting up a compost heap from all our vegetable rubbish in the opposite corner. My interest in gardening started increasing after having reached the unusual state of owning the property. Gardening, household tasks and little children were delightful experiences for me. Later, it was possible for me take over a vegetable plot on a nearby local council area for more gardening. As the plot had to be prepared for planting, I only managed to plant some potatoes. I also started playing hockey for some Wednesday games with the RAF team at Scampton and then ended up also running the station team as a secondary duty. Close to my house near Lincoln Cathedral there was a local hockey club called the Lincoln Imps which enabled me to also play hockey there. The construction of the little imp could be seen in the walls of Lincoln Cathedral that had been constructed before 1100 AD. It was a delight for me to be having a flying job, loving children and pleasant life activities.

Later, when my children were older, I ended up buying a motor-caravan and drove to various places around Britain. We motored up to the Lake District on our first excursion. One day it was starting to get dark when I decided to park the van beside a lake. It was only the next morning that I found that the left wheels of the van were in the water of the lake. It was a good job that the lakes did not have tides. The Lake District was not only beautiful scenic countryside, it also held a great affection for the poetry of William Wordsworth that I had read during my school days in Mombasa. It was a delight for me to be picking up his book of poems from his cottage in Grasmere in the Lake District. His lovely poem of *Daffodil'* I remember from my school days is in Addendum 2.

Pacific Ocean operations from Midway Island

During 1975 we started flying to Midway Island to collect some scientific information from the ash of two Chinese nuclear explosion tests. Those trips to the Pacific Ocean turned out to be great treats as well as alarms. We flew out from Scampton to Midway Island with stops in Goose Bay in Labrador and McClellan AFB in California. We refuelled in Hawaii on our route to Midway Island. Then, at Midway we waited for the Chinese to carry out their planned nuclear test explosion in the air and our task was to bring back some readings from the ash over the Pacific Ocean. The two Vulcans based at Midway were fitted with attachments for picking up some readings from the nuclear explosions. A couple of men from the nuclear test organisation had flown with us to operate the extra kit that had to be fitted. We would fly without any extra protection on us as those radiation levels were not going to be that high. I was told that it would be no more than taking in small radiations from our X-ray tests in a hospital. However, after we had arrived and settled down at Midway, we were told that there happened to have been a delay in the Chinese test. We ended up being stuck in Midway for three weeks and had to find something to do.

That long wait for the Chinese nuclear test became a rare holiday for me at Midway Island in 1975. Initially I had been fully awake in the middle of the night as there was a time difference of eleven hours between Britain and Midway Island. That resulted in me taking a walk along the beach before sunrise. There were a variety of birds flying around with many different take-offs, landing and flying modes. On the north side of the island there was the only beach that we could use. There was another smaller island on the east side. The islands were part of a large reef circle around a shallow sea. During our long wait for the Chinese nuclear test, that little island of Midway gave me a chance to experience some new activities in my life.

Even on the tiny island of Midway there was a nine-hole golf course where we were all required to turn up for a day of golf. That was the first time in my life I swung a golf club, but it would be no problem for me as I played hockey with a stick. We were all given a chance to hit a ball for practice. After a big swing at a golf ball I could not see where it had gone. The onlookers told me it was still on the tee peg! In all the sports that I had played there never had been the difficulty that golf was giving me. Unlike the other sports, in golf there was no interference from any opponent when we were playing the ball. Sometimes, no one would know where the ball had gone after it had been hit it. Even when the ball was seen to have landed on the normal fairway, we could not find it. That was because the fairways had big holes in them which some seabirds had dug deeply to lay their eggs. We tried to pull the ball out by sliding our club into the hole and pulling it out. That is when I found balls that had been lost by other players. Then we had to use different clubs on the greens for putting the ball into a hole. That was a totally different skill. Another problem in golf was to remember the number of swings a player has taken for getting the ball into a hole. I had only seen people gently walking around side by side and talking when on a golf course, so golf had never really seemed to be a sport to me. The introduction to golf on Midway Island had hit me with a totally different human pastime activity.

We Brits would gather together for a game of volleyball on the beach. We even played some games with the Americans. What surprised the Americans about the British was that we were all slim. Strangely for me, the mode of volleyball we played was different to the mode that I had played in Kenya. Still it was good fun for me. A lot of the time we would lie on the sand and jump into the sea. My swim trunks were worn for most of the day and my body got really tanned. For the first time, I became dark brown all over, almost. One day as I was lying on my towel on the beach when there was a pounding sound. It turned out to be a young albatross flapping its wings and running downhill straight towards us. I rolled away, and the albatross continued his run over my towel and down the beach. It must have been his first go because he was still running when he hit the water. Then he was floating instead of flying. He turned back and strode up the beach back to his start point. The strangest sight of that bird was that it looked clumsy walking on the ground, but once it was airborne it became a creature with graceful movement.

The Laysan albatross was the main occupier of Midway Island. The Americans called it the Gooney bird. During the last world war, the Americans had collected them and flown them away to another island, only to find that they flew back to their original home. The birds were everywhere on the island, including being close to their original locations on which buildings had been constructed. Those birds could not understand the strange humans in their home territory. Whenever we came across the Gooney bird on the path, we had to give way. The bird would never move over and would always stop and give people a queer look if we didn't move out of its way. They would build a nest with sand anywhere and sit there on their eggs. On my walk one day I went close to a bird on a nest and it raised its head and clicked its beak to frighten me, but then ended up falling backwards out of its nest. That resulted in me not bothering them again. One day on the golf course, a Gooney was lying dead with its tongue sticking out. That was the result after a fight with another male that had managed to grab the tongue and hold it until that bird had died.

During one of my days on the beach there was a bird hovering over the sea and wiggling its tail feather in the water to attract fish that it would then snap up. That bird was the long tailed Skua. On my walk around the island another day it was a thrill to be close to that bird who must have been hiding from me. The end of its long red tail was sticking out of a hole in the ground where it was hiding. It would have been great to have picked up such a feather, but the tail I was seeing was attached to a bird. As soon as it was touched, the tail disappeared deeper into the hole. Another day there was an unusual sight of a smaller bird called the arctic tern. They fly in pairs at high altitudes and it seemed that that their flying was for fun and not looking for food. It was unusual to see a bird sitting on its laid egg on a branch without any nest. Even when the bird moved away, the egg remained on the branch because it was glued to the branch. I was also told that the hatched chick would automatically grip the branch with its feet to prevent itself from falling off. My sightings of many new birds on a remote island in the vast Pacific were a real delight for me.

On the island of Midway there was an old aircraft that the Americans flew around for pleasure. One day we had the privilege of being taken on a flight around the atoll. It was the first time that I had stepped inside the tail-wheeled piston engine of a Douglas Dakota aircraft. The Americans called it the DC 4. During our flight we orbited around the Midway atoll. From there we could see the surface remains of a volcanic land mass that had originally been over the location where the current Hawaii islands are being created. During the flight, I also had the privilege of sitting in the co-pilot seat and to my surprise the pilot even allowed me to fly it. We had some lovely patches of low cumulus clouds and it delighted me to fly around them. When someone standing beside us was trying to look ahead, I pushed the nose down gently to enable the sight of the scene below. The pilot was happy to let me manoeuvre the aircraft around the area. That flight on the Dakota was a great delight for me. Then in the bar we were talking to the American pilot and I told him about my task in the Vulcan flying. He was shocked to realise that he had allowed someone who was not a pilot to fly their vintage aircraft and advised me not to tell anyone about it. I didn't tell any Americans in Midway about it.

Sailing was another new activity for me in Midway. The Americans had a few small sailing boats that could be hired for the day for one dollar, which was less than half a pound in those days. The sea inside the atoll was usually calm and I went through a few lessons. It surprised me that controlling the boat in the wind was natural because the direction of the wind could be sensed through the behaviour of the boat. It was a great delight for me to be doing some sailing on my own. When I was walking back to my instructor on the beach, one of my colleagues came running out to me and asked me if he could be trained to sail. Sailing within the atoll was very safe. However, a couple of times an American came up to me in a motor boat to advise me not to sail too far out.

When we went to Midway, I had taken my deep diving kit with me. Amazingly, that kit was stolen from my room that had not been locked shut. In addition to the Americans on Midway, there were also some Philippine workmen. The loss of that kit not only prevented me from doing any diving at Midway, but also resulted in me not re-equipping myself for deep diving again. My deep diving experiences at Malta ended up being my first and last experiences of the hobby that gave me the experience of coping with higher pressures. That was the opposite to my experience of lower air pressures outside my body when I went flying.

Golf and sailing had been activities that I had commenced during my time at Midway. One day the Americans were having a golf competition and asked us to join them. I decided to have a go and found myself teamed with an American for the competition. That day some of my golf shots were okay and we did reasonably well during the round. At the end of my first golf competition game it surprised me that we had the best score for the day. After my very first competition I was asked to step forward to select the first prize from a pile of prizes. That enabled me to pick up a new putter. However, the weird game of golf was only going to be a prime free time activity in a much later life.

While waiting for the Chinese test we flew once a week over the vast Pacific Ocean. That was the only time in my life that I had crossed the International Date Line and had flown around the global area that was experiencing the next day. Finally, after about three weeks the expected nuclear explosion did take place. All we had been waiting for was to collect some specimen of the radiation fallout. That was done by a crew on the next programmed flight and we all prepared ourselves for a return home. My crew returned home by transport aircraft. First, we flew to Hawaii in an American Hercules cargo plane and then by an RAF transport aircraft to Britain. After our return home in September we went on some leave from work to have time with our families. I had missed being with my delightful little children.

Faulty nuclear explosion in 1976

Seven months after our last trip to Midway Island we flew out again in March 1976 for another sampling collection from a Chinese nuclear test. We flew via Goose Bay in Canada to Offutt AFB in Nebraska to collect some equipment. From there we staged through California, refuelled in Honolulu and flew to Midway Island. On the last stage of our flight we suffered a loss of our HF radio communications, but I managed to relay our messages through an airliner using VHF radio.

Shortly after our arrival at Midway, the Chinese nuclear explosion took place and a crew flew out to collect the radiation sample. However, that time there was a near disaster for that Vulcan crew. As soon as the radiation started getting picked up, all the detection meters had suddenly swung to the maximum. The aircraft was rapidly swung round and was flown back to Midway. The radiation level was unknown as the meters had passed maximum levels. That nuclear explosion had not followed the expected pattern and had resulted in a very radio-active discharge being released into the atmosphere. The aircraft and crew were quickly dispatched away from Midway for safety. Shortly afterwards we departed from Midway on our transit back to home base without having flown any task flight. During our return we had to stop in Honolulu for refuelling.

Hawaii emergency

On our final approach to Honolulu airport we had a problem when lowering the landing gear. Our normal hydraulic system seemed to have totally failed and we had to use gravity to lower and lock the three wheels. As the two main wheels dropped down backwards, the airflow then pushed them into their locked positions. On the other hand, the nose wheel dropped down forwards and was prevented from locking down due to the airflow. We then had to break away from our landing approach and perform some aircraft manoeuvres to allow gravity to push the nose wheel into its locked position. That's when we were alerted to our special drill of sliding out from the aircraft if the nose wheel could not be locked into position. That involved me grabbing one hydraulic jack to deflect my fall away from the nose wheel and preventing me from slamming into it. Fortunately, the nose wheel did lock down and we continued with the approach for an emergency landing. The aircraft was initially slowed down by reducing the engine power and extending the electrical airbrakes. However, after landing the aircraft was slowed down initially by our rear parachute, but to stop us rolling off the runway, the emergency pneumatic braking system had to be engaged. Fortunately, all these worked out and we could taxi off the runway to the USAF Hickam side of the airport.

To me, that landing gear problem had been a puzzle. Then my experience of an unusual occurrence during our flight enabled me to fathom the cause of the hydraulic system failure. During our flight, I happened to have noticed some unusual movement of a control cable that was under the table beside my seat. I had mentioned that to the captain, but he told me to disregard it. Later, I realised that he must have been doing something to deliberately create a hydraulic failure, just to have some free days in Hawaii. As we had landed safely, I could not propel myself into reporting to our authorities about my experience of sensing the unusual movement of a cable in flight that must have been done by the foot movement of the captain and had resulted in the hydraulic system failure. That was the first and only time that I had lost respect for a flying companion.

Our aircraft was being repaired in a USAF hangar and after it had been repaired, we watched it being taken out of the hangar the day before our flight. There were many Americans watching our Vulcan being towed out of the hangar. Someone standing next to me said that the aircraft being pulled out must be the new American B1 bomber. When he was told that it was the B2 bomber that Britain had built and flown for more than twenty years, he was dumbstruck. On our return flight, we stopped at USAF McClellan in California for two days. There we sighted our other Vulcan parked well away at an isolated spot. It would remain parked there until its radiation levels had declined to a suitably safe level. During our weekend stop we had the opportunity to visit the lovely city of Sacramento. I was impressed with the sights of old European fittings inside buildings that also looked old. A night stop in Canada and a final flight got us home after a period of nearly three weeks.

One day my flight was with our squadron commander, John Willis, on a maritime exercise. After our long period of high-level work, we flew down to almost sea level to say goodbye to a warship. He flew straight for the side of the ship. Just short of the ship he pulled up to almost a vertical flight that must have blasted off any loose articles on the ship. The ship crew did give us a cheerful goodbye. Another day he took us up beyond our limited altitude of 50,000 feet. I had to ask the air traffic control for a climb to 55,000 feet and the controller calmly said that there was no aeroplane there. That was the highest level I have ever been at and had the delight of looking at the slightly more curved horizon of our planet.

Dramatic low flight over the Atlantic Ocean

One day we were sent on a flight to go and locate a couple of Russian warships that had been lost by the NATO forces in the northern Atlantic Ocean. We had to search a vast area and initially we flew up to our highest level of 50,000 feet to scan the ocean with our radar. Numerous radar contacts were detected and then we found a pair sailing together. To visually identify those radar signals I contacted air traffic control for clearance to dive down to almost sea level. There we sighted the Russian warships and flew past them at some distance. The Russians have been delighted, because they had a chance to detect, track and attack an intruder. Their guns were tracking our movement and we saw some flares flying out towards us. As the Vulcan bomber was only going to be used in anger at low-level against land targets, we did not need to display our tactics to the warships and flew past them with friendly waves and did not reveal any of our abilities in a real war. Then we set up in our climb to our high altitude on our return track. During our climb to the high level we had a real shock.

Suddenly our aircraft started rumbling with a loud noise. As there was nothing in our checklist for that problem, I shouted out to the crew to check all their systems. I also looked out with my periscope for the sight of any damage at the top and bottom surfaces of the aircraft. There was no sign of any damage. There was nothing wrong with any of the systems that we used. No one had found anything to be wrong with their systems. Then we all went through shutting down our normal systems in turn to see if we could identify where the problem was occurring to create the noise. When we had dived down to identify the warships, we were all fully strapped up with our parachutes and dinghies in case we had to jump out over the ocean. I was also ready to make an emergency call in case we had to jump out. Then suddenly, the noise stopped when the pilots had switched off the pressurisation system. We stopped our climb and levelled the aircraft below ten thousand feet for our return flight. I was sure that the Russians would not have been breaking the rules of our war game when we flew past them, but I did feel uncertain for a short period. Our pressurisation system was run by an electric motor that was situated right behind our pressure cabin and had come loose from its mountings. That is why the noise in the cabin was a real alarm for us. I experienced more frights during my high-level flying than I ever experienced during low-level bomber flying.

After my tour of duty with 27 Squadron I only had to enter another door at the same hangar to transfer to my next posting. My last posting in the RAF was to 617 Squadron, the dam buster squadron, for the nuclear bombing.

Chapter 10
Final RAF service

No 617 Squadron

My final period of RAF service life started in March 1977 on 617 Squadron (the dam buster squadron of WW II) that was also at Scampton. Those Vulcan flights were to be mainly for their nuclear bombing role, but we ended up being engaged in some other roles as well. My new captain was Gerry Margiotta who had bought from me a small Austin-Morris estate car earlier in 1969 when I departed from Scotland for Malta. He had married a French girl who I had met in Madagascar in 1966. The first flight of our new crew was to Akrotiri on some maritime training that gave us a lovely weekend stay in Cyprus. From our home base, we flew regularly on low-level flights and one day we suffered an engine failure due to a bird strike. As there was no major problem with aircraft control we flew around at a higher altitude and burned off fuel to avoid doing an overweight landing.

In July we flew several times on formation flights, practicing for the fly-past over Buckingham Palace on the silver jubilee for HM the Queen. She became the Queen when she was in Kenya in 1952 while I was there in school. The fly-past involved a formation of three Vulcans in a row accompanied by various other aircraft in formation on the sides of the Vulcans. During our later practice flight, we had a small problem with an undercarriage door and had to drop out of the practice flying group. That also resulted in us becoming the reservists for the fly-past on 30 July. It was disappointing for me to be missing the opportunity of flying past low-level over Buckingham Palace and to have waved to the Queen in her house in London. Four decades earlier she had driven past close to our house in Mombasa and waved to me beside the road.

During out flights in August we would first do some simulated high-level bombing for our conventional bombs that seemed to me to be completely out of date in the age of nuclear bombs. After that we would carry out our real task of low-level flying and entered various sections of the route that avoided built-up areas. The low flight to a target required the combined activities of all the crew. Our compartment behind the pilots would be blacked with curtains while the aircraft would be bouncing through the hills and valleys. I had to concentrate on various equipment operations and not bother about the scenery. Due to the intensity of the low-level flying operations, the only opportunity of sighting the outside scenery was for me to occasionally look backwards and sideways through my periscope. I would have no idea of our position from the views that would be flashing past. Low level flying required great concentration.

Meera Bala 'moonan'

After my daughter Meera Bala had reached her second birthday, I decided to give her the Hindu treatment normally given to the boys. She was given a '*moonan*' in which all her hair was cut off and then deposited in the sea as part of the Hindu custom. Little Meera responded very well during the ceremony. Her hair then had to be deposited in the sea during a suitable flight. During that period our flights were mostly to the west over the Atlantic Ocean. It was in September 1977 that I planned to drop her hair into the Atlantic Ocean when we set off on a flight to Goose Bay in northern Canada. Once again, we taped the packet of hair to a lower airbrake and I called for crew actions to eject the hair bundle from a high altitude into the ocean, south of Greenland. That experience had again puzzled some more of my friends over strange Hindu traditions, but for me it was solely an act of love for my child. I had been very fortunate for having had another loving child in my life.

Nebraska in the USA

From Goose Bay in Canada we flew to an American base at Offutt in Nebraska to carry out some low-level flying in that part of America. Flying at low level in the open areas of the USA was less stressful than our flights at home. One day we also carried out a practice diversion to the airport at the town of Lincoln in Nebraska. During our weekend stay, Gerry and I decided to visit Lincoln and drove there from Offutt. My city of Lincoln in

Britain had been named two thousand years ago, even before the Romans had arrived in Britain. The American city name must have been linked to the first American President. We had a nice look around the place and ended up in a café where a girl from the university was serving. Gerry asked her about entry requirements at the university for his daughter. The attendant said that all foreigners would have to sit an English examination before their entry. When he told her that his daughter would be coming from England, the attendant said that all foreigners needed their qualification in English, regardless of which foreign country they came from.

After our low-level flying in Nebraska we set off for Goose Bay. Just as we were entering Canada our VHF radio failed and we lost contact with air traffic control (ATC). I was then able make a contact on a HF channel and asked them to relay our messages to ATC. That HF channel then relayed back to us a clearance for landing even when we were not even in sight of the airport. When we arrived at Goose Bay the ground controllers were flashing a green light to give us clearance for a straight-in landing. During our return to Britain we flew out over the Atlantic at 62degrees north and passed over Greenland, which had plenty of ice in view. The name for that country was a mystery to me. The other country along our route, called Iceland, showed us more land than ice.

1977

During the autumn we had a 617 Squadron reunion gathering and I even had the pleasure of housing a member who had been flying in that squadron during World War II. He also brought his wife with him and it was a privilege for me to have hosted them in my house. At the squadron building and in the Officers' Mess it was a delight to be with more people who had been in a major war. It was a privilege for me to be in the armed forces of the country that had enabled me to go around the globe on which we exist. My RAF life was supposed to be a working life, but to me it was a delightful state of existence.

Later that year it was necessary for me to do a very unusual trip. Another crew that was in Goose Bay could not fly back because their AEO was unwell and the aircraft could not be flown without one. So, that required me to jump into a Vulcan as a passenger and fly westwards over the Atlantic to Canada. The next day my jump was into my normal position in the other Vulcan in Canada where I flew back home eastwards over the Atlantic. My neighbouring friends could not believe that I had been to Canada as they had seen me at home all week.

Ground duty

During most of my RAF period, my working periods were related to flying duties, but there was one occasion in winter when I was given the job of investigating damage to one of the RAF married quarters. When the young airmen had gone away on holiday, there had been a water pipe burst in the roof that had completely flooded the house. My new task took me a whole week to investigate that occurrence. I called various people for interviews at our administration building, visited the location and viewed the property in detail. The following week I submitted a report that did not find the young airman guilty for the failure as he had turned off the water supply at a pipe that came into the kitchen. The failure was caused by the channelling of the main supply. The main water supply control in the house was hidden behind a screwed-up panel beside his fireplace in the sitting room. The young airman and his wife were greatly relieved not to be punished for that accident, but they had to suffer the loss of their possessions that had been damaged. Some of my friends were surprised that I had managed to investigate and report my findings in just a week when it had taken them a lot longer during their investigations.

Flying exercises in 1978

My flying in 1978 was with a new captain, John Hills, who had to be trained to fly in the Vulcans. That resulted in me flying with him during his training period at Scampton in 1978 doing only the training flights at high level. Then at the squadron we had to go through the low-level flying exercises over the next three months. That is when he became fully qualified as the captain. After that we flew out to Goose Bay to carry out low-level flying over the uninhabited countryside. We had flown across the Atlantic, done three days of flying operations over Labrador and returned home on the fifth day. That tight period of flying in Canada had been done to enable us to be back for a major flying exercise at home.

From Scampton we flew on a major NATO bombing competition in which the American B52 bombers also took part. The B52s would not fly as low as we did through Scottish valleys, but they did have more sophisticated equipment to protect themselves. We went through the intense motions that would prepare us well for participation in a war that was most unlikely. Our squadron had managed to get the highest points for the first phase of the NATO exercise. Later in May we set off for another NATO exercise, but found that we could not carry out our attacks in Germany due to low level cloud. During our peace time flights, we were also concerned about our safety. Only during a real war, would we be using our radar systems for maintaining very low flight through cloud.

During a NATO exercise in June we dispersed to RAF Leeming in Yorkshire and camped beside six Vulcans parked and protected off the runway edge. After our usual practice jumps into the aircraft, we had the final launch on the third day for flights to different targets in Europe and Britain on return. After our high-level and low-level flights, we entered the bombing range at Tain in Scotland and dropped several 28-pound bombs. Then we flew to Stornoway on the Outer Hebrides Islands in Scotland for our usage of some electronic countermeasures against ground forces. During that exercise our squadron won the best bombing competition and several other prizes for the competition. When there were trophy presentations in July, we happened to be in Goose Bay in Canada for some more flying experiences. During one low-level flight in Canada we spotted a local fighter aircraft flying past us and then we noticed that the fighter turned to get behind us. Although that was not part of any exercise, I decided to give the fighter a challenge and got my pilots to do a sharp turn where I ejected out just one box of metal flakes to blot his radar. After that we never sighted the fighter again and the pilot would have been puzzled by not being able to get behind us.

In the middle of 1978 we had a nice squadron open day for our families and friends. I had been given the task of setting up the activities for the open day and made some announcements during the day. There were numerous static displays of the Vulcan aircraft, flight safety equipment, airport protection guns and missiles. For flying displays we had various aircraft in addition to the Vulcan. They included the Phantoms, Buccaneer, Gannet and Beagles. The final period was the barbecue outside the hangar where we had our squadron offices. Fortunately, the weather was fine for the day and it all went well. My neighbouring friends were surprised that setting up the day had been my task.

Some of my relatives in England came and stayed with me in Lincoln. During our walk around the city centre we had done some shopping. Little Meera seemed to be interested in carrying my little bag from the shop and it was hooked onto her shoulder. A little further down the street she was not carrying the bag and I asked where she had put it. She told me that a man had asked her to let him carry the bag for her and we never saw that bag again. The loss of the bag did not bother me, but it was a great relief that my daughter was still with me. One day at home little Meera was being shown my old black and white album and it surprised me when she said that it is good to be having colour in our lives that I did not have in my earlier days. My little Chetan used to spend time with me at my council vegetable plot. One day I told someone that I had planted forty potatoes when Chetan corrected me to say forty-one as he had planted one as well.

USA activities

In 1978 we crossed the Atlantic, stayed a night at Goose Bay and flew to Offutt AFB in Nebraska for some flights at low level. On our first flight, there was a failure of our radar system which is vitally important when low flying to a target. We then continued flying at a high level before finally returning to the base. As we waited for our radar to be repaired, we flew a couple of flights at higher levels. On one of our trips we flew at medium level over the Grand Canyon. That flight gave me the most fantastic sight in America. The ancient natural creations of our planet provided a beautiful scenery.

As we had to wait for nearly a week before the aircraft radar could be repaired for our proper training flights, I decided to contact some Indian friends from Nairobi who lived in Kalamazoo, Michigan. As there was no direct flight to Kalamazoo, I took a flight to Chicago. There the Sharma family picked me up in their car where I experienced a delightful long drive over an uninhabited area that took me to their lovely location in Kalamazoo for a few days. Vishnu was teaching at Kalamazoo University and took me for some golf at a course nearby. The Kalamazoo trip turned out to be a good holiday while I was supposed to be at work. After our aircraft was serviceable, we flew our low-level exercises from Offutt and landed at Goose Bay in Labrador for a night stop. The next day our flight across the Atlantic took us back home where it was a delight to be with my loving children.

Vulcan crash in America

A year before retiring from my RAF life, it was a shock for me to hear news of an air crash in America of a Vulcan flown by my own squadron. Even more devastating was the news that all four crew on board had died. That was the first time that I attended a Christian funeral service. The prospect of a death on a war mission never frightened me, but its occurrence on a display flight was very saddening. During the three months before the crash I had flown more than a dozen times in that Vulcan XL390 aircraft. It had been flown out to the USA by another crew for a display at Chicago. The Vulcan was based at the nearby airport of NAS Glenview. The crew carried a display flight for the press at that airport. The next day they took off early enough to do that display again at Glenview before going to Chicago. The aircrew had been reduced to four as the plotter navigator was not required. Shortly after the start of their practice display the aircraft was doing a tight turn to descend and do a touch-and-go on the runway. Just before completing their turn they realised that they were far too close to the ground and tried to fly round. It was too late for them and they crashed into the ground; the co-pilot even tried to eject out, but he did not survive. None of the crew survived that crash. The cause of that crash was unknown, but my own experiences during some of my display flights in Britain enabled me to fathom the cause of that crash.

A few times during my flights on displays I had been reminding my pilots to set the correct altimeter pressure setting after we had arrived at our display aerodromes otherwise, instead of reading our altitude above the aerodrome, we would be reading our altitude above sea level. That sea level reading is used during transit between aerodromes. As the airport of Glenview was at an altitude of 653 feet, I wondered if the cause of the accident was an incorrect pressure setting for the display. They would have taken off with the pressure for transit to the next aerodrome. In the display the aircraft would fly at 1000 feet above the aerodrome, do tight turn round 180 degrees and descend for a touch and go on the runway. With the wrong altimeter setting there was little chance of avoiding a crash during a 180 degree tight turn from only 350 feet instead of 1000 feet.

1978

During the latter period of 1978 we carried out various flights in Britain as well as in the Mediterranean. From Malta we flew some low-level sorties over Italy and a high-level radar reconnaissance flight over the sea. That weekend in Malta was spent on a yacht together with our navigator who was also a qualified sailor. We had a couple of lovely days of sailing, jumping off the boat and swimming in the sea when we had anchored off the island of Gozo. After our return to Britain I did apply to go sailing on the RAF yacht and waited to go on an exciting sailing trip somewhere. After our break in Malta we continued with some more Italian low-level flying as well as some flights at high level. At home it was a delight to be spending time with my little children, in the garden, in a very close tennis club and in our pleasant city.

That year we flew on numerous operations from our base. A couple of flights required us to carry out RAT (ram air turbine) lowering into the air flow. The RAT was an air driven AC generator tucked inside the bottom of the left wing that would be lowered into the airflow at very high aircraft altitudes in the event of multi failures of normal AC generators as the AC power was vitally important for flight control. The test required a pull on a tucked handle in front of the pilots. My periscope enabled me to view the RAT that had been lowered. After the handle pull by the pilots a flap would open under the wing and the RAT would lower into an airflow position. After that, I would check the RAT electrical output on my displays. During one of our flights we had a very unusual experience during a test of a RAT over the North Sea. When the RAT was lowered into the airflow, I saw it appear and disappear. That had occurred because the ground crew had failed to bolt it to the aircraft during the replacement. It had ejected out from the aircraft completely. We had effectively bombed some location with a

RAT from 45,000 feet up. It must have been like a meteor hitting the earth. Thankfully, nobody on the sea noticed that meteor crash.

English Channel sailing

After my delightful Mediterranean sailing I took part in some ocean sailing from Britain during the winter period 1978-79. From Portsmouth, we sailed south to Le Havre in the RAF yacht with a crew of eight. We bounced across the English Channel towards France in cold, windy and damp weather. My stomach started throwing out and the vision of the gentle sail in the sun in the Mediterranean was completely wiped out from my mind. We finally arrived at the French port and had to stay in the harbour for some days because of the high winds. Luckily, we spent some time on land in the French town.

After a few days of rest in France we set sail for the Channel Islands in much better sailing conditions. My stomach had settled down and I enjoyed contributing to various sailing activities. Just like flying, I found sailing to be good fun and challenging. The RAF yacht moved fast through the sea and we finally got to St. Peter Port on Guernsey Island. Later, we sailed pleasantly across the channel back to Portsmouth. There the crew decided to go to a restaurant for a meal. Strangely my body seemed to be rolling when I was standing or sitting down. As we had entered an Indian restaurant for a meal. Although my experience on that sailing trip was nothing like what I was expecting to embark on, it was still great to have had the opportunity to experience it. The challenge of doing a sail around the globe was never going to be in my head again.

My final RAF year

It was in January 1979 that I teamed up with another captain and we went through a session for our preparedness for a war. Several Vulcans flew away from their bases and met up in small groups at various aerodromes spread around the country. We flew off to Leeming in Yorkshire and set up together with four more aircraft from our squadron beside one end of the runway where the aircraft would be parked and guarded. We also needed to spend time putting up sand bags around our accommodation vans. As it was bitterly cold, we had to use pick axes to break up the frozen sand into rock pieces that were then dropped into sacks to construct walls around the caravans. There were a couple of men in a private car on the public road looking at us through binoculars. I was told that they were likely to be Russian agents, but they were not doing anything illegal during peacetime as they could claim to be bird watching. We were making up and putting sand bags around caravans to hide ourselves from spies. Our preparedness for a war was to launch off before any Russian bomb could arrive at our location. Then during the third night we were alerted for a rapid launch. We all jumped out of bed, rushed into the protected aircraft and all took off rapidly behind each other. After our take-off, we all flew in different directions to our individual targets that were in European countries. After the exercise encounters, we flew back to base that day. That was the period that made me feel that I had had enough of playing war games. It was a great relief to be home again with my children.

Strangely, I had a lovely farewell flight in a Vulcan on the first of June 1979 that was completely unplanned. After we had landed on my last flight, I was asked to help transfer a Vulcan from Scampton to Waddington that was positioned south of Lincoln. As we were going to be flying low over Lincoln, which was our privilege, I got the pilot to fly over my house close to Lincoln Cathedral. Some visitors at my house said that they had seen the supersonic Concorde flying over the house. That totally unplanned flight was a delightful farewell flight for me. After that, I had two months to prepare myself for my total retirement from the military services.

My decision to retire after sixteen years of service allowed me to retain a very delightful memory of my service life and allowed me to look forward to other life experiences. My retirement from the RAF service was going to provide me a pension at the early age of only thirty-nine. My decision for an earlier retirement was to enable me to experience civilian employment as well as carry on working for as long as I wished. My time in the RAF had been a delightful experience, but I also felt that I should be experiencing a life in the civilian field.

Life frights and sadness

In June 1979, I went on a motor caravan holiday trip with my children. We were walking on a hillside in the Yorkshire Dales. We met some people with whom I had a chat. After we walked away from those people, I found that little Chetan was missing. I shouted out for him and did not know whether to look for my son on my own or to run down and find helpers. It was my greatest relief when he was spotted sitting in a dip in the ground, not knowing what to do. After that shattering event, I felt never let him move out of my sight during our countryside walks. Another day we were in the Tower of London when suddenly a rain shower came down and everyone around us ran in different directions. To my horror my little daughter Meera was not in sight. Only after everyone had cleared the area in the rain did I spot my little darling, standing in the rain on her own. That shattering event made me feel that I could not afford to lose sight on my little children, even in town.

After returning to Scampton to finalise my departure procedures there was news about a tragedy that had struck a close friend of mine, Russ Todd. He had a car accident and died together with his son at a crossroad junction in the countryside. I had known Russ since my first posting to Aden in 1966. In the early 1970s they had lived in the same block of flats as me in Malta. Later, they also turned up at Scampton in Lincolnshire where I was on my retirement posting. That was one of the longest close relationships I had had during my RAF life. Russ had managed to survive the more dangerous life in the armed forces, but sadly lost his life on the road.

Plan for new life

Well before my final year of RAF employment, I had started preparing myself for my retirement in August 1979. My initial plan had been to become a flight engineer. Before the launch of the supersonic Concorde, the airlines had looked at the prospect of employing the Vulcan air electronic officers as flight engineers. However, the flight engineering branch of the RAF had given a negative reply. At an interview for a job as a flight engineer with Laker Airways they readily offered me the job and asked me to go and get my licence from the CAA. All that was required for me was to sit some written examinations related to flying for which I would

174

have had no problem after a short course. Then to my surprise the CAA said that the applicants for the job should have been an RAF pilot or a flight engineer or a ground technician for two years to qualify for even sitting the examination. As they had no idea of my job as air electronics officer, they told me that it would take probably a year to amend their ruling. Strangely, my RAF station commander at Scampton had told me to give him a call if I had any problem with my civilian job. There is no doubt that would have enabled me to become a flight engineer, but then I had second thoughts about another flying career. A flying job would have resulted in me having less time with my children. I decided to go for a peaceful technical job that would provide me with plenty of time with my children.

My final decision was to go into an electrical engineering job and I started doing a part-time study of engineering at the Lincoln Technical College. The engineering jobs required me to be familiar with the latest developments. My final decision was to take on a job of teaching engineering at a technical college. That seemed to be something in my capability. I went through a year of teacher training that enabled me to settle into preparing myself for a new life in the teaching environment that would give me more time with my children.

Chapter 11

New life in Devon

Life change in 1979

After finishing with my military life, my new civilian career was directed into technical teaching. Before I could teach, I had to do be taught how to teach. The start of this course was at the Huddersfield Polytechnic. Before that I set off with my children on a motor caravan holiday tour of Britain. In the beautiful area of the Lake District in England we walked on the hills beside lovely lakes. That was followed by a drive around some scenic lochs and glens (lakes and hills) in Scotland. At the mountain of Ben Nevis, we went up on a gentle walk along part of the track going up towards the highest point in Britain. My little Meera was on my shoulders for part of the way and was having a great time out in the open.

When we were walking up the hill there was a terrible occurrence on the path. At one point in the climb we were waiting for some people to step down a tricky path. Right in front of us, a man tripped and fell to the ground and did not get up. I went and helped him to sit up beside the path and to rest for a while. Later that man suddenly slumped to the ground and was found not to be breathing. His wife shouted out to people around to get some help from the base. A runner going up the hill turned back and ran down for help. I laid him down to force him to breathe through his mouth but could not manage to do it. Another helper pushed me aside, turned the man over onto his stomach and pulled him upwards. That made the wounded man vomit out and then he found that there was a clear passage to his lungs. He started pumping air into his lungs but also found that the heart of the man was not beating. That is when I joined him in the process of continually alternating between forcing air into his lungs and pushing down on his chest to try and restart his heartbeat.

It was nearly an hour later that the rescue service arrived and found that they could not manage to restart the heart or the breathing. I later learned from the woman that her husband had suffered a problem earlier when they were higher up the slope, but he had insisted in not calling for any help and had been stepping down himself. When he fell in front of us, it was his heart failure that had caused him to fall. That made me feel disappointed with my own ability. The next day I went to see the woman and she told me that her husband was taking her on a walk to show her where he used to climb during the last world war. After that terrible incident my journey continued northwards via Loch Ness to Inverness and Findhorn where I had stayed thirteen years earlier and ended up meeting some old people who were still living there. After my return home, my house had to be prepared for sale when I would be moving out of Lincoln for a new job.

After the death of my father at my early age in 1949, my life was protected and maintained by my uncle, Chanan Ram from my mother's side. That gentle loving man had some health problem in his later life. In October 1979, he passed away in Slough. That was another rare occasion when I ended up seeing and walking around someone who had passed away. Later, I attended the cremation ceremony to say my final farewell to my dear *Mamaji* who had been a great protector and supporter for us during my young life. He had been helping all my family and enabled us children to grow up and experience satisfactory lives after the death of my father in 1949.

Teacher training in Huddersfield

During my study for the certificate of education at Huddersfield Polytechnic it was necessary for me to stay at some college accommodation during the weekdays. The very first week of study turned out to be very stimulating. The instructor, Ted Duggan, was very keen and helpful. In our group of students there were some other people who had been in the armed services. One day when we were walking between our hostel and the college, someone walking beside me started talking to me and I was wondering what language he was speaking. It turned out that he was speaking in English. What was even more astounding to me was the fact that he was a local Yorkshire lad. Earlier in my life I had not understood what a Yorkshire man was saying when he had given me road instructions for my drive. Yorkshiremen do speak in English, but their local accent makes it sound like a foreign language to a foreigner.

The first two months of my learning taught me how to teach and then we were sent to some other college for some practice teaching. They sent me to a college in my home city of Lincoln. That teaching experience made me realise that there was more to teaching than what had been given to me. It was very difficult to maintain the attention of the students and getting them to absorb the knowledge. I realised that teaching was not just about delivering information to others, but also helping them to absorb some knowledge. Back at Huddersfield in December 1979, there was a review of my teaching practice and for my own further training. Later, we had another two weeks of practical teaching in Lincoln and during that period we were assessed for our job by a Huddersfield lecturer.

Back at Huddersfield we were given more information about the creation of higher education and the practice of delivery. During the lessons on the philosophy of education it surprised me that other trainees at the back of the class were having a private chatter. It also surprised me that the lecturer delivering the course was totally unable to control the behaviour of his students. That's when I interrupted the lecturer, turned around and told the other trainees to shut up or go out of the classroom. After that, the lesson then continued normally. What I learned from that episode was that even some people who were teaching us how to teach, did themselves not know how to maintain control during their teaching.

During our final term in 1980 we posted out our job applications. That was something I had not done since 1962 in Kenya. After having sent out my job applications, it was disappointing not to receive any replies. That is when my instructor looked at my applications and told me that the colleges would not be interested in my military activities, but only in my teaching connections. My job applications were reworded to focus on my secondary activities during my military life that were associated with some training. To my surprise, four invitations for interviews arrived. My first interview was at Rotherham in South Yorkshire. Strangely, the selection for that job had already been decided and the interview was only for some official procedure before the job could be given to some local man. That was a relief for me as I did not fancy the industrial location.

My second interview was at Exeter College in Devon that had sent me an incredible welcome and was also given a very receptive interview. It turned that they had already selected me for the job as they had earlier spoken to my instructor in Huddersfield. I liked the location and readily accepted the job. All my other appointments were cancelled. Surprisingly, during my first visit to Exeter I found a serviceman companion of my Malta days to be working in Exeter after his RAF retirement. He was running a business involving house sales in Exeter and Devon and ended up helping me find a suitable house in and around Exeter.

At home in Lincoln I had painted up a small earlier bicycle and taught Meera to start riding in our little street. One day there was a real fright. Meera was missing. After running around to see where she might have gone by cycling out of our street, I telephoned the police for help in locating my daughter. Thankfully, the police said that someone had rung them about finding a little girl cycling on her own. It was a great relief to have Meera back with us. Meera did not seem to realise that she was lost. She said that she had been cycling on our route to the allotment plot. The Renault 4 car that had been serving me since 1969 in Malta was having many problems in 1980. When driving beside Lincoln Cathedral, my car conked out and I was worried about having to stop driving in a tight spot. Strangely, my son Chetan who was with me told me not to be worried about the car problem. It amazed me that my little son saw that I was not relaxed and was giving me comfort. That experience was another eye-opener for the thinking that could be going on in the mind of a child. During that year, I replaced the brake pads for the car myself, but had to arrange for a garage to do some floor welding on the car. That resulted in me using my Honda motorcycle for my trips to Huddersfield during the final term of my teacher training.

In 1980 my cousin from my father's side was getting married in India. I sent some money to him via another cousin from my mother's side in Chandigarh with whom there was good contact. After the death of my uncle in India in 1966 my auntie and her children in the Indian villages had been continually supported by me. It had been very satisfying for me to have helped my relatives because during my own life in Africa I had been helped by my relatives after my father had died when I was still in primary school. Far from being a financial problem, helping a relative had always been a great privilege in my life.

Start of new life in 1980

My job in Exeter started in September 1980. During the first week of college, the staff had time for suitable preparations before the students flooded in. There was plenty of friendship and support from other lecturers and other staff in the engineering department in a new working environment. It surprised me that the staff members were not familiar with the new structure for technical qualifications that was being introduced. Strangely the new system was what had been taught to me. That resulted in me being involved in helping our college setting up the new system. The college staff had to set up and process the examinations in the colleges themselves instead of examinations prepared nationally. The college examinations would then be checked by inspectors to maintain the national standards.

My first year of teaching was very demanding as the notes for the courses had to be prepared by myself. It was after the first term that my house in Lincoln had been sold and my children came and stayed with me in a flat near the college. The strange experience at the college was that I was being programmed to be doing some overtime work because all of the instructors loved doing that for the extra money they would be receiving. The programmer was amazed that I was not interested getting more money. My main purpose of teaching was to deliver some knowledge to the students to help them in their working lives. It surprised me that a trade union in the college would make the lecturers go on strike in their demands for higher pay and ditching their attention for the students. To me, the process of going on strike from work seemed to be suitable only for the illiterate workers in the old days when they were not even asked for their opinion, which resulted in them being dragged out by their leaders to go on strikes for more pay for everybody.

In our staff room, there was a variety of behaviour amongst the staff members. It was good fun to be talking with an enthusiastic man. One day he came up with a concept of a perpetual rotation of a cylinder. However, he could not manage to get his construction to rotate perpetually and could not get any member of the engineering staff to identify what was wrong with it. After I asked him about the exact construction of his device, he told me that he had a cylinder drum on an axle plugged into the side of a water tank. He expected the layers of water at the upper and lower sides of the drum to be producing different forces to make the drum start spinning. He was expecting his cylinder to start rotating just like the blades of a water mill. I had to tell him that his device was nothing like the water mill that was in moving water. His concept of forces did exist, but they were acting horizontally against the screws that were holding the drum in position. Without the screws the drums would have been pushed out sideways and the water would be lost. It was clear that he had little concept of physics. Later he had tried to weld a leaking water pipe in his house without draining out the pipe and was surprised that the pipe had burst open. It was apparent he was teaching science without having any idea of what it was. I had fun talking with that man.

In our room for some staff members there would some smoking done without any regards for those that did not smoke. I could not stand the smoking that was done inside the room and they did not want me to open the window and let the cold air come in. That resulted in me leaving the staff room and moving into the storage room beside the staff room that was cleared out for me. The earlier staff room was used by me for making cups of tea and coffee. In fact, I took over the task of collecting the money and managing the provision of the items that we could use anytime in the room. During lunch breaks the staff could go to a restaurant that supplied food prepared by the students and there it was nice to meet up with many friendly lecturers from other departments of the college.

At the end of the academic year in July 1981 there was enough time to move into my new house. During the first long break from my job there was time for me to take my children on a drive in the south west peninsula of Britain in our motor caravan. We swam in the sea bay in Cove and saw an old castle at Tintagel on an island connected by a bridge. The long summer holidays were a great break from work and enabled me to have delightful outings with my children in our beautiful countryside. In addition to that, there also were breaks at Christmas, Easter and half-term periods. It also meant I could start engaging in new life experiences.

Start of pilot flying in 1981

A problem that my body had developed during the period of my employment change-over was a pain in my back. On reflection, I think that my back problem had been created when I fell off a tree onto some steps during my youth. That resulted in me having to give up playing hockey or having any physical leisure activity. Then, during our first summer break I had taken the children to the air show at Exeter airport and found that my spare time could be used for fun flying. That realisation made me join the Exeter Flying Club (EFC) at the airport. During my training period, the handling of the aeroplane in flight was no major problem for me as I had done some gentle handling of large aeroplanes including the RAF Shackleton as well as the American Dakota. However, handling those aircraft had been well above the ground level. My flight training with the club in the small two-seater, single engine Cessna 150 aeroplane with very basic flying instruments was very exciting. The training for a private pilot licence is mainly done by flying in good weather conditions and by keeping out of the cloud.

When it came to landings, I had only seen other pilots do the descent paths and landings, which were a totally critical aspect of flying. One day we went on a flight for my first approach and landing during my training. It was normal practice for the instructor to carry out the first circuit for demonstration, but I asked her to let me handle the aeroplane and she could do the talking. She let me do that. My major problem with aeroplane handling started occurring on the final descent path for the landing. That was because the sight of the land target would start to speed up as we flew closer to the ground, although the aeroplane speed was not increasing. Then the handling of the flight path in three dimensions required immediate operations of the flight controls that had to be well coordinated. On my first approach, the aeroplane started zigzagging because my control inputs could not be coordinated well enough. My instructor let me experience the need for the training and took over control. I felt I had behaved as a child jumping on a bicycle for the first time and expected to be able to ride it because he had seen other people doing it. It didn't matter how brilliant a mind the person could have; it was the body that needed to sense the three-dimensional movements created by the flight so that landing could be controlled to land on the runway in the right direction and not somewhere else. The main problem was that the wind direction would be affecting the direction of the flight path over the ground.

Developing the skills for flying an aeroplane are like driving a car, except that in the air one cannot stop the flight and have a look at a problem that one could do at a roadside. There were numerous checks we had to do outside as well as inside the aeroplane before starting the engine. Then brake checking had to done during taxying. At a holding point, full engine power had to be checked before take-off. During the flight, there were many other aspects of flight control that one had to be aware of to maintain safety. The major aspect was the loss of power from the single engine where speed could only be maintained by loss of height. First, one had to maintain control of the aeroplane without power and then one had to locate some area where a forced landing could be carried out only once. In the wild terrain we would have to immediately select some area for the landing, but we would only descend to five hundred feet during the training. However, over our airport we would go through the whole process of landing without engine power.

Another feature of safe flying was to have an alternative airport for landing in case there was some problem at the airport that required a diversion for landing somewhere else. That required us always to retain enough fuel and have details of the diversion aerodrome. I had not realised that the training for the flying licence was going to be stressful. My military flying as a crew member had been comfortable because there were other people handling other aspects of flying. On the light aeroplane the pilot was the only person in control of everything in all circumstances. All I wanted to do was to go flying for fun.

On one of my solo flights from Exeter I landed and took off at the airports of Lulsgate near Bristol and the Compton Abbas grass aerodrome in Dorset. During my return to Exeter on a westerly heading the sun was low and there was a haze in front of me. The terrain could not be seen well enough to be sure of the position. Then the sight of the railway line going past the airport prompted me to start following it. Suddenly, the railway line disappeared into a tunnel. That railway line did not appear in my sight again. Just when I decided to turn southwards to spot the coast towards Exmouth, the aerodrome appeared on my left. That made me contact the airport for an approach for landing. Instead of having done a flight straight in for a landing, my approach to join the circuit was from the opposite side. My training flights did make me experience some periods of tension. It took me nearly a year of strenuous flying to finally get my pilot licence. After getting that licence in July 1982 it took me time to recover from the tensions that I had been experiencing. Although my flying experience as a crew member had been comfortable, my flying experience as a pilot turned out to be far more challenging. I ended up having a break from flying for a whole year.

South West of Britain

From my house at the edge of Exeter city there were several footpaths to the city centre. They turned out to be a great delight in my life. As I lived uphill from the college it was easy for me to rush down to work, but there was no rush to get back home. There were a variety of paths away from traffic and through the big beautiful areas on route, including the wide area of Exeter University. I could also walk back through totally unlit areas at night to stop and look at the stars. Being on the edge of the city there were sights of foxes, badgers and deer during my walks to and from work that would be spread over different hours of the day, as we taught in the evenings as well. There were times when I would put on my boots after returning from work and go walking in the nearby hilly woods on the north side below which the river Exe was flowing. It was nice to be living in a scenic environment around a city that also had some peaceful wildlife around.

Although my house had four bedrooms it was necessary for me to put an extension to enable accommodation for my mother and visitors. After designing a two-storied extension I got permission for its construction. The electrical wiring, painting and decorating would be done by myself after the construction by the builders had been completed. However, there was a problem with the roof construction and the builders only completed their work at the end of our summer holiday period. That resulted in the extension not being used until the following year because there was no time for me to do my task for the extension.

The social contact with some of the lecturers was very pleasant. At home, I had plenty of time in the garden and with my children. It was pleasure to have long holiday periods together with my children. Teaching was a very satisfactory life for me. The beautiful countryside of Devon in the South West peninsula had scenic views and bird life. Close to the estuary of the River Exe there are numerous birds and it was a delight to see the avocets that are used by the RSPB (Royal Society Protection of Birds) for its symbol. The society took me on a boat trip in the Exe estuary when the avocet numbers had been only about forty, but later continued to increase every year and got higher. In the valley beside my house there were cuckoos singing and were occasionally sighted. There were many wild birds, foxes, badgers and even some deer in my back garden.

Falkland war in 1982

Less than three years after I had retired from the armed services, some of my RAF colleagues were engaged in a war against the Argentinians in 1982. After my training on the Vulcan bombers I remember stating in my report at the end of the course that the training for the use of conventional bombs had been a waste of time. The training for use of nuclear weapons would be the only useful status for the Vulcans for maintaining the peace on the globe. We had been deterring the Soviet Union from engaging in a nuclear war against us. It was only after my retirement that the Vulcan bomber would be used for some real conventional bombing and would be flown in anger for the first time.

The retiring old Vulcans would be used for their real purpose by dropping several one thousand-pound bombs on Stanley airport on the Falkland Islands that had been illegally occupied by the Argentinians. That was the only time that the Vulcans were not only going to be bombing in a real fight, but they were also going to be flying for extremely long periods. During my flying days in the Vulcans we flew the bombers for no more than five hours for our bombing role and we had never used the refuelling probe during our flights. For the Falklands war, the Vulcans needed to be refuelled several times for their total attack run of about 8,000 nautical miles on a flight that lasted for more than three times the maximum hours I had flown on those bombers. A dozen tankers did some combined refuelling of a single bomber several times to enable it to have one go at dropping its bombs on the Falklands, as well as flying back to base.

Amazingly, the creation of some holes in the runway at Stanley airport had deterred the Argentinians from operating their aircraft from the islands. The Royal Navy and the British Army managed to push the Argentinians off the Falklands. It was a massive achievement a long way from home with the use of conventional weapons only. The Britons became very proud of their armed forces. The Argentinian government had been trying to divert the attention of their public away from their domestic problems and tried to show power by robbing some islands away from another country and expected to get away with it. I am glad that some armed forces on the globe could counter the pathetic motives of some stupid countries.

1983 Tour de France

Added to the delight of my teaching profession, the long holiday breaks in my employment were delightful. After my second year of teaching in July 1983 I set off on my longest holiday together with my children. We jumped into our motor caravan and set off to tour around France for five weeks. We crossed the English Channel to Normandy. Initially, it was uncomfortable for me to be driving on the right-hand side of the road with my driving wheel also on that side. At the first campsite we stayed there for a couple of days before starting on an adventure trip. At the back entrance of the van a canvas extension could be attached. The car could also be detached from that tent and we could drive around with more free space in the van. We set off on a long anticlockwise tour of France.

We visited the very scenic island called Mont St. Michael in the Gulf of St. Malo and then drove south to stop at St. Hillaire de Riez for a few days in a campsite for French teachers. It was a great delight that there were a lot of people with young children at the school campsite. There we went swimming and I had a go at wind surfing. Chetan had his eleventh birthday and we went to a funfair park. Although my Meera was three years younger she had grown up faster and was nearly the same size as Chetan. At the campsite somebody trying to speak to Meera in French was surprised that she only spoke English. As it happened, it was an Englishman who was trying to talk to her in French.

One day we ventured out of France and drove south to the little country of Andorra la Villa in the Pyrenees between France and Spain. From a camp site beside a river we took a cable car up to a high lake. We returned back on foot and Chetan and I even had a race running down the slope. Back in France a drive took us down to Port la Nouvelle on the coast where we spent a few relaxed days. My children had their first swim in the warm Mediterranean. My little Meera even managed to swim for a hundred metres.

After an eastward drive through some beautiful hilly scenery we went along the coast and entered the luxurious town of Monte Carlo in the small country of Monaco. There we spent the day on the luxury beach. Once again it was a delight to be swimming in the warm Mediterranean with the children. Strangely, that day we even saw Prince Rainer of Monaco in a car. It was a delight to drive around on the roads that are still being used during the Formula One Monaco Grand Prix. After a drive past the big casino palaces we went out of the town to a hillside location and parked beside the road with scenic views below. Some of our items in the van were placed outside and we settled down for a comfortable sleep in the van. Then a strange singing sound could be heard outside the van. A drunken man was fumbling into our pile of belongings outside the car. As expected, he found nothing useful and walked past us and continued with his drunken singing.

During a drive through the high Alps, amazingly we saw the remains of the earlier sea floor of our planet. On the way to Paris there was a clanking noise in the engine beside my driving seat. While I was looking for a suitable place to stop, the noise strangely stopped sounding and there was no problem with the driving. At the campsite I found that the drive belt for the cooling fan was in a twisted state. It had been so loose that it had started slipping and knocking, but then had strangely twisted over, shortened itself and allowed it to function without noise. I had no trouble in fixing the problem myself. At the city of Versailles, we stopped and looked around the French palace.

In Paris we went up the Eiffel Tower and then took a boat trip along River Seine. At The Louvre we had a look at the Mona Lisa painting. Seeing all those sights and having taken my children to those locations had been a great delight. From Paris a drive took us through some heavy traffic to get to a camping site. Another motor caravan was beside me at a roundabout and at some traffic lights. I suspected that those people were trying to get to the same camping site. However, from the next lights that van set off on a different road to mine. Then on my route to my campsite that van again appeared in my sight, but it was going in the opposite direction to mine. What was most unusual was that when we got to the campsite entry, the other motor caravan also came to that location from the opposite direction. We both got out of our vans, walked towards each other and shook hands as if were old friends. We struggled to find a space to park at that campsite as it was nearly full of caravans. The next day a drive took us back through Normandy to Cherbourg for the ferry to Weymouth. After five weeks in a motor caravan we came back to a home that was an enormous carpeted house. After that we had another three weeks away from work and the children had time with their friends. The teaching profession had lifted me into a state of satisfaction in my life and with my children.

Private fun flying

After gaining my flying licence I had stopped for about a year. That was the sort of period when a lot of people would be terminating their flying after they had been through their rare experiences of flying in light aeroplanes. However, I restarted my flying activity by going through some advanced training for radio navigation systems during the college break in July 1984. Then a conversion to flying in a four seat Cessna aeroplane enabled me to start taking friends as passengers around the delightful and interesting countryside around us. Flying from Exeter around Devon, Cornwall and Dorset provided a lovely variety of sightings during flights of only about an hour. There was plenty of countryside area in the south west that was free air space for light aeroplanes, but the pilots could still have radio contact with Exeter or Plymouth for help and advice. The beautiful sights of the hills and coast in that part of Britain also made it easy to navigate around, as well as provide numerous delights to the passengers. Initially it was not legal to share the cost of flying with the passengers, but later the CAA (Civil Aviation Authority) did legally allow the pilots to share the cost of their flights with their passengers and not for any other arrangements.

Even after getting my flying licence it was difficult for me to be able to do a straight-in approach and landing. I would sometimes fly past for another approach if there was any doubt about the landing. With the other aspects of flying there was no problem for me due to my RAF flying as a crew member. It was a delight for me to be doing low flying over Dartmoor areas where there were no buildings. I would even wave to people on the tors by waggling the wings or my passengers would wave their hands. Strangely, some people on the ground were waving back at us. The more regular flying that one did, the less tension there would be during preparation for the flight. Many friends and their relatives enjoyed their low-level flying around the lovely sights of Devon. Exeter is situated at a location with beautiful views in three different directions with continual changes of scenery and numerous old human locations. Some people had never flown before and found it to be delightful. There were times when people would find it difficult to spot their house, even in a small village, because they had never looked at it from above. That resulted in me circulating around the town or village where people came from and got them to identify their homes and wave to their people below. Then I would roll the wings of the aircraft quickly to say goodbye to them. Flying light aeroplanes in lovely countryside has been a real pleasure for me. The delightful experiences of only one hour remained in my mind for several days after the flight.

My new college principal, John Capey, lived close to me in Exeter and I invited him to my house on New Year's Day and found out that he had been an airline pilot during his earlier days. He started flying with me for fun around the scenic countryside in 1984 and continued doing that for the next ten years. He too was enjoying an earlier working life experience which was now becoming a hobby in later life. I flew some people from Exeter to Plymouth via Dartmouth port on the coast and then some other people on my return flight from Plymouth over Dartmoor hills back to Exeter. After I had taken a college friend around Dartmoor and Plymouth, he later presented me with a little wooden tail wheel aeroplane that he had made and labelled it as Sharma Airways. That friend also encouraged many people from his village to go flying with me for the enjoyable experience of seeing the beautiful local area from the air.

As many of my teaching friends triggered their friends to experience the delight of local flying, my flying times started increasing and there was an increase in my friendships. That resulted in me also taking friends on flights to other airports in our area of the South West. My flights would be along the scenic south coast and inland countryside. We landed at the small grass airfield at Bridport and Compton Abbas and then returned via Axminster to Exeter with different views of our countryside. Some additional flight training for myself enabled me to fly on instruments so that I could fly through clouds. That would be very useful for me to fly higher up above clouds and to find the aerodromes below clouds. Professional pilots of airlines had to have that skill, but for the private pilots it was an option which required regular checks for that acquired skill. During my RAF flying I had experienced being flown through clouds many times by my pilots, but in my private flying that had to be avoided until the skill for handling the aeroplane in the cloud and navigating without any autopilot. Also, that sort of flying could only be done in the summer as small light aeroplanes have no ice protection systems.

Around Devon there are many valleys with which I was familiar with on the ground and was aware of numerous ancient sites that were the remains of human locations of more than three thousand years ago. Flying over those familiar sights was a delight for me. The sight of the coast and the hilly countryside made it easy for me to be aware of my flying position. I started taking many colleagues from Exeter College to go flying over the rapidly variable scenery and above some homes in the villages. One day there was a real surprise for me when I was low flying over Dartmoor because two RAF jets from behind us flew past below my aeroplane on either side. Those pilots could even have been some friends that I had flown with during my flying days in the Vulcan bombers when we flew only two hundred feet above the terrain.

On some of my flights I took a school teacher, Chips Barber, who was also a writer of books about the ancient sights of Devon. He got me to take him flying around the areas that he photographed for his books. He managed to do that a few times, despite the fact that he would end up throwing up. That friendship resulted in him getting his book photographs cheaply and it was a delight for me to be doing the flying. I would always be prepared to do an orbit around any sight that my passenger friends wanted to see. It was in July 1985 that my first flight overseas was to Guernsey with an instructor. After that I could fly out of our mainland with passengers, but that did not happen until a lot later. Most of my local flying was around Devon and even during those flights there were few landings at other aerodromes in Britain, mainly because of the added costs for landings.

Walking and home life

My new friends in the college went on long walks during the period when the college was closed, but the schools would close a week later. It was a delight for me to join them for the walk that they had already started. That group were on a walk along the longest footpath of seven hundred miles in Britain that covers the whole of the southwest coast between Bournemouth on the south coast and Minehead on the north coast. All of the planning was being done by another electrical instructor. Each of our walks were for about a hundred miles of the coast path that went through Dorset, Devon, Cornwall and Devon again. The walking distance would be further as we would also have to walk off the coast for accommodation. It was in July 1984 that I joined the group for a walk on the south coast of Devon from Salcombe to Looe. Despite my back problem the walks enabled me to maintain certain physical activities. Walking along the varied coast was a great delight.

As my walking group had already done the eastern part of the route between Bridport near Bournemouth in Dorset and Salcombe in Devon, I joined up with another lecturer to cover that part of the total coastal path. We had a nice long walk between Bridport and Swanage in Dorset. That covered the long Chesil Beach which has sea on one side and fresh water on the other side. We walked on the circular Lulworth Cove and passed the Isle of Portland and Kimmeridge oil pumps. It was a privilege to be having such beautiful sights close to our homes and walking through scenic sights along a path that was open to the public. On another day we walked from

Kimmeridge Bay to Poole Bay that was the south-eastern end of the longest footpath in Britain. That was the point from which our walking group had started earlier. Later during the summer of 1985, we joined up with the walking group for the up and down south coastal path between Looe and Falmouth that took us through Fowey and Mevagissey. It was a coastline of many different formations.

During one of our holidays it was a shock for me to see a mess and damage around the house created by some riotous activities when I was out. My drinks cabinet had been emptied and there were drink splashes on the carpet and the curtains. My hats had been thrown out of the house onto the roof and the trees. My children had done their best to clean up the messy house. It seems that the mess had been caused by a bunch of strange children who seemed to have strayed into the house. I just advised my little children never to allow strangers into the house.

My adventures with open learning

After the start of the academic year in 1984 the head of department directed me to attend a meeting at the East Devon College in Tiverton about the start of a system of open learning being created for the colleges. Tiverton is about ten miles north of Exeter and that college was looking for lecturers for some additional part time work for a new form of learning. The new course had been prepared by the college at Tiverton by a setup called the Microelectronics Open Learning Unit (MOLU) that was planning to set up the teaching for a later qualification from the City and Guilds (C&G) institution. Tiverton open learning was part of the new national setup called Open Tech that was trying to emulate the higher qualifications that the Open University had achieved at university level. The initial setup was solely for people to learn something without having to sit any examination at the end because the qualification had yet to be set up.

I decided to join in and to have telephone contact with people in Devon who would buy the books and electronic equipment for the course. That new work required me to use my own private time to do some technical teaching from home on the telephone to people in their Devon homes. The establishment then asked me to be engaged in the process of establishing a qualification course in liaison with the C&G of London. All that work

192

needed to be done outside my normal hours of work with Exeter College. That was a pleasant teaching task for me where there was friendly contact with various people around Devon.

Although I arranged to be by my telephone at home for one evening a week, none of my dozen students called me. That resulted in me making the calls that turned out to be social conversations because the students were not preparing for any examination and seemed to have reduced their initial interest in their search for more knowledge about electronics. There would also be some meetings with the learners at the Tiverton College for some practical electronic work, but even that did not produce active participation in their learning. I took some electronic instruments including the CRT (cathode ray tube) display from Exeter College to Bicton Agricultural College to teach electronics to some agricultural students because microelectronics was starting to affect all works of life. Even that failed to get them to become engaged in learning more about technology. The main problem with those initial Open Tech arrangements had been that there was no examination or certificate later. On the other hand, it was pleasant for me to be having some social contact with people around the county of Devon.

During 1985 there was a new setup for the start of the Devon Open Tech (DOT) by Devon County Council. As I was enjoying the new teaching experience in my association with MOTU, I was keen to get involved with DOT, which was trying to match the Open University. It was a delight to have been selected from Exeter College to join the new setup. Initially we started receiving immense management training and then became involved with the setting up of the new learning institution. However, when we arrived at the situation of delivering the learning we were amazed that there was only a few administrative staff and we would only be trying to sell products that had been created by people in numerous colleges in Britain. Some products that I saw were rubbish. My job was not going to be about teaching technical subjects, but about selling subjects related to numerous other aspects of life. That was not what I had wished to get involved in and decided to ditch it at the end of the academic year. Although the new job came with a higher salary, it gave me no satisfaction. Fortunately, the Exeter College could not find someone to do some part-time teaching for the Microelectronics Level III that I had been doing and asked me to do that some evenings. Strangely, that was a relief for me.

My part-time job with the college at Tiverton was also pleasant because it involved subjects that I could teach, although it had not achieved very much with the people who were only doing it for fun. With the college at Tiverton I became heavily involved with setting up the examinations for the issue of C&G qualifications for the course that would be studied at home by the students, together with help from their lecturer on the telephone. We had a representative from the C&G who would regularly come and talk to us about their examination system and it also resulted in me making some visits to their London offices to extract some of their examination questions that we could use with the new examination. On top of that I created questions applicable to our course. In those examination questions the sitters were only required to select one of the four multiple choice answers. That part-time job was done totally in my own time. However, my access to the bank of C&G questions that Exeter College was preparing our students for their City and Guilds examinations enabled me to understand the system. After my completion of setting up the examination questions for the Tiverton course with the C&G qualification I found that the open learning venture in the whole country had totally collapsed. My enjoyable work was to end after four years because there was no proper national structure for the Open Tech.

Holiday tours in 1986

In 1986 we had a long holiday break. The first week for me was with five colleagues on a coastal path walking from the place where we had finished walking the previous year. We took a train to Falmouth in Cornwall and started our walk from there all the way to Land's End, which is the most western area of the mainland. The rocky coastline is very different from that near Exeter. We had some very fast exciting walks along beaches near Praa Sands, continued through Penzance to Land's End, which was the most western area of our walk. There were many casual walkers on those paths who were surprised at us rushing past them. Land's End was the final point of our walk that time and we would later be walking north-eastwards to eventually finish at Minehead in north Devon.

After the schools had closed, I set off in the motor caravan on our second tour of Europe over five weeks. We toured parts of France, Germany, Switzerland, Austria, Italy and the small independent country called Liechtenstein. An overnight ferry from Dover took us to France. A clockwise rotation over Europe took us into the area of the Black Forest in Germany. Beside the road on our route we saw some hang gliders jumping off a hillside to go flying in the valley below. That was an aspect of flying that I never experienced during my life. Through the Liechtenstein scenic countryside, a drive took us along a minor road on a hillside to a small parking area by the roadside where we spent the night. A car had passed by slowly one way and then the other way. Then during the night there was a thunderstorm above us. Later in the night there were some bells sounding beside us. We jumped out to see what on earth was going on. Strangely, it was a delight to be seeing a herd of cows with bells on their necks going past us as they were being shepherded downhill at night by people carrying lamps. In the morning, we again saw a car go slowly past us without stopping to say anything. I don't know if they were looking at us for some illegal parking or our safety from transiting cows at night.

Our next drive took us through beautiful sights of Austria and at a place called Schruns where there were local people dressed smartly in traditional colourful clothes. There was a free evening concert of folk music performed by a big band in the evening. A delightful uphill hike took us up to a cable car that took us further up to the panoramic scenery of the Alps. A drive through more scenic countryside took us to Innsbruck where there was a small parking area in the town. Some Greeks who were parked there told me that they were parked there for the night, which is what I also did and did not get bothered by anyone. We walked around the beautiful city and ate in a local café. The sights of the beautiful, old European cities were a real delight for us.

Venice

A scenic drive from Innsbruck took us through the Dolomite countryside with beautiful sights of the jagged peaks of the Alps. A short walk at Belmonte took us around the hills and we even found rocks with seashells in them. After eventually getting to our destination, we parked the van and visited Venice, the most unusual city on our planet. To me, Venice had seemed to be a vision of life on another planet and I was fascinated by the unusual residence that humans had created in the water. That must have been on a trading route between Europe and Asia.

In the city of Venice there are special boats that are push-driven by local people in their traditional dress taking visitors around. We did only one trip on those boats as they were costly. My walk around Venice was a real delight as it had been a dream of mine since my school days. It was a thrill to have been to the most unusual city with my children. However, when we got back to the van the parking area was flooded with flies and a local vehicle had been spraying chemicals on our vehicles. The next day we again visited, but after that I drove out to a coastal parking area for tourists at Marghera where there were free buses to take tourists to Venice. At the camping site, our van accommodation was extended with some canvas as we were going to stay there for a few days. In addition to the bigger cushion bed in the middle of the van, another bed was created by flattening the backrest at the front bench. Many people passing by looked at our setup as they were surprised to be able to see through the extension and the van interior. As the children felt that they had seen enough of Venice, they decided to stay behind at the camp and amuse themselves while I was away in Venice for another delightful walk around the unique city.

Rome, Florence and Pisa

A scenic route took us through Italy all the way to Rome. After a drive around the city of Rome we went out to a camping site. Just when we reached the site, the motor caravan engine beside my seat had started to push out smoke. That turned out to be a leak at the head of the engine and a breakdown service had to be called. They came to our campsite and arranged to tow the van away from the campsite the next day for repair. We went by bus to Rome and wandered around various sites including the Vatican. The van was back when we returned from town and we set off for Florence on the motorway. We spent nights out in the open near Florence and visited the city. There I visited the Uffizi Gallery while the children amused themselves outside. Then they joined me in the Academy Gallery where we all had the delight of seeing the historic statue of David by Michael Angelo that has been a wonderful human creation.

A drive took us to the coastal town of Livorno near Pisa where we relaxed for three days by the seaside. From there I took the children to see the famous leaning tower of Pisa. That was a sight of something which was only an image in my head during my childhood. It was good fun taking photographs of the children posing in positions propping up the leaning tower. Strangely the main attraction at that location was the tower for the bell beside the big old cathedral that was only of secondary interest to the numerous visitors. After that, a drive on the motorway along the coast took us past Geneva, through some very scenic area with panoramic views and along some winding roads all the way into Switzerland.

Switzerland and France

At the Swiss border, the customs people seemed to be puzzled by our entry and checked my passport and car contents thoroughly before letting me continue to my home in Britain. They seemed to have been surprised at seeing Indian people touring for pleasure. We drove through very scenic views and stopped for the night at a small parking area in the hills that had beautiful views. A couple of high-speed military jets flew past us well below our level. A drive through some more panoramic views took us to France where we visited the beautiful Fontainebleau Palace. Then we staged through to Cherbourg in Normandy for a night ferry back to Britain. That long trip had been my second driving trip around Europe with my young children. Being together with my children was a delightful period during my life. The delightful trips with children around Europe were easier and cheaper than going overseas.

Return to delightful days

After my disappointing year with the open learning I returned to the college in 1986 and had satisfying engagements in technical teaching. My work and pastime activities drifted back to a state of delight. My college teaching even included some overtime work to help the department for the teaching of microelectronics. With computing systems being integrated with numerous engineering practices, the engineering companies needed their older employees to update their knowledge. During that period, ordinary humans did not have electronic computers at home or in their pockets. Although it was a struggle for me to keep with the new advances in technology, I enjoyed doing that.

By the end of 1986, I had passed my first hundred hours of flying as a pilot in light aeroplanes. Strangely, it took me five years to do 120 flights for those 100 hours of flying. That engagement in life had turned out to be a real delight for me and my friends. In 1987 some additional flight training enabled me to fly in clouds using basic flight instruments. That enabled me to fly to destinations in France. However, most of my fun flying in Britain was done in clear conditions to enable my companions to be sighting the lovely views of our countryside and coast. In 1987 some of my friends came flying with me on a beautiful day trip to Land's End. We flew along the south coast via Plymouth, Falmouth and Penzance to land at a grass airport near St. Just. After a lunch break, we flew out north and east via Tintagel, Okehampton and Crediton over the western countryside to return home to Exeter after flights of about one and a quarter hour each way.

It was in 1987 that I started venturing into flights over the sea for which we needed to carry the additional weight of a dinghy and life jackets that we wore. Additional flight briefing about safety had to be given to the passengers before taking off. Getting out of an aeroplane after ditching in the sea would be a big problem and I ended up putting the safety dinghy at the feet of the rear passengers instead of placing it behind the seats. Thankfully, we never had to do the safety drill for real, like my safe RAF flying days.

My flights over the English Channel were initially only to the Channel Islands. As John Capey had become hooked on flying again, I took him with me south across the sea to Guernsey Island in October 1987. From Exeter we flew southwards over Berry Head that has a radio beacon that enabled us to fly in a straight line over the sea towards Guernsey. As the air traffic control held me out over the sea while controlling commercial aeroplanes, the island disappeared from my sight in some clouds. That meant I had to do my first instrument flying approach for my landing. It was good job that I had a professional pilot with me. On my final approach the runway appeared in view and there was no problem with the landing.

We stayed the night at Guernsey and toured around the island the next day. Then the flight back to Exeter resulted in me doing an instrument approach for the landing. Strangely my handling of the flight in clouds was more difficult than that for an airline pilot who would have an autopilot handling the aeroplane most of the time. The manual handling of my flight inside the clouds was a great achievement for me.

My daughter Meera was going to become a teenager in March 1980 and it was a delight for me to be having her interested in astronomy. Some people at the Astro Society even started talking to her as if she already knew a lot about astronomy. My interest in birdlife in Devon made me make a visit with my children to the Slimbridge reserve at the top of the Bristol Channel. That was a real delight for me, seeing numerous varieties of birds that were being supported by us humans and not being caged.

Chapter 12
Tour of India in 1988

Bombay

I had been planning to do a tour of India during our summer break of eight weeks. Placing a map of India over that of Europe on the same scale made me recognise that India was bigger than the whole of Western Europe. As the Indian transport was going to be much slower my planning had to be vastly modified. The only booking that was going to be made was for the flights to and from India. My anticlockwise tour over the Indian subcontinent started from Bombay (Mumbai) and went towards the south-western tip of India via Trivandrum (Thiruvananthapuram), followed by a north-easterly route to East India for visits to Madras (Chennai) and Benares (Varanasi). Then there would be a north-westerly train journey to our relatives in the capital, Delhi. From there a flight to Kashmir would take us to the most northern area of India. That was to be followed by a southerly flight to Chandigarh for a stay in that region. From there we would move to Delhi for a return flight to Britain

I contacted my relatives in Bombay, Delhi and the Punjab province to arrange approximate periods for staying with them. My accommodations during the trip would be chosen only after our arrival there. During my earlier life there had been only two trips to India and my next trip was going to be the first one for my children. My first trip was in 1945 when our dhow sank in the ocean and my second trip in 1973 was when I said goodbye to my aging grandmother. However, my contact with my relatives in India and Indian life remained to be very much part of my life.

My adventurous son, Chetan, was confident to go on his own before us because he was finishing school before my college break and I arranged to let him go alone on his first flight to some new relatives in Bombay. He set off towards another continent, two weeks before us and was going to be reaching the age of sixteen a month later. Meera flew with me from Heathrow and we arrived in Bombay at night. My new relatives in Bombay lived in a flat. The sight of massive numbers of people everywhere took some time to get used to. My tour of India had been planned to go south from there because the monsoon rains would be moving in the opposite direction.

In Bombay we saw a hanging garden, a Hindu temple, elephant caves and the posh Taj hotel. On a hillside there were some big black birds flying around and my relative told me that we were going past a location where the Khoja people would be exposing their dead bodies to the animal life. That was for the humans to be giving food to the animal world that humans themselves had been receiving during their lives. From the flat we went out on delightful walks on pavements beside the sea where numerous people were strolling. However, there also was the presence of numerous poor people who would even be sleeping on the pavements between the road lanes. India was very different to other countries around the world.

South India

The monsoon rains started arriving on the day that we set off on a train that initially went north-east to the ancient temple sites of Ajanta and Ellora. The good thing was that the wet weather was not cold weather. My relatives had been puzzled by me booking second-class travel, which used to be the third class in the old days. For me it was going to be an adventure to be mixing with the ordinary people of India. All the windows had steel bars across to stop people creeping into compartments. Clinging onto the outside of the train seemed to be another common method of train travel in India. From Jalgaon we went on visits to the sites of ancient temples in the rocky hills over two days. Amazingly, the whole construction had been carved out of solid rock and included not only the temple but also the big and small statues around the building showing numerous human actions. Those creations had been used earlier for religious gatherings, but later they seemed to have become no more than tourist attractions.

At Aurangabad, there were some rare sights. There was a smaller version of the Taj Mahal which had a grass area that was being cut by women squatting on the ground. Beside a pond there were benches and a lovely gigantic tree with roots hanging down from high branches. From there we set off south-eastwards by train to Hyderabad and started moving out of the wet weather. There we toured around in a motorcycle taxi and saw really crowded areas. Around Golconda Fort on a hill there was a large walled citadel area. That also was the place which housed the world's most precious diamond, the Kohinoor. Now that diamond is in the British crown. We took an overnight train, southwards to Bangalore in the south-eastern state of Karnataka. In order to avoid paying extra for hotel accommodation as a foreigner we went around as Indians.

From Bangalore we set off by bus eastwards to the site of a huge white stone statue of a naked Hindu god. There we had to climb up numerous steps to the foot of the massive god statue. The toe of the statue was as big as a human standing beside it. That amazing sight was the statue of Gomateswara at Sravana Belagola. From the top of that hill there was a scenic view of the beautiful countryside. We stayed in a nice guest house beside a secondary girls' school and were delighted to be seeing crowds of girls coming and looking at us with smiling faces. We seemed to be a novelty to them. That night, Chetan and I both had stomach problems despite all the trouble we had been taking about what we were eating and drinking. Buses took us southwards to Mysore where we stayed for three days and looked inside the Mysore Palace, a bird sanctuary and some lovely hill temples. It was amazing how much skill people had in the old days for making intricate stone carvings around those temples. There is no trace of their methods of construction.

A coach then took us over the hills that are part of the Eastern Ghats. We stayed at the high town that had been named by the British as Ooty. The Indians have reverted to calling it Udhagamandalam. We stayed in a hotel at a high, cloudy location where the electricity had failed. That day also happened to be Chetan's sixteenth birthday and he was enjoying the experience of life in India. Meera was already thirteen and had been carrying a thick English book to enable her to deflect herself from the very different life around her. A steam train from Ooty took us southwards and downhill. It was a delight to be chugging down beautiful countryside. To our surprise we stopped at a hilly location and many people had got off the train and were wandering outside the carriages. The train had stopped because there were wild elephants on the track. Chetan got off the train with me and we walked forward to see those elephants gently stepping off the track. We then returned to the train, but some people were still outside when the train had started moving. They had no trouble jumping back on the train.

After the steam train trip, we continued in an ordinary train overnight to Cochin on the south-west coast of India. In the morning, we had delightful sights of the scenic coast. The route took us to Trivandrum, which the Indians have reverted to calling Thiruvananthapuram. A taxi took us to the tourist seaside location of Kovalam where we relaxed for three days and spent most of our time on the beach. There, Indian women who would try and sell things to us on the beach. Beside the beach we saw a young girl drawing water from a well and met two young girls who invited us to meet their parents in a nearby hut. It seemed that the locals relied on tourists to help them with their living. We were there when there were hardly any tourists and had very good service in our hotel. Kovalam was the most southerly location during our visit to India.

After a relaxing period in the south, we went back northwards by road to the town of Quilon on the west coast to catch a train to take us eastwards. At that place, there also was a sea canal that went north along the coast and there were boats that were being used as buses for carrying people and going up and down the calm canal that was not being affected by the tides. Before going eastwards, I decided to set off on a boat trip from Quilon on that rare mode of transport which was normal to the locals. It was for only a small fare that we had a ride on those boats that gently went north through the scenic views. There were numerous coconut plants and we saw people making the coconut shells into roofing material. We stopped for a basic Indian lunch beside the canal, but I did not eat much as my stomach had not fully recovered. During our return trip to Quilon I even had the chance to sit on top of the roof of the boat. Surprisingly, the driver of the boat bus refused to take a tip that was offered to him for our delightful trip. That bus boat trip of six hours showed us beautiful coconut scenery. It had been a very delightful experience for me, but for the local people it was their normal travel. Later we took a train journey from Quilon that went eastwards to inland Madurai.

Middle India

Near the town of Madurai there were fantastic temples with numerous carvings. A place called Belur had several old temples in good condition and covered in numerous delightful stone carvings around the outside of the temples. There were steps in a square that went down to the water in the ground where some people would even take a dip. After that we got onto an overnight bus to take us to Madras on the east coast. That city has been renamed as Chennai, but I prefer to keep calling it Madras. It was a heavily populated city with pollution in the river. There were masses of people in town around the cinemas in the evening and there was a theatre that was presenting the beautiful Indian classical dance. To my surprise, the classical music was free and there were only a few educated people in that theatre. It was a delight for me not only to see the dance, but also to meet the Indian girl who had even been to Britain performing those dances. The next day we went to a snake and reptile park. However, during a later visit to a temple we ended up being in a very crowded area and we got squashed. We struggled to exit and finally managed to get out without seeing the attraction for the masses.

From the heavily populated area of Madras we went south to Mahabalipuram to rest in a seaside hotel for three nights. A group of small temples by the seaside was a nice sight. The strangest one was the temple that was partly in the water. The local people said that there was another one that was totally in the water, although it had been built on dry land earlier. Strangely, I ended up doing an unusual rescue operation at that location. From the top of a coconut tree a nest with crow fledglings in it had fallen into the sand. The local people were surprised to see me deciding to place the nest back up the coconut tree by climbing a tree that had no form of steps. It meant that I had to hug the main stem and creep up to the top with a rope tied to me. After getting into a secure position the rope was let down where the people tied the nest with the chicks to it and pulled the other end, sending the chicks up to me. The little crow chicks were then placed back securely, and I slid down the tree. Although my legs got bruised, I was delighted to have returned the chicks to their home location where their parents had returned. That then resulted in some local fishermen taking me out to sea with them on a delightful fishing trip on a thin long boat that they pushed along with poles driven into the ground that was not too deep.

Our longest train journey took us from Madras northwards to Varanasi that used to be called Benares. That was the only time that we went on an Indian train in a sleeper compartment. As all seats of first class for local people were fully booked up, my British passport enabled me to acquire a whole compartment as a foreigner. The Indians on the train thought I was an Indian working for the railways, especially as I was travelling in first class. Food was brought to our compartment. When an attendant was asked to take away the waste, he picked up everything and threw it out of the window. The sights out of windows were very unusual. In the early mornings and evenings there would be people sitting beside the railway line, passing out their waste. That had been a puzzling situation when I first came to India in 1945 but found that some things had changed very little in forty years. The slow train had many stops on the way. After our departure from Madras on Saturday we arrived at Varanasi on Monday.

Varanasi is the most religious place in India. We stayed in a government tourist bungalow and went to the riverside location of the Ganga where the cremations and ash deposits took place. The availability of wood for the cremation was not enough to fully cremate some bodies and the river had masses of ash, flowers and parts of bodies. It shocked me to see someone who was not fully dead to be laid there on a stretcher. He must have asked his relatives to take him there. Many people were dipping themselves in those waters and praying. The bodies of those people must have become incredibly resistive to illness. Every twelve years there are masses of people from around the world who go and dip themselves in that religious water. Around that area there were yogis and a very fit looking man doing incredible exercises. We went across the river in a boat with a local guide who told us about various activities in that area. That visit revealed to me the Indian participation in returning the human body to nature after life termination.

The next day we took a train towards Delhi, but we got off at Bareilly and stayed with a friend and his family who had been at Exeter University studying chemistry. Beside their house, someone on a flat roof was using a wooden pole and fumbling with the electrical contact of his own house line with the supply lines. He had been doing that to improve the connection as he must have been getting dim lights. My friend then showed me his biochemistry working location. An overnight train trip took us to my relatives in Delhi. Being the capital city of India, Delhi was immensely populated, but also had some new open sites. We stayed with my relatives from my father's sister side and ended up staying in different accommodation to my children. It was a delight to see some classical Indian Katha dancing for free. Later, it was a delight to meet the young, enthusiastic and friendly dancers. They invited me to come and see them the next day during their early training exercises before they embarked on their normal jobs. From Delhi a flight took us to Srinagar in Kashmir.

Kashmir and Punjab

Our flight to the Kashmiri capital of Srinagar from Delhi only took an hour. During our approach and landing there were delightful sights of mountainous countryside. We stayed a night in a beautiful houseboat in which I was amazed at the accommodation because it looked like an English house. Then I learnt that those houseboats had been built by the British who were not allowed to own any property in Kashmir. However, they could have boats in the canal for their summer breaks away from the hot areas at lower altitudes. A coach then took us along the beautiful countryside to a higher location called Pahalgam. The next day I set off with Chetan on a three-day mountain walk together with a guide and a mule handler. Chetan was happy to carry a rucksack and we set off to reach the altitude where the ice was commencing on the edge of the Himalayas. We saw lovely Kashmiri children on the way up, but to my surprise some of them were begging.

We got up to ten thousand feet altitude and spent the night in the tent that had been set up where a meal had been prepared for us. The next day we set off through beautiful scenery, which included lakes. When we got to the point of seeing the ice, the guide said that he would not be going any further. So, Chetan and I continued going up until we reached the ice. Our highest point was at thirteen thousand feet with beautiful scenery around. For me it was a real delight having touched the foot of the Himalayas together with my son. We then trekked back to Pahalgam over two days and there we were shocked to hear of what had happened while we had been away. Kashmir was in a state of emergency because of a religious conflict that had been triggered by the death of the Pakistani president in an air crash. The buses to take us back to Srinagar had stopped travelling.

The next day a bus had been set up to go via a different route and we managed to return to Srinagar. The shops were shut and there were Indian soldiers everywhere, which was a consolation. We found a hotel to stay the night and were directed to a Chinese restaurant for an evening meal. We walked through quiet streets and met soldiers who were amazed at seeing us being out in the open, but I was happy to see them there. The next rainy day we flew out of that beautiful area that was in a sad state. We flew via Jammu to Chandigarh where we got off to spend some time in the Punjab where our family life had originated.

The new city of Chandigarh was beside the Punjab area where a lot of my relatives lived. We stayed in a big house with the widow of my cousin who had died from an electrical accident at home. The next day I was ill and weak and had to have a doctor come and give me some medicine. After recovering from my stomach problem we started visiting my relatives in various villages. A taxi took us around the villages in the Punjab where my relatives were living in a mud house and we spent time with them. It gave me a chance to show my children where my grandparents used to live and where my auntie still lived. That was the village of Shamespur. I had been supporting that auntie since she became widowed in 1966. My children had the rare experience of seeing the locations of their great grandparents. After meeting my many relatives in the Punjab, we returned to Chandigarh for a couple of days and then took a train to Delhi.

Centre of India

We spent time in Delhi with relatives from my father's side and then set off on my final tour in India together with my children. A taxi from Delhi took us out on a triangular route to Jaipur and Agra over three days. We motored through crowds of people on roads and stayed the night in beautiful Jaipur. The next day we had a lovely tour around that red city and the Amber Fort. On the way to Agra we stopped and looked around a beautiful but abandoned area of India. That was *Fateh Pur Sikri* that used to be the palace grounds when there used to be water in that area. When the water disappeared from that area the palace had been totally abandoned. In Agra I took the children around Agra Fort before going to the Taj Mahal for the final delight on our tour of India. The children had a chance to see a world heritage site. I too, was delighted with that sight. Back in Delhi we visited the Red Fort and then went on our final shopping trip.

My longest holiday trip

Eight weeks after we had arrived in India, we said our goodbyes to our relatives and flew to Britain the next day at midday. At Heathrow, my cousin in Slough came and collected us. From there I drove back to Exeter late on a Saturday before the start of college which opened on the Monday. For me, it was a delight to have engaged in a teaching career that enabled me to have time for thrilling experiences. It had also been a real delight to have taken my children to the land of our ancestors. My son, Chetan, would be leaving home to join the Royal Navy and it would not be long before Meera would also be venturing into her own life. That holiday trip was to give my children a taste of the country and culture of our Indian origin.

Chapter 13

Later years of college teaching

Fun Flying

On the second of January in 1989 there was a public holiday when our Exeter airport was officially closed, although there was Air Traffic Control (ATC) staff on duty for emergency response to airliners. Strangely, it was possible for private aeroplanes to go flying without any response from the ATC, an arrangement that had been agreed with our flying club. There would be no rescue service, but we had to make blind transmissions on the radio for movements on the taxiway, take-off and landing. I went flying with three friends over the scenic hills of Dartmoor, along the river Dart, over Dartmouth and back along the coast. In March 1989 three colleagues joined me on a flight to Jersey on a lovely day. We flew south to Berry Head near Torquay that had the only available navigation aid for me when flying out over the sea. From there a straight flight could be made on a bearing for Jersey and later we could detect the distance and bearing from a beacon at Jersey as well. A visual sighting of the island enabled me to take a shortcut route to the approach path for the runway in use. It was delightful to land on a long runway and taxy to the parking area for light aeroplanes. That flight only took us an hour and a quarter. We drove around Jersey and stayed the night. After more sightseeing, on the next evening we flew back to Exeter. It was nice to go overseas with friends just for a night stop.

Some friends came with me on a hop across the Bristol Channel to Cardiff that took us only thirty minutes. We flew over the lovely Exmoor countryside in North Devon from where we could see the Welsh coast and Cardiff, hopped across the channel at a good altitude and landed at the airport for a cup of tea. After that we took off and headed on a south-easterly direction along the coast to Bridgewater with beautiful sights of the

209

Somerset coastline. Shortly after that we were back over the familiar terrain around Exeter. That had been a delightful short hop for a cup of tea.

One weekend a college friend and his companion came with me on a flight to Jersey Island where we had a lovely drive around the island. The next day the weather at Exeter was going to remain out of limits for the whole day. We let our college know that we would not be at the college on the Monday morning. The next day the weather in Exeter was fine, but in Jersey there was fog which prevented me from taking off. Finally, the weather was fine on Tuesday and we returned to Exeter after a much longer break in Jersey than planned. Fortunately, our college was very good with arranging cover for our duties and relieving us from the pain we were suffering with being stuck in Jersey.

Some young college students had been stimulated by their staff to go and experience the fun of flying. Three students came with me on a flight to Guernsey and back on the same day to do a trip overseas. Two of those students had never flown before. That had been on a good day and the flights only took an hour each way. It was a delight for me to be giving young people a delightful taste of air travel, something which was a novelty to them. During our college midterm break in May 1989 my college friends came with me on a flight to France and an overnight stay. We flew south in beautiful conditions over Guernsey and then used a radio beacon for a straight flight to Dinard near the northern coast of the Brittany province. After a stay in that beautiful, old French city we flew back on a winding route that took us over the beautiful occupied island of Mont St. Michel in the Gulf of St. Malo. A northerly flight along the winding western coast of Normandy took us straight over the sea back to Exeter. That lovely return route gave us two hours of delightful sights from the air. The flying of light aeroplanes was giving me a great delight in being able to hop across the sea to a new environment, even if it was for just a one-night stop. Sharing the cost of flying enabled me to engage myself in a delightful activity, as well as give a delight to my friends.

Life delights in the south west

At the seaside hotel in Exmouth I bought a week of summer accommodation that could be used for the next 25 years as well as the use of their gymnasium, sauna and swimming pool that could be used throughout the year. The hotel staff even allowed me to take friends with me to the pool. Also, walking along the beach at Exmouth was delightful for me. It was like the delights that I used to have on beaches in Mombasa as a youngster. Depending upon the timing of the tides we could continue walking on sand eastwards from Exmouth and return on a path on top of the old cliff.

In 1989 the beautiful Devon countryside also dragged me into going for long walks with family and friends along the coast, as well as the hilly terrain of Dartmoor and Exmoor that had become national areas and had been opened to the public for scenic healthy walks. It was a delight to be exploring many of the tors on Dartmoor. One day, I had a surprise view with my binoculars from one of the tors when I saw a building that was at the Exeter University near my home. From Exeter I was able to identify numerous tors on Dartmoor that could be seen from upstairs at home. Although that area had been a long way in the car, it was not out of sight from our home as we were located on a hilltop with lovely countryside views.

On Meera's fourteenth birthday in 1989 we went to the Double Locks on the canal; after lunch Meera walked back with me for about ten miles along the canal. On a sunny day Chetan came walking with me up the river Exe from Exeter to the old village of Bickleigh in a lovely valley. Part of that walk was along the disused railway line path. At Bickleigh we stopped for lunch at the Fisherman's hotel that was beside an old bridge over the river Exe. In the southwest peninsula of Britain there is enormous opportunity for getting involved in coastal path walking. That year my children walked with me from the mainland coast to the island of St. Michael's Mount that had been shown on some detective film. A visit on foot could be done only when the tide was low.

My Indian friendships

In addition to having many English friends I had contact with some Indian people, including some who were born in East Africa. We held a Diwali celebration in November 1988 together with them. North of Exeter there is the old Grand Canal between Sampford Peverall and Tiverton. A canal of six miles happened to be at the end of the canal building in Britain because the railway lines had taken over the transporting of goods around the country. Before that the goods had been transported by barge boats that were towed by big Shire horses on a path. Currently that method of transport continues to be used on the Tiverton canal where the barge is towed by a Shire horse for taking people on pleasure trips along the beautiful countryside in the summer. A big Indian party was held at the university where we ended up forming a group for gatherings during Hindu religious days, as well as normal friendship gatherings.

One day, the world-famous Indian *sitar* player, Ravi Shankar had come to Darlington in Devon for a presentation in June 1992. It was a delight for me to hear Ravi Shankar playing the *sitar*, accompanied by a *tabla* (drum) player. It was during the interval that an English woman started talking to me because she considered me to be one of the Ravi Shankar team as I was wearing the Indian clothing of *kamiz* (long shirt) and *pyjama* (trousers). In north India, the men normally wear that and the women wear the *kamiz* and *salwar* (fancy trousers) during the day. It seems that the early Englishmen in India had taken to wearing a short *kamiz* and *pyjama* for sleeping in, instead of using their long English frock.

Although I was not a very religious person, some of my English friends got me to give talks to English school children about Hinduism. At the primary school in south Devon I went dressed in my Indian clothes. It was thrilling for me to see interest being shown, not only by the children, but also the staff. My presentation of the Indian view of God to Christian people had a loving response from the crowd. During my presentation of the concept of Hinduism to secondary schoolgirls it surprised me that they were desperately trying to write down what was being said about the Hindu God trinity pairs that represent creation, preservation and termination of life. The girls were delighted that the trinity Gods were both male and female. At another primary school in Thorverton village in the countryside the children were delighted with the loving and peaceful Gods in Hinduism. I also had to tell the children that they could only be a Hindu if they had Hindu parents. However, there was nothing stopping them from having fun with Hinduism.

Teaching and life activities in 1990

My technical teaching job was primarily to do with the electrical engineering that was advancing with new technology. The HNC (higher national certificate) was for the students who were employed in engineering work and came to the college for just one long day per week. The students for the NC (national certificate) were full time students who would be looking for employment later. There were also similar courses in electronics that received qualifications from the City and Guilds institute in London with whom I had liaised closely during the unsuccessful Open Tech period.

There was someone in Exeter who had set up a group for helping people in Ethiopia and I started spending time with him. We went on enjoyable walks around our lovely countryside. We also set off on a night walk on the hilly countryside over Dartmoor. The full moon was in sight and the terrain was beautifully lit up without any interference of city lights. We did not even use our torches. It was great to be in a natural environment in natural lighting at night. The small clouds passing rapidly over us gave us new sensations. The sound of some night birds called nightjars was unusual and exciting. For me it was a great delight to be able to be out in our open countryside at night.

My son, Chetan, had finished his training with the Royal Navy in April and it was a delight to be at the ceremony of his passing out into a service life. My female cousin from Delhi came to Exeter with the son of her younger sister. I took them around the English countryside and even took the boy to Lundy Island on a ferry trip in the Bristol Channel. There we had some lovely sightings of sea birds and scenery. The beautiful countryside and sea scenery of Devon was a delight to my Indian relatives who lived in the densely populated area of Delhi.

During the last week of the college year in 1990, I joined a group of staff who took eleven boys and girls on a climbing expedition up the three peaks of Britain. The trip was planned and controlled by a college lecturer.

We were going to the peaks of Snowden in Wales, Scafell in England and Ben Nevis in Scotland. Up Snowden, on a cloudy misty day, we scrambled up some rocks to get to the peak in a cloud. When we arrived at the peak it became windy. The next day we walked up to the peak of Scafell in the Lake District and had a gentle walk back in good weather. Then our final climb up Ben Nevis was done on the fourth day in good weather. We went up a route to the peak that took us on two rocky scrambles up streams. Then a climb through snowy ground took us to the peak in mist. There, snowballs were being thrown at each other and during our return some of them skidded down on plastic sheets. It was a great delight to have taken enthusiastic youngsters on physically challenging activities. We drove along Loch Ness and had an unusual sighting of a big twin engine army helicopter flying very low past us. Then we saw that the helicopter had landed in a field that had cows in it and I met the aircrew who had walked out. They told me that they had done an emergency landing because of some failure indications during their flight.

With only a day of rest after my college three peaks trip, I joined my walking team to complete the long coastal walk of 600 miles that had been started seven years earlier. We walked from Combe Martin to Minehead over three days and completed the walk on the longest footpath in Britain. I felt like giving myself a medal for that achievement. Instead, we took a steam train to Bishop's Lydeard.

My son, Chetan, who was in the Royal Navy was back home celebrating his eighteenth birthday in July 1990. I followed that by arranging the purchase of a house in his name and contributed to a life policy in his name. My bank was happy with the arrangements that I made with them for the house payments. I would look after that house in Exeter until he could take it over himself.

RAF reunion

At a reunion of 27 Squadron at Marham, near King's Lynn in November 1990 we had a formal dinner where the officers' wives were the guests. It was a delight for me to meet up with John Willis who had reached the high rank of Air Vice-Marshal before retirement. It amazed me to meet someone who had joined the armed forces even before the RAF was created in 1914.

We had Stanley Thomas, aged 99, who amazingly gave us a talk after dinner. I decided to initiate a fly-past on his 100th birthday in Cornwall where he lived and spoke to the new squadron commander, Nigel Elsdon. The commander was interested and said that he would be contacting me after returning from his task in the Middle East where Iraq had invaded Kuwait. Unfortunately, there were some subsequent catastrophes that terminated my drive for that display flight. In 1991, Nigel was shot down during the Kuwaiti war and did not survive. Together with him, there was a navigator who had been in my squadron when I was on the Vulcans. I found it hard to fathom that ordinary stupid wars could continue to infect our lives.

Hockey with Isca and college

After a break of ten years my body was starting to revert to its fit state which enabled me to begin playing hockey. The Isca hockey club was situated close to my home, but there was little chance of me joining them because I was not very fit. However, there were more people interested in playing and we created a fifth team for the club that started playing against many other clubs in the county. In fact, some people from higher teams volunteered to join us. We ended up playing against the first teams of other clubs in the county. It was a delight for me to be back in my delightful sporting life after passing the age of fifty.

My flying and walking activities had been triggered by a back problem that had made me give up playing hockey. After my recovery, my hockey and other physical activities continued. Isca had decided to start running a youth team and asked me to take on the task of running that. That resulted in me starting to coach the young players at the Exeter School pitch on Saturday mornings. Then in the afternoons I would be captaining my adult team. The size of the youth team increased a lot and other players started helping me on that pitch. On Wednesday evenings Isca could use the floodlit hockey pitches at a school in nearby Ottery St. Mary. That resulted in me going there often to do some training for myself.

The delightful engagements in hockey also stirred me to become trained as a coach and an umpire. My hockey coaching training took place in July 1991 at Lilleshall and there were people doing many other sports including a professional footballer. Strangely, the Exeter college, where I was teaching engineering, asked me to take over the task of handling the college hockey team events for the boys. My Wednesday afternoon periods in the college then became devoted to taking the hockey teams to matches around Devon. To my surprise there were many well-trained hockey players from the sporting school at Ottery St. Mary who had just joined the college. That resulted in me forming two teams to play hockey matches on Wednesdays and had other members of staff from our Physical Training department help me out with weekly matches. As it was necessary for me to be doing the umpiring in our friendly matches I ended up attending some talks, sitting an examination and getting my certificate for umpiring. In addition to the regular friendly games with other colleges in our region we also went to some national competitions. Our team even reached the semi-final of a competition. Sports had unusually become part of my teaching engagements at the college. Strangely, it was difficult to identify which of my activities was for leisure and which was for my working life. That was further highlighted when the college principal asked me to fly him to France to extend our college activities in France.

Flying for Exeter College in 1991

In 1991 the college principal asked me to fly him to France for an official visit because that would be the quickest, cheapest and easiest way of getting to Normandy in France. The college was looking at buildings for use as educational locations in France. I ended up doing three flights from Exeter to Caen in Normandy to enable the principal to make some short trips to France at a low cost. That enabled him to go and look at various locations in France where Exeter College teachings would be carried out. My restriction was that my flights would only be in suitable weather conditions because of restrictions to my instrument flying qualification: in France were different to those in Britain. Strangely, Britain was the only European country that provided a reduced certificate for instrument flying for private pilots to fly in uncontrolled airspace and make landing approaches in bad weather in Britain. The French qualifications for instrument flying in bad weather conditions were given to professional pilots only. As it turned out, my flights in France were in good weather conditions and I would not have restrained myself from doing instrument flying in France if I needed to do it for safety.

Our first flight was in March 1991 and we flew eastwards along the English coast to Bournemouth and then turned southwards over the sea channel to Cherbourg. We landed at Cherbourg to go through customs because the air traffic staff in Caen would be having their lunch. A flight along the Normandy coastline gave us a view of the floats at Utah beach that had been used during the D-day landings in 1944. We landed at Caen; the next morning we were taken by cars to look at sites for a suitable college extension. Our return flight was in a westerly direction to a Jersey beacon over the small Sark Island and to Berry Head in Devon. Then a descent and approach path brought us back to Exeter after a delightful outing to France. Those routes avoided long flying over the sea.

As the cost for the flights had been paid for by the college principal, I had a letter from one of the club instructors telling me that I was breaking the private pilot rules about payments for my flights. He sent me a copy of the aviation authority rules that laid out the payments for flights flown by private pilots. The instructor had highlighted the paragraph stating that rule. To my utter delight, the paragraph that had not been highlighted was stating clearly that the flight by a private pilot could be fully paid by his employer. Strangely, that stupid instructor had issued me with even better evidence of me having my employer officially pay for the total cost of the flights.

My second trip to Normandy was with the principal and two others. We flew the route via Bournemouth and went nonstop to Caen despite the fact that the air traffic controllers were having a break for lunch. That was possible because France allowed that to be done. It was up to me to determine the runway for landing and after landing we went through customs. We had flown for two hours to get to Caen in the early evening and then we were driven by car to some more sights of possible college locations. The next day air traffic control (ATC) said that I had not filed a report of my landing the previous day. The French authorities provided a computer system that had to be used by pilots to pass their message to the central ATC after landings if the flight had been from overseas when the French custom officials were having their lunch. All I could do was apologize to them and we set off on our return trip. We flew towards Jersey and routed homewards to land after a flight of two and half hours.

On our third flight to Normandy in July 1991 the college surveyor joined us. We flew on a countryside route to Dorchester, then headed southwards over Isle of Portland, across the channel and along an inland Normandy route to Caen. From there we drove to another location in France. After our visit and inspecting a big majestic building, the surveyor reported that the woodwork in the roof was rotting and that building had to be ditched from the final selection. One of the earlier sighted locations was selected for our new setup in France. My return flight was westwards via Alderney and then straight to Exeter. Because of cloud around Exeter I ended up doing an ILS (instrument landing system) approach to finally have the ability to see the runway at one thousand feet, which was well above the minimum altitude of five hundred feet that was my limit. It delighted me to be flying comfortably with flight instruments on a very basic and manual aeroplane.

An adventurous day of flying in 1991

During the start of our long college break in July 1991 I set off on a flight to France to swap the crew on a yacht at Quimper in the south coast of Brittany. Initially my plan was to fly back the next day, but because of bad weather my return flight had to be on the same day. That turned out to be a day of flying tension for me. I took off with a lecturer friend from the college and another sailor. Over Brittany the cloud above the airport required me to do an instrument flying approach, but to my horror found that the French air traffic officials were at lunch. The weather situation made me divert my flight to Brest, which provided air traffic control during lunchtime.

After contacting Brest airport, it dismayed me to be told that their instrument landing system was not functioning. From their information about the cloud levels I was able to continue my approach on a simple navigation aid that required a break from approach at a higher level if the airport was not sighted. We flew through cloud on the crude NDB (non-directional beacon) approach and flew out of the cloud at a safe level and had to locate the runway visually. It was one of my passengers who first sighted the runway. That was followed by properly lining up with the runway and safely landing. The French control staff were puzzled at me having landed there in those conditions. It had taken me more than two and quarter hours of flying to land there.

After clearance with the customs people it was not possible for me to get refuelled as the staff were out for lunch. We jumped back into our aeroplane, took off and flew visually at low level through the coastal countryside and did a visual landing at Quimper after another thirty minutes of flying. There, the other boat crew members were relieved to see us. After refuelling, they jumped in with me and we took off for a straight return flight to Exeter. My three sailor passengers were amazed that the aeroplane had crude navigation aids because they used satellite navigation kit that helped them know exactly where they were. My return flight was fine all the way to Berry Head, which the boat crew could recognise, but they were surprised that from there we were descending for a landing at Exeter. It had taken me only two hours for the return flight. Although I felt physically weakened, it was a delight to have done an adventurous day of flying. Strangely, that day's flying turned out to be part of the requirement needed for upgrading my flying certificate. Flights and landings on two different qualified airports on a long-distance triangular route had to be done on the same day.

Goodbye to my mother in 1993

My mother had reached an unusual state of existence in her life. One day she was smiling at me and I asked her why she was smiling. She said that she knew that I was her uncle. That made me realise that her mind had reverted to her childhood days. She was losing awareness of what she was doing and I even saw her having another bowl of breakfast cereal just after she had finished eating one before. Her behaviour in the house was starting to become confused. It got to the stage when I would have to come back home from work to attend to her during the day. Eventually, nurses from the health centre attended to her and were surprised that I had been doing that myself when her health had deteriorated.

One day my mother was rushed to hospital and was looked after and later transferred to a care home near my house. Her body still maintained itself, but her mind had faded. Although I realised that she had passed her state of existence it saddened me when she finally passed away peacefully in January 1993 at the age of 84. She had brought me into existence and had been a loving mother. I had been delighted to have cared for her during her final state of life.

Flights to France in 1993

One day I was surprised to be contacted by a friend of a friend who asked me to fly him and his new wife to Paris where they planned to spend their honeymoon period. That was a rare challenge for me. I planned to take them along different routes to and from France with scenic sights from low level flights. We set off together with another friend of mine for the airport of Pontoise that is close to Paris. We flew eastwards along our scenic south coast to the Isle of Wight which had low cloud below us and I encountered a problem of flying through the clear sky airway ahead of me because the ATC (air traffic control) in Britain only allowed pilots with a commercial pilot instrument rating to cross the airway even in visual conditions. Had I lied to them, there would have had no problem in flying across that airway. As they were told that I did not have the commercial rating, it was for me to decide on my flight path. Strangely, that would have been no problem for me in France as they allowed private pilots to cross the airways in visual conditions. All I could do in Britain was descend into cloud, fly on instruments at a safe level to cross the ten-mile airway and then climb up again to a clear sky. That was a path of flying that I had not planned to do, but was also confident of doing my instrument flying.

After crossing the Isle of Wight in cloud at a safe level I went on a south-easterly direction to a higher level above the clouds and flew across the English Channel towards the port of Le Harve where the river Seine flows into the sea. Some very helpful air traffic control service in France enabled us to fly freely along the river all the way to the Pontoise airport. We had lovely views along the very winding river, flew south of Rouen through which the river flowed and finally contacted the Pontoise airport and landed. That flight of two and three-quarter hours was my longest flight time on light aeroplanes. The delighted couple took a train link to Paris and me and my friend spent the night in a very quiet area that was not heavily populated during the weekend. The next day we took off and flew westwards past Caen and Jersey and then turned northwest for Exeter where we landed after a relaxing flight.

A week later I flew to Pontoise again to collect my passengers the next day. Joining me on that trip was someone who was prepared to pay for that flight as the captain. On the flight she was not confident with her flying. We had flown over Alderney and she was concentrating so much on the map that I could see us flying into a cloud and was ready to take control. When she looked up and discovered that the land had disappeared, instead of commencing instrument flying, she started panicking. I took control and finally flew out of the cloud, but still on our programmed track. She started saying that she wanted to return to Exeter but I assured her that there was no problem. Then a break in the layer of stratus cloud below us enabled us to dive down to a level below the cloud with clear views of the countryside; she was happy again and took over the flying. We landed at Pontoise, had an evening meal in town and later met with the pair returning home.

The next day, my other pilot said that the weather conditions were not suitable for a flight. I told her that she either had the choice of coming with me or making her own way back. She did not say anything after that. We set off on a north-westerly direction over the countryside to Dieppe, across the channel to Seaford and then over the beautiful English countryside and some ancient sites on the route to Exeter. I let the other pilot do an instrument approach and landing, even though the weather was fine. The couple on their honeymoon had been delighted with their trip. For me it was great to be having other people sharing the cost of some adventurous flying.

My son, Chetan, had turned twenty-one in July 1993 and came home a couple of times during his break from the Navy. It was nice to be with him and to hear about his experiences in his first job before reaching adulthood.

Hockey and golf in 1993

My hockey activities continued until the Achilles tendons on both my legs started to affect my running. Then a hockey ball hit me in the face and cracked my nose, for which I had to go the hospital surgery for a check-up and a repair later. Then another hockey ball hit me on the mouth and one front tooth fell out into my hand. Fortunately, that day I was playing with my dentist and he advised me to place my tooth back into the mouth immediately. Then at the end of the game he took me in his car to his surgery, put it back into place and had somehow glued it there. Incredibly a tooth that had fallen out, had been replaced and has been serving me perfectly well for twenty-five years and has remained white. It was a much better outcome than putting in a false tooth. The dentist's son who has taken over tells me that the dentists at their annual meetings are amazed that I was having normal usage of the white tooth that had fallen out of my mouth years earlier. My physical problems eventually resulted in me quitting playing hockey. I started playing golf and ended up having a complete break with hockey in 1993.

My college friends took me to the golf driving range at Fingle Glen near Exeter where I started whacking golf balls. The more time I took to hit the ball, the more it seemed the ball tended to go in the wrong direction. Then we started having a go on the small hilly course. At that time, it was not easy to join a golf club because they all had waiting lists. That required people paying a deposit to be placed on a waiting list. It would be a few years before I was offered membership at a local club. During the college summer break in 1993 I drove to Dartmouth to play on a new golf course that was offering temporary membership. One day I was standing on a green when another player was putting his ball. Suddenly, a big church bell toll was heard, followed by a shout saying 'Fore'. My head started spinning and made me drop to my knees. Then some people walked down to our green and apologised for their ball that had swung in a semicircle, bounced off my head, crossed a small lake and landed in some grass. There was a bump on my head that was the size of a golf ball. Strangely, that did not stop me from continuing to play and complete the round of golf. The next day the bump on my head had disappeared and there was no pain. That made me realise why we have a shell of bone around our delicate brain. That year my face had been hit twice by a hockey ball and then a golf ball had bounced off the top of my head. This made me feel as though my life activities needed to be revised.

After a few months at Dartmouth I had the highest handicap of 28. After a competition it dropped to 27. That club invited me to play in a friendly competition at another club. Golf was enjoyable, but I needed a golf course near Exeter. That is when I joined Woodbury Park Golf Course, which only had a shed for the club house. After a round of golf with a group of friendly people, they said that my handicap would be dropped to 24. When asked how they could say that, they told me that they were from the club committee and had decided that on the spot.

Normandy D-day ceremonies in 1994

In June 1994, that there was a special gathering at Normandy to commemorate the fiftieth anniversary of the D-day landings in France. I flew out together with some friends to land at Cherbourg to clear the French customs. There we parked beside a vintage aeroplane, cleared the customs and then continued our flight southwards with only one passenger as the other two people had hired a car from Cherbourg. My flight continued to Granville where we landed and parked the aeroplane on the grass where there were numerous aeroplanes. From there we were picked up by the others in a car and went to Caen where various D-day celebrations and ceremonies were taking place.

There were many formal ceremonies and displays by aeroplanes and ships, which was also attended by the French president. These sights were from a distance because of security. Then we drove to the famous Pegasus Bridge where the British soldiers had achieved great success, as well as numerous life losses. A lot people around were in old wartime uniforms and vehicles; it was a delight to experience the feeling of relief after a war success. The sights of numerous cemeteries made me admire the courage of humans, even if we cannot understand the stupid motives of the wars. Finally, we drove back to Granville, jumped into our aeroplane and flew back to Exeter.

My family life

My son, Chetan, had always been a great delight in my life. After his engagement in a new life with the Royal Navy he was away from me most of the time. My daughter, Meera, had been the most special creation in my life. She was the only one in the family who had learned to play the big piano that I had bought. My life with that delightful girl began to have some problems during her teenage years. She wanted to be allowed to do whatever she wanted without any interference from me. My own creation was drifting away from me. I hoped to recover my loving relationship with my daughter when she got older.

Chapter 14
My life collapse and recovery

Loss of family life

After more than a quarter of a century of family life, I was to experience an inconceivable termination of that existence. My wife and my children walked out of my house and my life in 1994. For me it was the termination of my prime purpose of existence. All my other efforts and achievements in life seemed to have been totally wasted. During my married life, I had felt that my family had been part of my body. A total detachment with my family made me feel that I had lost, not only a part of my body, but also my desire for life. My mind and body had been split apart. It felt like I was in Hell and not being able to terminate my own life.

My slow recovery

My family disaster made me retire from my job. My mind was in a daze and it was difficult for me to fathom what to do with my life. My life drifted to learning to become a flying instructor. The new European system ruling required every flying instructor to have a fully professional pilot licence before becoming a flying instructor. That made me go to Bournemouth and sit through the ground-school preparation for some written examinations. Instead of listening to what was being said by the instructor in the classroom, my mind would constantly drift to my family disaster. All I wanted to do was fathom how to terminate my life.

One day at Bournemouth, a lovely pigeon wandered into our training centre and walked around us without any fear, looking for something to eat. The next day the bird was inside the building again and was looking for food. However, at the end of the day it dismayed me to see that the lovely pigeon had been run over by a reversing car. That disaster also made me feel that I too had lost the path for my life. Only when the thoughts of my family life disaster were to be flushed out of my mind, would there be any path for my life.

The ground school examinations were only one stage of the preparations required for achieving the flying instructor licence. The flight training would be carried out in Exeter over a long period. At the Bournemouth training centre, I teamed up with two new friends for study of the course. Neil Madden had retired from his engineering career and lived in Marston Magna in Dorset, where we three spent time together in his house in preparation for our examinations. We sat the two examinations after separate one-month periods of study each time. One day he invited me to a special birthday party at Marston Magna. There were a lot of people at the party who dressed up quite smartly. When I was talking to my friend it shocked me to see another man with the same face appear in front of me. It turned that my friend was celebrating his birthday with his twin brother with whom I had been talking. My friend had been having a problem with a woman companion that resulted in a split in their relationship. Somehow my contact with him had helped me to start coming to terms with my own life disaster. My contact with that new friend had helped me to regain my desire for continuing with my life. It felt as if I had been lifted by a wave that gave me a sight of land during my disaster period.

In February 1995 there was an exciting experience for me on the last hole of the golf course when I was playing on my own. After hitting the ball from the tee, I lost sight of where it had landed. Then there was some commotion. There were workmen on the top of the clubhouse being built who were cheering and waving to me. To my amazement my ball must have disappeared into the hole. Then there was another surprise. The new owner of the club came running out of his hut to see what disaster had happened at the building site and was delighted to see that there had been a hole-in-one on the course that he had recently bought. He congratulated me and offered free drinks in our tiny bar for the few people around. To my surprise he later presented me with a prize putter for the first hole-in-one on his course. The new manager of the course was Nigel Mansell, the world champion of Formula One racing cars.

On another day at the golf course our club manager drove up to me and my friend after we had played our shots to the seventh green. He asked us to stand aside and let the boss go through with his companion. We stood aside as two long shots went past us and Nigel drove past with his friend, Greg Norman, the world champion golfer from Australia. As our balls were already on the green, we waited to let them finish the hole and move on. To my surprise, Nigel brought Greg over to us and told him that I was the one who had scored the first hole-in-one on his course.

Having passed the age of fifty-five, I could play as a senior player in the golf club, but our club did not have that arrangement. One day the president started such a group and it was a delight to join that group. At the group meeting it surprised me to hear the president say that I was going to take charge of running the new program. That then became the centre of focus in my delicate life, although golf was an activity that I had only recently started. Even the main club team invited me to play in matches with other clubs. Golf turned out to have great social connections with other clubs. After our friendly matches around the county we would dress up and dine together with new friends in a great social get-together. Golf started providing me social contact with numerous new friends from very different walks of life. There were times on the dining tables when I talked to people who had been flying in the RAF and we exchanged our experiences. Also, golf was an activity that a person could even enjoy well into old age. During my life, sports had been enjoyable activities, but golf also turned out to be a great social activity as well. As we did not normally have a referee with us and it did not take me great effort to understand the basic golf rules. To my surprise, many golfing people did not understand even the basic rules of golf, although they had been playing for years and even been the captain of a golf club. That resulted in me giving talks on the golf rules to the club and giving out some handouts to raise the level of understanding of the basic rules of golf to others around me. My golf life started to bring me back to a normal life.

My life started opening-up again

As well as going through all the written examinations I went through flight training over a period of nine months to obtain my basic commercial pilot licence (BCPL) in 1995 through my flying club. Flying was an activity that completely captured my mind and it was a delight to take other people, for whom it was also was a delight to be pottering around in the sky. My professional pilot's licence enabled me to teach people how to fly, but I also continued doing fun flying with my friends.

One of my friends from the college asked me to fly him and his friend on a photographing flight along the south coast between Plymouth and Land's End. That was for them to capture the scenery for the training of ship crewmen on a simulator. We flew to Land's End for a short stop and then eastwards along the coast to enable the cameraman to photograph the coast that the trainees would be seeing from their ships. As the aeroplane had the wings above our heads, the sight of the coast was being blocked by the left wing. I ended up tilting that wing up to clearly display the coast. Then, to enable flight in a straight line ahead, the rudder on the tail of the aeroplane had to be pushed to the left to enable us to fly straight ahead. Some extra engine power had to be applied for that abnormal form of flying that could also be done only for a short period on the approach to the runway when there was a strong crosswind during landing. In that attitude the photographer could take clear pictures all along the coast of Plymouth over a period of about an hour. To me that flight was a delightful experience. For the cameraman, it was a lot cheaper than doing it on a helicopter. Later, he sent me copies of all the scenic photographs that he took during that trip.

My college friends came flying with me to France for a whole week. Our first flight was to Rennes in Brittany, but we had to land at Dinard because of the weather conditions at our destination. After a short wait at the airport we flew to Rennes and met up with members of the Rennes Flying Club, because the city was twinning with Exeter. Members of that club then took us out to a delightful French dinner. The next day my aeroplane was inside a hangar where the French had parked it and they pulled it out when we got there. A south-easterly flight then took us to the small town of Saumur where we were cleared for landing by an advisory air traffic controller who also helped me to refuel the aeroplane. After parking the aeroplane, we walked out to a youth hostel on the river Loire and stayed there for five nights. The French countryside and villages were delightful. One day we went by train westwards along the river Seine to Les

Rosiers where we had a lovely walk around the woods. For me, the biggest delight was the sound of nightingales in those woods, where we heard three nightingales. My companions felt that they were being dragged into listening to the nightingales for long periods. In addition to that we saw many other birds including the orioles and the lesser whitethroats. Another day we took a train for a day visit to the city of Tours to the east, but one person decided to visit some cathedral in St. Nazaire where he would be spending the night.

After our delightful stay at Saumur we walked from our hostel back to the airport, took off and flew westwards to St. Nazaire where the river Loire enters the Atlantic. There we met up with the other friend and early the next day we set off on our return flight after our long outing of a week. Over the land we flew at two thousand feet altitude to look at the French countryside. After passing Dinard, I climbed up to five thousand feet for our flight over the channel and used radio beacons for navigation across the channel. We passed the Channel Islands to Berry Head in Devon and home to Exeter. I even ended up playing golf that evening. My friends on that outing were amazed at the low shared cost of the flights and the places we had visited. Flying became the delight in my existence that was lifting me out of my phase of life collapse.

My friend Neil kept in touch with me and we decided to get involved with professional flight training. It was in February 1997 that I was offered a job at Bournemouth where I had been studying for my professional licence. Unfortunately, my participation in that teaching environment did not fit in with the requirement and that job was terminated. At the British European airline in Exeter I met up with the ground training manager and had a nice chat with him, although they had no job to offer. Then at the end of the year, Oxford Aviation Training offered me a job for the ground training of professional pilots at the start of their flying careers. To my surprise my friend Neil also got a job at the same location for flight training to helicopter pilots.

My full recovery

During my life there have been disasters. As a child, I had been in a dhow that sank in the Indian Ocean. That disaster had threatened my life very closely, but that had been just for a short period. However, after our return to Africa, my father lost his life three years later. That loss did strike me with pain for a long period. My family survived only because of help from my uncle. Fifty years after our dhow sinking in the Indian Ocean, I had been struck by the worst personal disaster in my life. My wife and children had walked out of my life. It took me a long time to dampen out the pain from my wounds.

During my recovery from that life disaster, I had started to see that humans who survive a disaster are the ones who would continue suffering unless they could ditch the memory of their disaster. Although it took me a long time to do that, my life then slowly started returning to a joyful state of existence. My children, Chetan and Meera, had been the greatest delight in my family life. It felt as if I had earlier vomited out all the food when there had been only one item that my stomach could not hold. Although the sole purpose of all life forms on our planet is to reproduce, we humans are the only creatures on our planet who have the added advantage of some bonus state of existence in addition to reproduction. My life has been a rare experience of existence on a rare planet that has been giving me delights as well as pains. Every human, animal or insect can have an experience of a life only once. I decided not to ditch the rest of my existence. It was only after my life recovery that I became aware of the fact that our thinking and behaviour could be affected by the genes in our bodies.

Chapter 15

New world at Oxford

Professional pilot training

I started work in Oxford in January 1998 with a long-established organisation called OATS (Oxford Aviation Training School) located at the airport, for training people who were starting to become airline pilots. Their one-year training included both the ground school as well as the flying aspect, and my job was solely for teaching the technical aspects of flying. It was a delight to be working again with people with whom I had been flying in the RAF with, as well those who had been at my RAF locations. That process of training new pilots was delightful and stimulating for me. Even after work time it was stimulating for me to be at my empty workplace for lesson preparations. After my initial lessons, some of my pupils brought me regards from their parent or employer who had been flying with me during my RAF days in the 1970s. My new working life and my working environment was lifting me into a better existence. The residence during the working weekdays was with an English family in the delightful village of Combe near Blenheim Palace. However, all my weekends were in my home in lovely Devon.

My friend Neil started working at Oxford to train helicopter pilots and had started a new family life in a big new house in a nearby village. The year I had started to work in Oxford there were repeated telephone messages on my home telephone from the British European airline based in Exeter asking me to join them to train engineers and pilots. Strangely, there was a choice of jobs for me. My final decision was to continue with my delightful new life in Oxford.

Pilot ground school

At Oxford, the staff had started preparing new notes for pilot training for the new European qualification for professional pilots. My job at Oxford was to prepare the new notes and lesson plans for some of the subjects. For me, the vocal radio communications for airlines was not difficult to set up as I had been carrying out various forms of communications with the military and the civilian linkages during my RAF flying days. We had the support of computer men to help us prepare and set up delivery of our new lessons on screens in the classrooms. Also, a new set of examinations for the new system had to been written by different participating countries. Many youngsters and some middle-aged people came in for airline flight training for themselves. For British Airways (BA) there were youngsters who were a delight to teach and who also engaged themselves in other activities.

The initial examinations turned out to be chaotic as different subjects produced widely different results. Although radio communications and electrics did not create any problem, I found that immense work needed to be done in many other subjects in the system. However, the job was providing me with a delightful situation of engaging my mind in activities that were for a good purpose. My mind was drifting back into a pleasant state of existence. Our ground school building was close to the hangars and air traffic control. That enabled me to take my students to the small aeroplanes in the air traffic control areas that they were going to be flying. A visit to the vintage tail-wheel RAF aircraft in the hangar delighted many of the youngsters. Even for me it was a delight to be shown other aeroplanes at the airport. The modern cockpit of a business jet, the two engine, Hawker Sidley 125 gave me a chance to look at the modern instrument displays in the cockpits. For me it was also a delight to be inside one of the few Twin Otters with turbo-propeller engines that were used in the Antarctic during the summer time there and returned to Oxford during our summer time.

My job also gave me the opportunity to fly in the cockpit of a BA Boeing 737 for a return trip to Rome from Gatwick. The captain turned out to be an ex-RAF man who had also flown in Shackleton aircraft. We had a nice chat along the route to Rome and they showed me the operations of the modern flight displays. During their turnaround at Rome, the pilots went to their operations room and let me wander around the airport building. However, during my return to the aeroplane from that building the customs people would not allow me to proceed to the aircraft because I had no passport on me. Eventually, they allowed me to proceed to the aeroplane, but the flight had to be delayed. Those were the days when even the passengers had the option of visiting the cockpit during the flight and the pilots were happy to show their cockpit displays to the passengers.

Varied activities

During the time of their earlier period at Oxford, the BA trainees were also required by BA to carry out some other activities. The course that I was tutoring had decided to carry out a challenging mountain climb at a weekend, during which they intended to climb the three peaks of British mountains in a period of 24 hours. After they heard that I had helped my college students many years earlier climb those peaks over several days, they asked me to help them on their trip. That resulted in me driving one of their minibuses to Scotland where we stayed the night in a hostel. As two of the students were not going to be doing the climbing, it enabled me to join the group climbing up the Cairngorms and let those who were not climbing to do the driving. We commenced the climb early in the morning for Ben Nevis, got to the snowy peak and then rushed back down to get in the vans to head south. That evening we got to the location of the highest English mountain in the Lake District called Scafell Pike. It was during that climb that my hip started to pain me and stopped me from doing any more climbing. The other van had already shot off for Wales in the night. By the time that we got to our base for Mount Snowden it was starting to get light. Some of the athletic people in the earlier group had managed to get to the peak in time to claim their climb within 24 hours of the start. The others took their time to get to the peak that day and returned to base in the mountain train. It was a delight to have been with an adventurous group of youngsters of the BA who had a great achievement climbing the three peaks of Britain in a weekend. Although I had been with the BA group voluntarily and just for fun, BA asked me to write to them about my impression of the exercise carried out by their trainees. My association with the airline started becoming closely interlinked.

At the flying club in Exeter there was a person who was working on a postage service that flew a small twin engine Seneca aeroplane for delivering mail between Exeter and two other places in the evening and night. One evening that solo pilot took me on two flights. We flew to St. Mawgan in Devon and then to East Midlands. He allowed me to do some of the flying during those flights. At Oxford in September some student pilots came with me to Farnborough for the bi-annual air show. We had the opportunity of seeing a variety of aeroplanes and various flight displays. At a display of the Bombardier airliner, the Dash 8 Q400 the presenters were happy to take us into the aircraft and allowed us to have a good look around that new aircraft with powerful turboprop engines.

India excursion

All through my life I had kept in contact with several relatives in India where my parents had originated. It was in December 1988 that I visited that country for a month to meet up with my relatives as well as do some sightseeing. A British Airways flight on the Boeing 747 took me to Delhi. It was possible for me to visit the cockpit and I had the delight of chatting with the crew about the modern flight instruments and controls and my flying experiences. On coming out of the cockpit, the attendants gave me excellent treatment and offered me a drink in the luxury lounge behind the cockpit. However, when I was leaving, the attendants told me that they had thought that I had a seat in the first-class cabin. Our landing at Delhi was almost in fog as there was immense smoke from ground traffic. In that heavily populated city my stay was with my cousins from my father's side.

From Delhi I set off eastwards to spend three days at a tiger camp in Ramnagar at the foothill of the Himalayas. It was thrilling for me to be taken around the big park on the back of an elephant. The sights of other animals, birds and even insects delighted me. My guide was amazed when I asked him to let me get off the elephant to have a closer look at the enormous ant hill. It was even more thrilling to have seen the wild tiger that had killed a deer. There were several other visitors and we sat together beside a camp fire. The clear night sky presented us with a beautiful sight of the stars and galaxies. On another elephant ride the next day we saw that another deer had been killed. Then we heard some rushing noise in the bushes, but no one caught sight of the tiger that ran away. When we were being driven in a minibus through the woods we had to slow down because there were some wild elephants on the road. After they had crossed the road we slowly moved on, but behind us one of the elephants was charging us from behind and chasing us away from his territory. Later, a long stop beside a river gave me a chance to look at some crocodiles that were lazing in the sun beside the river.

In Chandigarh I stayed with the widow of a cousin who had started staying with us in Africa in 1949. She had been helping me to channel financial support to my widowed auntie in India for three decades. It was nice to meet my cousin who had accompanied me to the Taj Mahal during my earlier visit. He had retired from his medical work and took me with his whole family to visit an unusual rock garden in Chandigarh. Strangely, the entire display setup at the park had been carried out using discarded and broken components of domestic materials.

Another adventure in India was a visit to an ancient site that was not damaged. A flight from Delhi took me to Khajurao in mid-India. That was near Chhatarpur where numerous old Hindu and Jain temples had not been destroyed during the earlier invasions by Muslims. The outside walls of those temples were covered with numerous statues of people and animals. There were statues that also showed various engagements in sexual activities. Beside our hotels there was countryside and a small village of local people. I wandered around that area for three days where some local children were playing. When looking at bird life with my binoculars, several children appeared around me to see what I was doing. They were delighted to be looking through my binoculars and ended up walking with me through the village. That walk gave me the delight of seeing people in their normal lives, such as pulling water out of a well with a bucket. I hired a bicycle and went on my own around the numerous temples in the region. A local guide even walked and talked with me although I was not looking for a guide.

My return flight from Khajurao to Delhi was in the new Boeing 737. I asked to go into the cockpit, but they told me that the pilots could allow me to do that only after the final landing. They did a short stop on the way and were then unusually taking-off in the direction of the wind flow instead of into the wind that all airliners need to be doing. After the final landing at Delhi they invited me into the cockpit and allowed me to look at the new electronic flight displays in front of them and I got them to trigger some of the tests for the displays that needed to be taught to the new pilots. After our exit they took me back in their coach and then I asked them about their unusual take-off direction. They seemed embarrassed at having to tell me about their reason. They had taken off in a hurry in the direction of their route just to rush back to Delhi and land before the time when their landing fee would go up.

During my final tour in India, an early morning express train took me to Agra for a short visit to the Taj Mahal. After that a bus took me to Bharatpur where I spent a couple of days in the bird sanctuary on a bicycle. It was delightful to be sighting wildlife birds that had migrated from other areas of our planet. After a stay with relatives for a couple of days in Delhi, a flight took me to London. It was after five weeks that I was back at work in Oxford. My life had started returning to a delightful state of existence.

1999

British Airways invited me to their Waterside Centre near Heathrow for the graduation ceremony of BA pilots for whom I had been the course tutor. The period of their training had been great fun for me and it was a delight to be at their final graduation ceremony in London. In March groups of Algerians needed to be trained to fly airliners. They were jolly, but some struggled to take in the technical information being delivered to them. During the practice examinations given to them they were warned not to talk during the main exam. Despite the warnings, some of the students were thrown out from their CAA exams because of their communications in Arabic during their exams. It was a shame that they could not be taught about examination behaviour. They all finally managed to get through their ground school training, but they seemed much happier to be doing the flying.

At the Kidlington airport, it was possible for me to go flying in a Piper PA 28 aeroplane around the local countryside. There was a lovely sighting of the ancient horse symbol at Whitehorse Hill near Uffington that was dated to have existed more than two and half thousand years ago. It was possible for me to do some circuits and landings at RAF Brize Norton. After my touchdown-and-go on the runway, I asked for another flight around the aerodrome circuit. The air traffic controller said he would only allow me to do that again if I did not fail to ask for a landing clearance on my final approach. Oops, I had previously touched down on the runway without having had a radio clearance for landing from the controller. The grounds of Blenheim Palace were close to the Combe village and had a side entrance that could be used for access to the lovely grounds of the palace where there were some small deer and other wild life, beautiful trees and lakes with various birds. One day the young boys at home came with me for a walk in the local area and they were amazed to see deer in the fields and the beauty and wildlife in the palace grounds near their home.

I started playing golf in the Oxfordshire area with another RAF man who had been doing the same job as me on maritime patrol aircraft. It was a delight to have his company and we spent a lot of time together at work and on the golf course. During that period, I ended up buying a new bag of golf clubs costing more than a thousand pounds to replace the ancient clubs that had been picked up from an American store in 1976. The new clubs were in the back of my car at Oxford. Then one morning, to my utter shock, my car was missing from the front of the house. It was not the loss of my old car that bothered me, but it was a shock to have lost my new golf clubs. Strangely, after my call to the police I was told that they had already found a burnt-out car that seemed to have been taken by some youngsters for a drive and then dumped and set alight in the woods without having opened the tail gate. All my golf clubs were burnt. Although the insurance enabled me to have new my golf clubs, there would be no restoration for the putter that I had won in Midway Island during my very first golf competition in 1975.

In August 1999 Britain had the rare experience of seeing a unique solar eclipse. My retired college friend Jim Sharman, who was living in Cornwall, invited me to his house. Although the day had started rather cloudy, we were extremely lucky for the clouds to open and allow us to view the start and finish of the unique sighting of a solar eclipse. The moon was hiding the sun, but the curling ejections out of the sun could be seen. That eclipse was a delightful sight for me. That even enabled me to look at the solar eclipse with my bare eyes for a short time. Although we can see the moon most of the time, the sighting of the massive sun being blotted out by our tiny moon also made me appreciate the benefit of the moon for our amazing existence on a small planet in a massive universe. In the past I used to wonder why the moon was always facing us the same way even though it is always rotating around our planet. Even after some small variations of the sightings the moon always returns to the same stable position. I wonder how many people understand why the moon going around the Earth for millions of years always shows us the same face.

2000 and 2001

British Airways invited me to two more ceremonies where their recruits had finally been given the BA wings to wear on their uniforms. On one of those ceremonies an American astronaut gave a talk during the event. He was being prepared for a launch into space sometime later. After his talk it was a delight for me to have a chat with him. My golf handicap had dropped to ten and I was enjoying events in Exeter and around Oxford. I set up a competition between groups at our Oxford institution. On a course at Lyneham we played a competition between four teams that were made up of people from the different departments of management, ground training staff, flight training staff and students. The prize was won by the students, who happened to have no official golf handicaps.

In 2000 my brother, Krishan, from Canada came twice and stayed with me to attend two weddings in our family in London. The second time he was with his young and tall grandson for the wedding. In Exeter they were delighted to be taken around the beautiful countryside and on a trip in a steam train to Dartmouth. After having worked away from home for four years I decided to transfer my job to Exeter in 2001 to the airline, British European had changed its name to *Flybe*. That training was for both aircraft technicians and pilots on aircraft technical aspects. I expected to stay with my *Flybe* job until my retirement age. My actual working life turned out to be quite different to my expectation.

Chapter 16

Training airline crew in Exeter

Dramatic start of Flybe training

My job with the *Flybe* airline started in September 2001. Just a week later I heard news that some aeroplane had crashed into one of the New York tower buildings and assumed that it would have been a small one. To my amazement, it was an airliner that had crashed into the big building. That was followed by another airliner crashing into the adjacent tower building. There were more crashes of airliners into major buildings around America on the same day. I couldn't believe what we were hearing on the radio in our staff room. It seemed to be some sort of fiction to me. The crashes had been carried out deliberately by some religious extremists. In America, that day of disasters came to be called the 9/11 (September eleventh). Those disasters were later going to be restricting me from sitting as an observer in an airliner cockpit.

My training tasks with *Flybe* were going to be associated with both technicians and pilots. As the engineering notes being used for technical qualifications were very old, I decided to write a new set of notes for some subjects. Also, during that period the aviation qualifications for engineers were also integrated into a European system. That resulted in mechanical engineers having to deal with electrical systems in an aircraft. I was given the task of setting up and delivering a condensed course about aircraft electrical systems to mature mechanical engineers who were disappointed with having to do that. Some even thought that they were unlikely to be able to sit through the whole course, but after the start, they got hooked and continued coming to my class. All of them sat through my classes and all the qualified technicians managed to pass through their first examination successfully and were delighted. That course about electrics turned out to be a great relief for the mechanical engineers who would welcome me to their aircraft whenever they saw me in the hangar. That also made it easier for me to show pilots the aircraft that were being serviced.

The ground training to the pilots was for the Dash 8-300, a 45 seat twin turboprop aircraft built by Bombardier in Canada. A turboprop engine has gas turbines driving propellers. After that training the pilots needed to go to Canada or Norway for some simulator flight training before starting their airliner flying. That was the first time that I started looking at every system from nose to tail of the aircraft, teaching the whole course to pilots on an aircraft that had no flight engineers on board anymore. During my RAF flying time I had flown on multi-crew aircraft. On the Shackleton aircraft, we had two pilots, two navigators, one engineer and one radio operator to deal with our transit flying. The Vulcans had two pilots, two navigators and one for air electronics officer. On the modern Dash 8 airliner there were only two pilots doing everything and who needed to be familiar with all systems.

That teaching task was going to be a challenge for me as I had to become totally familiar with everything inside, outside and hidden in the aircraft that the pilots needed to be taught to help them deal with any technical problem in flight. The new equipment, which was called avionics, involved the integration of aviation instruments with electronics and that resulted in traditional flight instruments being replaced by electronic screens. I attended a course for pilots on that aircraft in November 2001 to prepare myself for teaching those courses. One of the young pilots who had been taught by me in Oxford arrived at Exeter for his first flying job with *Flybe*. He came and stayed with me while he went through his initial Dash 8 training. In 2002 it was my turn to deliver the technical part of the course to Dash 8 pilots over a period of two weeks on my own. That course prepared the pilots to sit through a CAA examination for that aircraft. Those courses were delivered to people who were showing great interest in their learning and participated extremely well. It was a delight for me to be helping pilots through their professional training. They too were delighted to be taught technical aspects by someone who had also been flying. There was someone on one of my courses who had also been flying Vulcan bombers in 1973 from RAF Waddington where I had been based.

During all my courses at Exeter I always took the pilots to a Dash 8 aircraft on their first day, either in the servicing hangar or at the outside parking area. In the hangar, the pilots could walk on the wings, open the engine panels to peer inside, go up some framework steps to walk around the tall tail and then go inside the stripped cabin to see numerous components that they would never be seeing again. There was no need for any motivation or control during the teaching. In the first year, my teaching was for five groups of pilots, with each group having about eight pilots. That teaching association with professional pilots was a very delightful experience for me.

In 2002 it was a delight for me to go on some flights in the earlier Dash 8 cockpits. My first two return flights were to Dublin and Birmingham from Exeter. I sat with the pilots in the cockpit and watched their flying activities and got a chance to see their association with the other crew and passengers. It was a delight to be seeing the real world of work after teaching pilots about the technical aspects of that aeroplane. During the taxying after the landing at Exeter I stepped out of the cockpit and was preparing to step out of the aircraft when a passenger on a seat at the front happened to be one of my golfing colleagues. He was surprised to see me coming out of the cockpit. *Flybe* was in the process of expanding their flying operations and decided to buy the largest number of the new Dash 8 Q400 aircraft for 72 passengers that the manufacturer was building in Canada. The training for the aircraft systems of that aircraft had started and I sat in for the avionics (aviation electronics) courses being delivered to the maintenance technicians in 2002 and continued teaching another four courses to pilots for the older Dash 8 aeroplanes.

During my last training course for the earlier aircraft I caused an embarrassing situation for our maintenance team. While looking for an aeroplane to show two pilots the layout in the cockpit we could not find one. At an aircraft that was being spray washed, the technicians gratefully terminated their washing and let me spend some time with the electrical power on to show the instruments to the pilots. As it was rather hot inside the cockpit, the roof hatch for ventilation had to be opened. However, after we had finished, I had forgotten to close the hatch before leaving. The next day the engineers called me to report the dreadful event that occurred on that aeroplane. The technicians had continued with their washing after we had left and had ended up with a wet cockpit. All I could do was to apologise and was relieved that the airline did not punish me.

In August 2003 *Flybe* had started with a new apprenticeship scheme for producing aircraft technicians. That resulted in me setting up and teaching some of the subjects for that scheme, including the electrical and electronic aspects. Even from the selected group of starters in the scheme, teaching those youngsters was not easy. At the end of the lesson they could hardly answer any question that I threw at them about the topic that had been taught. The first year turned out to be very difficult with them, but somehow, they managed to stay on, got more interested and completed their four-year period of training. To my delight those crazy starters turned out to be good workers of aircraft systems. One of those lads even took me in the cockpit and taxied the aircraft to the engine test bay. There they slammed on full power with the brakes on and noted various engine indications for efficiency after maintenance completion.

Some qualified technicians would be going through further training for other aircraft types on their licences and required to be taught in classes. The mechanical engineers were only taught the basics of avionic systems on the Dash 8 aircraft and they showed a great interest it. One day, one of those mechanical engineers asked me to show him the outside components of the aircraft that he had seen me doing with the pilots and identifying numerous items that were related to the indications the pilots could see on their flight instruments. For me it was a great delight to be providing people with knowledge related to flying, an activity that had become a hobby for me after my retirement from the RAF.

Hole-in-one

Golf was another activity that had very much become a part of my later life. It was nice to have the company of friendly people and we also played matches with other clubs in the South West. During a competition at our club in May 2002, I experienced the most amazing delight in golf. A shot that I had hit from 240 yards got me a hole-in-one score. Strangely, even before the ball went into the hole, my playing partner said it was going into the hole. The players who had finished that hole were teeing off from the next hole said that they heard the ball hit the flag pole. That has been the only hole-in-one for me in a proper golf competition. My first hole-in-one had occurred over only half that distance when I was playing on my own and it was the builders of our new club house who had witnessed it. In all my golfing time, only twice in my life has the ball gone into the hole with one shot from the tee. These shots had been nothing but flukes.

Light aircraft flying

Flying in light aeroplanes had been a great delight for me for a long time as many friends and acquaintances would take up the three spare seats. There were many beautiful countryside sights close to Exeter. Flying low over colourful hillsides in the autumn, over snow covered white hills in winter and many old age dwelling sites in the south west were a real delight. We flew over our delightful coastline and landed at many small aerodromes as well as doing trips across the English Channel to France. My friends found that sharing the cost of flying made it easy for them to experience the delight of flying to our chosen sights and destinations.

One day I managed to position the aeroplane for a rare sighting. During my Shackleton flying days, I had seen a full circle rainbow that had been moving around with us. During one of my light aeroplane flights, there was the possibility of placing ourselves in a position where a circular rainbow would appear just for us. There had to be a suitable cumulus cloud with a rain shower underneath it and no lightning flashes. The position of the sun was low enough for us to fly in the beam of sunlight that was illuminating the shower. I managed to position the aeroplane suitably and ended up sighting a full circular rainbow in the rain. The rainbow moved along with us until we flew out of the beam between the sun and the cloud. Then we flew back a couple of times to continue sighting the delightful display of the full circle rainbow all along the width of that cloud. During all my flying days, I had only occasionally managed to see those circular rainbows flying with me. My discovery of that sight had occurred in the Indian ocean from a Shackleton aircraft.

Later that year a friend came with me on a flight to the Isle of Wight, flying past the cliff arch at Lulworth Cove east of Weymouth and then the Needles on the western side of the Isle of Wight. Our return flight took us past the old wartime aerodrome of Stoney Cross near Southampton and the naked giant image on the hillside at Cerne Abbas. The ability to be able to jump into an aeroplane and pop around our countryside had been a great delight in my life. In addition to flying around in the south west of Britain my flights further away were mostly across the English Channel and I ended up doing more landings in France than in Britain. It was in June 2002 that two friends joined me for an early morning flight that took us almost in a straight line south across the English Channel to Lannion in Brittany, France. After the coast of Devon there was no sight of land until we got close to France. As we did not have any auto-pilot control it required concentration from me to maintain our heading as there was no scenery around us and the aeroplane was drifting to the left. In flight, we could only trim the up and down movement of the aeroplane, but the trimming for left and right movement could only be done on the ground. The control in flight became awkward if that trimming needed to be adjusted. As there was no radio signal from that location, we had to identify what we could see on sighting the French coast. To my surprise there was a big white dome covering a radar antenna that was near the aerodrome. That enabled me to find the aerodrome and we landed and parked the aeroplane. Then we took a taxi to some small French towns at the coast, had lunch and wandered around the coast before taxiing back to the airport. We then jumped into the aeroplane and flew back over empty airspace at about five thousand feet. On that flight the beacon at Berry Head enabled me to maintain our track. We landed at Exeter just before 8 p.m. when the airport would officially be closed. That had been a delightful day trip to France.

In July 2003, we flew in a Cessna aeroplane to an airport called West Wales with someone who wanted to meet a friend in that area. That airport was being created from an old RAF station and only had some advisory air traffic service. For our departure from there I did a take-off from near our parked position although the wind would be from our tail, which was not normal. Starting from a higher level would help us speed up our groundspeed during the take-off. For rotating the aeroplane into flight, the speed through the air had be a set at a minimum amount, but our speed over the ground would be higher because it would be the speeds of the wind and the aeroplane added up. That meant that it would take us a longer distance to rotate the aeroplane into flight. There would be no problem with a light aeroplane on a long runway which would enable me to take off in the direction that was needed. That was like the take-off I had experienced as a passenger in a jet airliner in India that was taking off in the direction of the wind to return to its destination before a certain time. That take-off and landing direction is certainly not a common practice for airliners.

New Dash 8 airliner

The new Dash 8 Q400 was more sophisticated and the passenger load had increased to 72. Our training manager had been to Canada to learn about that aircraft and then had started teaching it in Exeter. Then in December 2003 I was asked to sit in on a full course being taught by our manager. Halfway through that course the manager failed to turn up at the classroom as he had dumped his job with *Flybe*. Strangely, the company asked me to take over the teaching of that course as there was no technician who wanted to do it and my earlier qualification entitled me to teach that later version aircraft. Surprisingly, I managed to do it with great co-operation from the pilots who were delighted to have completed their training. After that there was plenty of time for me to prepare the delivery of the next course. As none of the other ground instructors were keen to be teaching pilots about technical details of flying, I ended up being the sole instructor for the pilot ground training, even beyond my retirement age.

On my second course in February 2004, there was also a man from the CAA (Civil Aviation Authority) who was keeping tabs on the airliner flying training standards. The CAA man turned out to be an RAF man that I had known during my Shackleton flying days in Scotland, as well as during my time in Malta when he was in Rome with NATO. We had liaised about the tasking for the maritime patrol aircraft in the Mediterranean. It was a delight to have him in my class in Exeter more than thirty years later and he was very enthusiastic and jovial. The teaching of technical knowledge to the pilots was enjoyable and fulfilling. There was great social contact with many pilots on those courses and they even took me out to dinner. Sometimes at our airport some pilots in uniform who had been taught by me would come and tell me about some system problem they had encountered during their flights.

In 2004 it became possible for me to start and run the engines on my own on a parked aircraft. Qualified technicians took me through the procedure of starting and running the engines and I was then certified to do engine runs. That gave me the opportunity to do engine starts with the student pilots on a parked aircraft. During that period, it was necessary for a technician on the ground to stand in front and signal clearance for the engine starts. As it was difficult to find a spare technician, those engine starts were done only a few times. When I was teaching a course about electronic instrument systems, referred to as avionics, to mechanical technicians, it surprised me that those technicians were delighted with what they were learning. My increased connection with training pilots for the Dash 8 aircraft resulted in me being not available for periods to teach engineering apprentices and technicians. Still, I enjoyed my relationship with many friendly technicians.

Friends and hobbies 2004

The sight of different rocks in the moors and our south coast started getting me interested in geology. Strangely, it was only after my association with The Devonshire Association (DA) that made me realise that I was living on the most interesting coast on the globe. Our coastal path displayed the soil and rocks that had existed more than 250 million years ago. We visited the South Croft tin mines in Cornwall and looked at the layers of very ancient rocks that had been formed when that land was well south of the equator. The ground beneath our feet would start to get younger the further eastwards we went along the coast towards the white cliffs of Dover. The bones of the later living creatures would only start showing up in the soil along the coast eastwards from Exeter. Near Lyme Regis people had been picking up bones of dinosaurs that had been around 100 million years ago. Our long south coast displays the longest period of the history of our wonderful planet.

In the Normandy area of France there was a big gathering for the sixtieth anniversary of the D-day landings. As we could not land at Caen during that period, I flew with some friends to Cherbourg on the fifth of June. There, we were picked up by my French friend and taken to his house near Caen. Together with the French family we went to various Normandy beaches on the D-day and viewed numerous gatherings and displays. We saw the Pegasus Bridge at Caen and the cemeteries at Arrowmanches. In the early morning of the next day, we were driven over to Cherbourg, jumped into our aircraft and flew back to Exeter. I parked the aircraft and turned up in the classroom on the aerodrome to start another pilot course for the Dash 8 aircraft at 9 o'clock in Britain.

That year I met my French friends a lot. Their daughter Emilie who I had known her since she was a child, started working in a Wimborne school in south Britain because she had learnt English at school. Before she returned to France, I picked her up from Wimborne and showed her around lovely Devon. Later that year I went and stayed with that French family for a few days. We visited the museum at Bayeux where there are the stitched displays of the Norman invasion of Britain in 1066. Strangely, my friends had never visited that museum near them. Then they were also surprised to learn that the stitching had been done in Britain. They accompanied me to the D-day memorial in their area. We had several delightful walks along the Normandy coast. Then in December the French couple arrived in England by car. They stayed with me for a few days before going to Cornwall. I took them to University Great Hall to listen to a musical concert by the Bournemouth Symphony Orchestra. They were delighted to have been to their first classical music concert. Despite our language problems it was a delight to be having their company.

In 2005 a fleet of four aircraft were on a combined trip to France for an overnight stay and persuaded me to join them. After drawing up the planned route and walking to the aeroplanes we were told that the route planned had been changed and we should follow the leader. We were going to be having different people becoming captains for the different sections of the trip. We flew over a long stretch of sea and finally got to Deauville. In our manoeuvre to get on the final approach the captain pilot ended up being badly placed. That made me tell him to go around again for another approach for landing. After another tricky approach manoeuvring, he finally managed to bounce on the runway and came to a stop with great relief.

At Deauville we found that all of the hotels were fully booked up due to some conference gathering. So, we all jumped back into our aeroplanes again and we all took off without any planning to fly along the Normandy coast to land at Cherbourg. That time I was to be in the driving seat and rather than following the others; on the shortest route, I flew to the cathedral of Bayeux where there was a dangling body of a parachuting soldier. Of course, that body up there was only a dummy and represented the event that had occurred there during the big invasion in June 1944. We landed at Cherbourg and had no difficulty with finding accommodation. The next day someone else took the flight and we returned home safely. Flying with a group was never going to happen in my life again.

Exit and return to work

Flybe was expanding its operations and I was happy to continue doing the job even after passing my retirement age. My work with *Flybe* in 2005 would then be on a very short-term contract. Strangely, that extended period of employment was to end sharply within that year due to some staff problems that we had. A new employee would use dreadful foul language during our conversations, and I stopped talking with him. He complained to the training manager about my detachment with him. That manager arranged a meeting between us. There we were asked to state our problems and objections. That resulted in me saying nothing. We were asked to report for another meeting after two weeks. That is when I handed in a one week notice for termination of employment.

Two months after my employment termination, a *Flybe* ground instructor rang me to ask for some help in teaching cockpit controls and indications to pilots. I refused to help him. It was during that period that I happened to be at a *Flybe* social gathering of pilots at the weekend and was asked by the pilots if I could run the new course for them as there was nobody from the engineers who was going to be doing it. I agreed to do it only if they could be employing me and not the engineering manager. They agreed, and I turned up at the training centre to surprise a group of pilots who thought that they had to teach themselves. After that course the engineering staff failed to sort out their problem of training pilots and contacted me more than once to come back for that training. In order to put them off, I said that I would only do it for twice the pay. Strangely, they agreed. The next eight courses for the pilots starting in February 2006 were run by me as a self-employed instructor. Later I found that after my completion of the courses, the future Dash 8 courses for pilots would be transferred to Farnborough where two Dash 8 flight simulators were being installed by the American company Flight Safety International (FSI). Although working away from home was of no interest to me, I was interested in working with flight simulators on a part-time job. I did write to the company about that prospect, but strangely heard nothing from them and stopped thinking about it. I continued with the delight of training another sixty *Flybe* pilots for their airliner.

Farnborough start

Surprisingly, in May 2006 there was a telephone call from the centre manager of FSI at Farnborough airport asking me to come for an interview. That company had not even acknowledged the job application that had been sent to them three months earlier. After their late call for an interview, I agreed to go there to check the training facilities and the job. FSI was a big American company setting up their first simulator flight training facility in Britain. After the interview in Farnborough for a job as a ground instructor, I had positive indications that they wanted me to join them.

It was a delight when they called me to say that they would take me on a part-time job, as I had requested. There was a very friendly welcome for me at Farnborough. People working for FSI had come from various countries in different parts of the globe. The new building was spacious and well equipped. There were fifteen different flight simulators in three blocks and there were two simulators for the Dash 8: that was the only airliner. All of the other simulators were for business aeroplanes or for small passenger carriers. There were numerous small jets taxiing past the building. It was a delight for me to be there during my later period of life.

Chapter 17

Flight simulators at Farnborough

New Employment in 2006

Two months before finishing my work with *Flybe* in 2006 I started working for Flight Safety International (FSI). Initially, both my jobs were interlinked as they both involved training the pilots of *Flybe* on the Dash 8 airliner. Flight Safety was an American company with dozens of bases in the USA. The three international bases were named as FSI and were in Canada, France and the UK. Despite me having passed the age of 66, FSI would be contributing into a pension scheme for me until the age of 75. My main interest in the new job was the opportunity to fly the simulator cockpit constructed with the very same components as the real airliner. The main FSI training centre for the Dash 8 was located right beside the aeroplane manufacturer Bombardier in Toronto. That was where pilots from around the world had earlier been obtaining their flying licence for that aeroplane. The new FSI training at Farnborough provided simulator training for the new Dash 8 for people from Europe, Africa and Asia. There were also many other business aeroplane simulators in the same building.

   The classrooms at Farnborough had no windows, so as to avoid outside distractions. The walls widely displayed vast diagrams and images of the aeroplane systems and two projectors displayed information on the front screens from computers controlled by the instructor. Some classrooms even had computer controls and displays at their desks. It was the most advanced teaching environment I had ever engaged in before. My main job was to deliver the technical information to the pilots about the airliner. Initially, there was an opportunity for me to use the flight simulator during my teaching to relate to the information that had been taught in the class. The cockpit in the simulator was the same as that on the real aircraft, but behind the cockpit there was a set-up that was used by the instructors to control indications to the pilots about the flight attitude, various system failures and weather conditions. The cockpit windscreen was a large screen that could display the real scenery for a lot of places on the globe. Behind the cockpit there were two more seats for observers. The outside of the simulator was totally different from the aircraft as it was mounted on jacks moving the simulator in many directions. I remember in my earlier days I had even considered paying for some fun flying time in the cockpit of an airliner simulator. My new job was going to pay me for being in a fun environment.

Half a dozen new staff pilots had already been sent to the FSI base in Toronto, Canada for their simulator training. It turned out that I was the only one at FSI who was familiar with the Dash 8 Q400. *Flybe* was the only airline in Britain who used the aeroplane. Hundreds of pilots had already been taught by me over three years. The Farnborough staff had many ex-RAF pilots. There was Duncan Ross with whom I had flown nearly thirty years ago in the Vulcans. In 1975 we had been on a trip to Midway Island in the Pacific Ocean. FSI sent me to Toronto for a course to enable me to be certified to teach the FSI course for the Dash 8. At a Holiday Inn in Toronto some of the others from Farnborough who had been there for months came to meet me. Toronto was also where my brother, Krishan lived. He took me on a great touristic trip to Niagara Falls and a hydraulic power station.

At our Toronto building I sat in a course taught to a group of pilots from the Far East. Several instructors were taking it in turn to present different technical topics to the pilots. That had been done by me on my own. The FSI course was set up differently to my *Flybe* course and was jammed into several days less than the one used in Exeter. However, at Farnborough they also taught the weight and balance as well as the aircraft performance that had been done by flying pilots at *Flybe*. Effectively the FSI ground training was done in two weeks, something which was being done over a period of three weeks at *Flybe* in Exeter. During the break on the course the pilots started asking me for information instead of asking their instructor during the rushed lessons.

During my time with *Flybe* in Exeter I had been talking on the telephone to the Bombardier people in Toronto about Dash 8-400 technical matters. The Bombardier location was right beside the FSI in Toronto. That enabled me to meet up with the person who had talked to me on the telephone. He took me around their setup to see a finished Dash 8-Q400 in the hangar. What surprised me was that all the other FSI staff from Britain had been told not to visit Bombardier that was next door to them. Our tension with the staff in Toronto must have been due to fact that Toronto was going to be losing some of their customers to Farnborough. Strangely, no one had said anything to me about going to the Bombardier location. My time in Toronto enabled me to sit in with some Toronto instructors in the simulators. There I noticed some incorrect display on the simulator that resulted in the staff calling in a Bombardier manager. After checking the cockpit display Bombardier accepted that there was a problem and agreed to modify the simulator behaviour so that it would relate to reality.

After coming back to Exeter, I went to France to attend the wedding of the older daughter of my French friends living near Caen in Normandy. A ferry from Portsmouth took me to Caen where they picked me up. For me it was a delightful experience of a French wedding, with the celebrations lasting until 4a.m. The next day the return ferry took me to Portsmouth where my car had been parked and returned to Farnborough for the forthcoming courses. Initially, it was the delivery of the *Flybe* courses that I had been doing in Exeter. The Flight Safety courses would start only after the Farnborough simulator had been checked by the British CAA. However, as things turned out, the CAA check was delayed.

My continued link with Flybe in 2006

After the completion of the FSI training our staff returned from Toronto to start training the Dash 8 pilots. However, the Civil Aviation Association (CAA) in Britain postponed the Dash 8 approval checks because of problems in some other simulators at Farnborough. That is when *Flybe* was asked to run their own courses at Farnborough with their own staff. *Flybe* agreed to do that, but they wanted me to continue doing their ground school training and FSI were delighted to allow that. As our companions in Toronto had failed to properly deliver the Dash 8 displays for our classroom, I transported *Flybe* displays from Exeter to Farnborough and was ready to continue doing my old job with them. There were many other courses that were being run by FSI and their instructors had to be trained for many months before they could start teaching their courses. They were surprised to see a new member of staff teaching a course shortly after joining. What they did not realise was that I was teaching a *Flybe* course to *Flybe* pilots at their location. Those courses continued to be repeated and I ended up working in Farnborough for nearly three weeks every month. During that time the FSI flying instructors had to be trained to use the *Flybe* course procedures to enable them to engage in the *Flybe* training program. We continued to work in that arrangement until the end of 2007. During my training engagements with *Flybe* at Exeter and Farnborough about 450 *Flybe* pilots had been taught about the Dash 8 airliner by me.

Strangely, I also ended up with private link with *Flybe* to train ground technicians for the Dash 8 aircraft maintenance at the FSI location because FSI did not train aircraft technicians at Farnborough. The simulator that had been booked for *Flybe* was used by me to train the technicians. FSI also had multi-screen set ups of two Dash 8 cockpits in one of our rooms for use by the students. Some of the technicians were happier with the activity in the stationary cockpits than in the simulator. Although in the simulator the purpose was to train the technicians for the handling procedures on the ground, I also took them on some flying trips which were a great delight for them. After training them, I signed their maintenance certificates. For me it was a great delight to have been involved with that training, although it was only for a few technicians. Then in 2007 the *Flybe* and FSI association had expired, *Flybe* resorted to doing its own pilot ground training in Exeter although the simulator was still at Farnborough. My delightful teaching association with *Flybe* finally came to an end.

2007

The FSI training programs were used for pilots from countries around the globe. My integration into the proper FSI process of teaching had been diverted due to my engagement with the *Flybe* training. For me to be integrated into the FSI system they sent me to Dallas in Texas for an introductory teaching course. The FSI course was designed to guide new instructors to the task of teaching, something that I had been doing for several decades. At an enormously spread out Dallas International airport the airliner even taxied above a busy motorway. There happened to be a major golf competition being held close to my hotel which gave me the chance to see some live professional golf on the Sunday. It was a delight for me to see famous golfers in action. At the FSI training centre there were two very enthusiastic instructors delivering very good teaching. Strangely, the black American instructor appeared to be like a priest preaching us. Then I discovered that he had been a priest and had become a devout instructor. During the course I had to participate by giving a short talk. After I finished my talk, there was silence in the class. The Americans had been stunned at hearing foreign English. Even the instructors said that they didn't have the heart to tell me that I had exceeded their time limit. For me it was a great delight to have been with the group of very friendly pilots from all around America.

Although my instructor colleagues at Farnborough had become familiar with the cockpit of the Dash 8 aeroplane in the simulator, they still had not been inside a real aeroplane. *Flybe* allowed me to show the FSI staff around an aeroplane inside their hanger at Exeter. My FSI colleagues came to Exeter over two days and I took them around the aeroplane that they were teaching, but they had never been close to one themselves in Canada. They had the chance to see the hidden insides of the aircraft cockpit, fuselage and the engines, as numerous coverings had been removed. They even had the opportunity to stand on the wings beside the opened-up engines and at the top of the tail of the aeroplane. They experienced being in the aeroplane that they had been taught a year earlier without a single visit to the neighbouring manufacturer at Toronto.

In 2007, I was involved in a car accident with a young woman who had just acquired her driving licence. My car had to be written off and the next day there was a pain in my neck that made me visit a local hospital for some treatment. Three weeks later at an auction near Farnborough I managed to pick up a Volvo. As the car was nearly three years old it had to put in for an MOT certificate. Whilst there I also asked the garage to look at the slightly tricky reverse gear selection. To my surprise they told me that the tricky gear linkage could be replaced for free with a redesigned linkage because the car had been guaranteed for three years. It was a delight to have had the problem sorted without having to pay for it.

In 2007 my auntie *(Chachiji)* from my father's side in India passed away. She had been supported by me since her husband had died in 1966. She had raised her five children and now they were all married. For more than forty years she had been supported by me. When my father had passed away, I was only nine years old and my mother's brother *(Mamaji)* had raised me and supported me through my young life. The Indian practice of supporting a relative had been embedded in me. Luckily my financial position enabled me to give extra support to my relatives.

It was in 1957 that I had the delight of being selected to represent Kenya at the boy scouts Jubilee Jamboree at Sutton Coldfield in Britain. Fifty years later I went to the Centenary Jamboree that was at Hylands Park in Chelmsford. Some young African scouts from Kenya were surprised to meet someone who had been one of the Kenyan scouts in the Jubilee Jamboree in Britain in 1957. At the Centenary Jamboree, there were some people who had been at the 1957 Jubilee Jamboree. Together we went to the earlier site that we had been on and tried to locate the position of where our camps would have been. It was a delight to be reliving the experiences that we had fifty years earlier and being together with the old group. We all gathered around beside the memorial that had been constructed to display the occurrence of that Jamboree.

2008

At the start of 2008 the Dash 8 courses at Farnborough began to be delivered at intervals of only three weeks. I would be engaged in the first two weeks of the course that lasted for about two months. The start of our training program turned out to be a very intense period. On the first course, there were two pilots from Austria and one from Luxemburg and I taught them all through the weekend as well. During those courses I also used the simulator for some cockpit procedures training in addition to the classroom time.

Immediately after that course, it was necessary for me start a short course at the weekend for two experienced pilots of the airline, *Skywork* in Switzerland. They were going to be the managers of the new aeroplane being acquired by them. Although both pilots had previously been instructors for that aeroplane, they had to have a short recurrent training program over three days because of their long break since flying it. At the end of our course one of them told me that, being an instructor himself, he used to go to sleep whenever he was being instructed, but he was amazed that I had not allowed him to do that. He was delighted to be kept attentive all the time. Instructing a lot of experienced pilots made me get them involved in delivering information to the others, based on their flying experiences. My simple technique locked everyone's attention to the lesson and no one had a chance to go to sleep. It also allowed some pilots to pass on their knowledge from their flying experiences. That technique helped me because I would solely be delivering the whole ground-school course continuously over two weeks. In Toronto that job was being done by half a dozen instructors who each taught only one aspect of the aeroplane.

My ground school teaching was only done during normal hours on weekdays. The simulator sessions involving flight handling would be carried out all week during day and night periods by flying instructors. Our training program was for pilots from around the world. We had four pilots from *Skywork* of Switzerland in February and later four pilots from Tyrolean and Croatia airlines. Then we had two groups of eight pilots of *Air Philippines*. The first surprise was the presentation of gifts from them to me at the start of the course. An ex-Boeing 747 captain joined that course two days later and struggled to get to grips with the aircraft systems. He even invited me for dinner to help him catch up with the technical aspects. On the Boeing airliner, he had an engineer to look after all the systems. On the Dash 8 he had to learn to cope with it on his own. I gave him additional time of training and managed to get him through the examinations. In aviation exams the percentage for achieving a pass required a minimum of 75%. As it turned out he managed to achieve passes for his ground school exams, but then found himself unable to deal with system failures in the simulator. In the first group of those pilots there were two who failed to achieve their type rating for the Dash 8. One of those packed it up, but the other one had another go for the whole course and eventually managed to get through.

During my drive to Farnborough on a Sunday evening in June there was a clutch failure in my car that would take a week to fix. While walking between the flat and my workplace at Farnborough I went past a cycle shop.

That resulted in me buying a folding bicycle for that travel, which encouraged me to start using the bicycle instead of the car. Cycling became a pleasant physical activity during the evening time because there was a cycle path beside the river close to the airport at Farnborough. Even in Devon there were many cycle paths that had been opened recently and many more were being laid out. A knee problem that had made me give up jogging a long time ago did not affect my cycling activity. Cycling was an activity that I hadn't done since I had left school more than fifty years before. Beside our Farnborough work location there was a golf course, which resulted in me using my golf clubs in the evenings. One day, our boss at Farnborough was also playing there and we decided to start a golf competition for all the people at the aerodrome. That year the first competition for people working close to us at the airport was held and it was a delight.

The Farnborough air show in July 2008 was a great delight for me. The Vulcan bomber XH558 in which I had flown six times in the 1970s was doing a display flight. During my RAF flying time I had enjoyed flying in many displays around Britain in other Vulcans. However, my most exciting flights on Vulcans had not been displays at aerodromes. There would be no spectators for our flights in which we exercised for possible war bombing. I am glad that our fighting posture had helped to block the start of a major world war. My RAF time is what had triggered me into flying light aeroplanes for fun. Living on my own had enabled me to engage in many pleasant activities both in Exeter and in Farnborough.

Air Berlin came to us for their training on their new Dash 8 aeroplane. We had four captains on the first course and four co-pilots for the second one. They were all very keen and talented pilots and must have been delighted as they continued to send many more crews to Farnborough. It was a delight for me to teach two African co-pilots for a firm called *Arik Air*, based in West Africa and I was hoping to hear from them about their flying in Africa. We had pilots flying for different European airlines that also included Croatia. During our break times a female pilot would be talking to her child at home on the computer link that they could link to in our classrooms. One day we heard a fire alarm go off in the building when we were on a break and I had to make sure that all the pilots on my course were out of the building. As the female pilot was not there, I ran back into the vacated building and found her sitting in the empty classroom and talking to her daughter on her computer. The fire alarm briefing that had been presented to the group at the start of the course had not sunk into that pilot at all. Fortunately, that there had been no major fire in the building.

Dash 8 air crash in the USA in 2009

The very type of airplane that I was teaching to professional pilots in Britain had crashed in the USA in February 2009 during its approach for landing at Buffalo. It was a fatal accident for all 45 people on board, as well as one human in his home. Although I was teaching the pilots to understand all the controls and the instruments in the cockpit, the actual handling of the controls in flight was done by flying instructors in the simulators. I wondered what had gone wrong with the flight controls and later found out the cause of the crash.

The pilot had been descending with reduced engine power to reach the lower flight level for the final approach to the runway. What he had failed to do after that was to increase the engine power to maintain a flight level until the flight was closer to the runway for landing. Instead, he had been talking to the co-pilot. The autopilot was maintaining the flight level, but because the engine power had not been restored, the nose had to be pushed up by the autopilot to maintain the altitude. That resulted in the airspeed continuing to decrease and finally sounded the stall warning. The pilot's response should have been to take manual control of the flight, slam on full engine power and hold the altitude to prevent a stall of the flight. Instead, the pilot immediately put the flight into a climb. That incorrect response resulted in the airplane stalling again a few times and finally coming down vertically on one house on the flight path.

2009 - 2010

During 2009 we ran nine courses for *Air Berlin* and in August we started training the *Olympic Air* pilots from Greece. Half the pilots were sent to Canada and half of them came to Farnborough. Their chief pilot had decided to come to Britain. On the initial course for that group of eight male and female pilots there was a great response and a very friendly behaviour from the group. Even before the end of the first week the chief pilot felt that he would like all his pilots to come to Britain instead of going to Canada. He could not arrange that as the training locations had been selected by the manufacturer that was located beside our setup in Toronto. The Greeks were staying in the luxurious new hotel built beside our airport. They invited me for dinner with them at the Aviator Hotel. My working life was giving me delight and respect. As I needed to prepare myself for the Kilimanjaro climb it was necessary for me to be fit. That resulted in me joining the Velocity leisure centre near the airport.

After the first two groups of pilots had finally finished their training they returned to Greece, but they then had to wait for their flight as their aircraft from Canada had not arrived in Greece. They were also going to be using pilots from *Flybe* to help them settle into operating their new aircraft. In 2010 I had started teaching some Greek pilots. The next day, there was some heavy snowfall, but I had managed to drive to work and was told that the centre had been closed due to the snow. Also, it surprised me that the company car could not be driven to pick up the pilots from the hotel that was right beside the airport. I decided to walk to the nearby hotel and meet the Greek pilots. The luxury hotel could easily set up a classroom and provide overhead projection. That is where I managed to deliver my course to the pilots for two days. The trainees were delighted to receive their training in the hotel. The Greeks showed great respect for the training they were receiving from me and ended up inviting me to several dinners during all my Greek courses.

Kilimanjaro

My second climb up Kilimanjaro was part of my attempt to get to the highest point in Africa, fifty years after I had first been there in July 1959. My first climb up Kilimanjaro had been through my college in Nairobi and had been done with the Outward Bound Mountain School at Loitokitok in Kenya. About two weeks before my departure for the trip I went to Mount Snowden in Wales for a couple of days for my final fitness training. The climb up and down the mountain was done with ease on my first day and I set myself a bigger target for the next day. I went up and down the mountain three times on different routes and then drove back home. My body gave me no pain or problem. However, my preparation in Britain had been at low altitudes and the mountain of nineteen thousand feet was bound to be far more challenging.

As I failed to establish contact with the Outward Bound organisation in Kenya, my second climb was to be through a business setup in Tanzania. A flight from Heathrow took me to Nairobi, which is at an altitude of 5,500 feet. During my stay for three days at Nairobi a young African who had first met me in 2007 at the Scout Jamboree in Britain came to be with me. He took me to the Rowallen camp where I had been selected to represent Kenya at the 1957 Jubilee Jamboree in Britain. There were various people associated with scouting at that location. During our drives to and from the camp we drove through a very big shanty town that had not been there in my earlier days. I also visited the university which used to be called the Royal Technical College during my study period.

A small coach took me to Moshi in Tanzania. It surprised me that there was a team of six African porters who would be helping just me in the climb. It was no problem for me to get to an altitude of nine thousand feet. That night there was a wonderful view of a night sky that struck me more than ever before. The Milky Way and constellations of stars appeared clearly. It was a delight for me to be seeing the Southern Cross constellation that is not in view in the northern part of our globe. We climbed to twelve thousand feet to the Horombo base for a stay of two nights to give myself better altitude preparation. During that stay we walked up a higher altitude in the area between Kilimanjaro and Mwenzi peaks. It was on the third day that we tracked up to the final base at Kibo that was at 14,000 feet. There were many people coming down from the peak and it was delightful to have stopped and talked to some of them. There was no trouble for me to get to Kibo base from where I set out at midnight with my guide, to get to the summit and then to return to Horombo.

The final climb suddenly became very steep and I used spike poles for support and a headlight to see the track. After passing sixteen thousand feet we stopped for a rest and I took something to drink, but then vomited it out. That made me restrict myself to water only and continued to stagger up the mountain, struggling and resting, but not giving up. We passed people who had given up. We saw the sunrise even before we had reached the rim of the crater. Some people were even returning from their climb to the highest point. It was a struggle for me to reach Gillman's point at the rim of the crater at 18,600 feet. That is when it felt that the worst part of the climb had passed. While going around the rim to the highest point we passed many people returning from the peak. We finally got to the top called Uhuru Peak at 19,340 feet. Uhuru is the Swahili word for freedom. In 1959 it had been called Kaiser Wilhelm Spitz. It was a great delight for me to have made it to the top again after fifty years. I enjoyed the sights around us, although there was no snow at the peak and the ice packs were much smaller than before.

On our return my body started feeling better and we finally made it to the Kibo huts for a short stop and had something to eat. During the descent to the Horombo huts at twelve thousand feet, the sun had set, and my body was feeling weak. On arrival at that base I went straight to bed and woke up the next day feeling fine. At breakfast, several people told me that they had been alarmed at not having seen me at dinner the evening before. That Kilimanjaro climb made me feel thrilled with having managed to repeat my greatest physical achievement after fifty years.

East Africa

After my mountain climb, I set off on a safari tour of five days in a vast wildlife area that also had human habitations. It felt strange to me that I was going around as a tourist in the region of the planet where I had been born and raised. It was a delight, again to be seeing many hippos in a pool and giraffes by the trees. After a night stop at a lodge beside Lake Manyara the safari took me to the Olduvai Gorge in the Rift Valley that was another delight for me. That is where ancient hominid fossils had been found by the Leakey family a long time ago. During the period of my study at the Royal Technical College in Nairobi, Louis Leakey gave us a talk about our ancestry. It felt great for me to be at the location where the homos had been nearly two million years ago and was then used by our ancestors, the homo-sapiens that originated less than two hundred thousand years ago.

A balloon flight was something I had not managed to experience before. It was a great delight for me to go over the Serengeti plains on a balloon trip over the wildlife area. Amazingly, the basket would house about twenty people and we had to enter the basket that was on its side. Only after there was a full inflation that the balloon righted up the basket and we started looking around. Instead of climbing high we continued at a low altitude from where we could see wildlife running around. There was a lovely view of the vast countryside and the sun just rising. A second balloon rose after and us and we drifted along the terrain in the same direction. There were times when we nearly brushed into a tree on our path. Herds of wild animals would be scattering away as we approached them. It was nice to see a group of lions underneath us jumping over a stream to get out of our way. The speed and position of our flying in a balloon was a totally different experience compared with my numerous flying experiences in aeroplanes.

Our basket landed safely beside a track and remained upright. Beside our location the other balloon landed and ended up with the basket on its side. That balloon flight had been a delightful experience for me. Then there was a surprising final farewell. Some cars appeared and set up tables on the grass. Food and wine was laid out for us by dressed-up waiters. I realised that the balloon flight was designed for tourists. After that early balloon flight, the driver took me down to Ngoro Crater that was packed with plenty of wildlife including wildebeest, zebra, hippo, hyena, bustard, cranes, lions, gazelles and cheetahs. It was nice to sit close to some herds and see them getting on with their lives. My night stop was in a lodge, at the top of the land. After returning to my hotel in Arusha I saw some young African lads playing football with great passion in a park beside us and wondered if they could end up playing for my Arsenal team. An African wedding crowd dressed very smartly in European style clothing was at a nearby park. When they saw that I was trying to photograph them, they came over and posed to let me photograph them.

In the YMCA accommodation in Nairobi there were many professional Africans who were astounded that I had climbed Kilimanjaro again after a period of fifty years. Someone looking for activity in retirement, got interested in going up Kilimanjaro. From Nairobi, a flight took me to Mombasa to be with my friend who had been in college with me, played football together and had also climbed Kilimanjaro in 1959. As a civil engineer, he had done very well in Kenya and was living in a huge luxurious house on the north side. The old floating bridge at Nyali had been replaced by a causeway linking it to the mainland. My friend decided to come with me on a trip to Antarctica which I was going to start planning. Then a flight took me to Nairobi and I returned home to Britain in an airliner the next day.

Passing the age of seventy

After my return to Britain in 2009 I was engaging well into my physical activities, as well as my aviation work at Farnborough and Exeter. For my professional flying activities, a special aviation medical test in London was required as I was approaching the age of seventy. The doctor was impressed by my Kilimanjaro climb. The medical testing for my body was fine. However, the medical officer was shocked to see that I had been taking *Terbinafine* pills for a toenail problem for about a year. Taking those pills would normally have resulted in me being banned from flying. As I had not suffered any problem and had even managed to have been up Kilimanjaro, the doctor decided to give me the health certificate providing I completely ditched taking those pills.

At the end of 2009 the two African pilots whom I had trained earlier returned for a Dash 8 re-currency course. They had not been used for flying by their employer and returned for a short course to maintain their licence. It was strange that some people could be trained intensively and would then only be sitting in an office doing nothing. In 2010 it was a delight for me to be instructing the chief pilot of a company that was flying the earlier Dash 8 200 aircraft from the Wilson airport in Kenya, the country of my birth and upbringing. He had come to sit through the entire course for the Dash 8 Q400 that he hoped to start flying. Although I had helped with the training of 150 pilots from around the world, most of the pilots came from the European airlines of *Air Berlin*, *Olympic Air* and *Croatia Airline*.

Flying had become part of my life by chance. In the RAF I had flown for sixteen years on 760 flights for 3,600 hours of flying. My flying in light aircraft was for forty years on 815 flights for only 800 flying hours. My delivery of ground training to professional pilots was to more than 600 airline pilots over a period of eight years. During the latter period of my life I had managed to fly in light aeroplanes, both for pleasure as well as for training people how to fly an aeroplane. Flying had turned out to be for me, a delight as well as a source of income, even after I had passed the age of seventy. I had been having great fun with my job and in my life. The American company would continue to pay into a pension scheme until the age of seventy-five. Suddenly, in 2010, I was hit by a medical problem that came out of the blue. My very existence was threatened by something that I could never have imagined.

Chapter 18

Forced retirement after age seventy

Near head operation

After having passed the age of 70, I was suddenly hit by a headache in June 2010. At my golf club there was a strange pain in my head when I was stepping out from the shower. That resulted in me driving home and going straight to bed. There were no pills in my house as there had never been any headache problem in my life. There were many times that I got up to pass and drink water with my head continuing to ache. Eventually, I woke up with my head not hurting and came downstairs. It was then I was astounded to realise that I had been in my bedroom for four nights. After having gone to my bedroom on a Sunday night, I came downstairs on Thursday morning. For four nights and days I had only been drinking water in my bedroom. There had been no concept of time passing in my head. Strangely, I did not feel like calling for any medical help during or after that experience. However, I started having problems using my computer and seemed to have forgotten some things.

The following week I made a call to my medical centre and they told to remain at home and a doctor would come to see me immediately. The doctor who came, did a blood pressure check and told me to pack a bag to be taken to the hospital for a medical test. Then an ambulance crew arrived, came to my door asked me to take them to the patient. They were surprised that I was the patient. They tested me during the drive to the hospital. The doctors kept me there for more than a week despite the fact that I felt okay. It was on a Tuesday morning that I suddenly realised that was the week when I was supposed to be at work in Farnborough and managed to make a telephone call to them. They were greatly relieved. They had tried to contact me at home and had ended up calling my next of kin about my whereabouts.

The hospital allowed me to go home and booked me to return for a brain check more than a month later. As my body was feeling fine, I went to Farnborough by train. The regular courses for the Dash 8 aircraft had dwindled and I sat in for a refresher course being delivered to another instructor. After my return to Exeter the hospital gave me a thorough brain scan to identify the problem. The hospital doctors then called me in to give me some shocking news. My brain problem required me to have a head operation in the Plymouth hospital. I couldn't believe it. That is when I felt that my life would be coming to its end if my brain was going to be cut out. That resulted in my brother and sister from London coming to see me in Exeter. My brother in Canada told me that he would be coming when he was medically fit.

Strangely, that month the chairman of Flight Safety in the USA sent me a letter congratulating me for being one of the three best instructors at Farnborough that year. Although that was a surprise and a delight for me, I was more concerned about my very existence. The termination of that job was not going to be a problem in my life. However, fifteen years earlier in my life, I had been through the worst state of existence. After that disaster, I was ready to accept whatever was coming my way.

While waiting for my appointment in Plymouth, the Exeter hospital surprisingly told me that they would be giving me another medical check in Exeter before going to Plymouth. That made me drive to Farnborough airport to say goodbye to my many friends and pick up my belongings in the flat. After saying my goodbyes, I returned to the flat to pick up my belongings and felt slightly unwell. That resulted in me staying there until the next day, but to my horror the head problem continued for three days. That made me call my companions at Flight Safety for help. They immediately arranged my safe return to Exeter, together with all my belongings.

The medical specialist at the hospital told me that my head was not any better. However, he also told me that my head was not any worse either. To my surprise they had initially thought that my head had cancer in it, which is why they had arranged for it to be chopped. After their latest test, they found that there was no cancer and would be checking the head again a month later. It surprised me that my head was going to be cut for a diagnosis that had been guessed. Then another head check was given to me a month later when it was feeling fine. A specialist in the hospital then told me told me something that I could not believe. They told me that they did not need to see me again. Not only was I cleared of my problem, but no further head checks were needed. I couldn't believe that my life was going to have a chance of further existence.

On reflection, my problem had been very strange. During the initial state I had not been feeling any pain or problem while the doctors were worried and doing their tests. After saying my goodbye to my companions in Farnborough I had experienced severe pain in my head and realised that there was a problem in my head. However, when I went and saw the specialist at the hospital, he told me that they would not be sending me to Plymouth for a head operation, but instead for further tests in Exeter. That was followed by them saying that they never needed to see me again. Life has been a very strange experience for me.

A life change

My head problem made me lose some of my memory and made me abandon many of my life activities. My flying on light planes and my ground school teaching of professional pilots for flying an airliner had to be ditched. My plans for a trip to the Antarctica and the dhow sailing across the Indian Ocean had to be abandoned. I had to accept an earlier state of retirement before I could have suitable activities in my life. One day an instructor at Flight Safety asked me something about some control in the Dash 8 cockpit. That is when I realised that mind could not even picture the cockpit, let alone give him the answer to his query. My head problem had completely drifted my mind away from my professional life activities. That made me feel lost in life and I started recollecting my life experiences.

The most amazing path in my life had been my linkage with flying by chance when I was looking for an engineering job in Britain. After my retirement from the RAF, flying also became my hobby and later became my employment with civil aviation. It was only after my life recollections that I found it difficult for me to identify which of my life activities had been work and which had been play.

My little robin

One day I had a rare experience with a little robin bird. While reading the paper in my back garden there was a fluttering of wings behind the paper. After putting the paper down, I saw a robin sitting on the grass in front of me. After I started to read the paper again, there was a fluttering of wings again. That robin was sitting there and looking at me, as if he was trying to say something to me. All I could do was to walk back into the house and collect some food for it. To my amazement the little robin turned up in the kitchen with me and started flying around in the house. That made me rush around and open all the windows so that it would not crash into the glass. Fortunately, that lovely robin flew out safely and I did not see it again that day. That close encounter with a little wild creature was a great delight for me.

Then on another day, the little robin gave me another surprise by coming into the kitchen with me when I had come in from my garden. It amazed me that the little bird could be having such a loving close connection with a human. Even when I was not at home my mind was attached to that lovely creature and its delightful behaviour. On my return home, my heart sank when I saw the body of a little robin in my backyard. The little robin must have been the baby of another robin that had also lost its life to a cat. The little robin must have been treating me as a parent and made me feel that I had failed to do my duty. It saddened me to see the life termination for a little robin at an early age. It also reminded me of having been close to a termination of my own life in 1945.

Did slaves ever retire from their jobs?

Slavery is a state that should no longer be seen to exist on our planet. Not many people will realise that we humans are still holding slaves. Just like the earlier practices of slavery, the current slaves, their children and grandchildren will be used as slaves until their deaths. I would like to see them be paid for their employment, retired at the national retirement age and given a pension like the rest of the population. It may seem strange that some people are still being enslaved, but the realisation will easily sink into the minds of people if they were to be told to continue working until the last day of their lives. In the earlier days, countries around the world had monarchs who owned and ruled the country. Later, the local people became the rulers of the countries and the monarchies were disbanded. However, in Britain the monarchs were retained to provide pride, pleasure and delight to the public. The country converted their monarchs into slaves who have been continuing to work until they say goodbye to life. I would dearly love to give them the opportunity of experiencing the delight of retirement in the later years of their lives that the rest of the population are granted.

Chapter 19

My dream world

Dreams

We humans have experiences of dreams mostly during our sleep. It was only in my later life that I felt that some dreams in my life had been unusual. I can place the dreams in my life into three different categories:

1. Normal dreams in our state of being in light sleep.
2. Abnormal dreams when we know we are dreaming.
3. Dreaming when awake.

Also, during our sleep some humans have experienced something that I do not consider to be a dream. That is the experience of walking in a state of sleep without having any recollection of that experience. I don't know what other people call those experiences. As I have previously not been narrating any of my dreams to other people, I don't know how many people would have had dream experiences like mine. Maybe, people might start narrating their dreams to others to expand our understanding of those experiences.

Normal dreams

All people must have experienced normal dreams and can see that it is the activity of the brain to sort out the experiences of the day for storage in the brain. Pet dogs may have been seen to be physically reacting during their sleep because even animals can be experiencing dreams. We humans also have some reactions during our sleep when we are dreaming. I remember during my childhood days when people have heard me making sounds in my sleep. It was during my college days that I was told by my companions in the hostel that they had heard someone screaming in their bedroom at night. Many had come out of their rooms and put on the corridor lights, but they could not see who had been having some trouble. I don't remember ever having woken up and may well have been the person who had done the screaming.

To me, a nightmare is also nothing more than a dream. During the time of being awake the brain collects from our sensors the vast amount of data piling in and stores it all in one compartment. Only during our period of sleep does the brain go through a process of sorting out and storing that information received during the day and storing it into the right brain compartments so that the incoming compartment would be free to store new information the next day. That is the period when dreaming takes place and people can sometimes remember some of those dreams that only occur during our light sleep periods. However, during our deep sleep the brain is at complete rest after having completed its transfer of information, dreaming does not occur. The timing and the number of those deep sleep periods is variable, both for humans and for animals. Some animals on our planet even go into a deep sleep for months in winter and I cannot imagine them to be dreaming anything during those periods as they would not be sensing any more life.

Abnormal dreams

I don't know how many people have ever been aware that they were dreaming during the dream. Those experiences have occurred seven times during my life. The first of those abnormal dreams occurred when I was very young, probably not even in my teens. It was only after a period of more than thirty years that there were more of those rare dreams occurring in my head. Just as normal dreams are hardly mentioned to other people, I also had never related my unusual dreams. Strangely, those rare dream experiences had remained in my memory while most normal dreams faded away. My experiences of those few rare dreams are spread over a period of about sixty years. During the earlier experiences, I had been unable to do what I wished to be doing. However, in my later dreams, I even managed to do in my dream what I could never do when awake. My 7 unusual dreams are presented in the order in which they had occurred.

1 Mangoes in Makupa market

I was standing just inside the side entrance at Makupa market near our house in Mombasa. There were fruit stalls beside me. In front of me, there was a pile of lovely mangoes. I suddenly realised that I was in a dream. Me being in a dream made me think that I could help myself to a lovely mango without having to pay for it. All I needed to do was to step forward, pick up a mango and walk away. It was then that I looked up at the stall holder and saw him looking sharply down at me. Then I thought that, being in a dream, I would not feel any pain even if that man was to smack me. That made me turn and look at the mangoes again. Still, I could not screw up enough courage to step forward, pick up a mango and walk away. I just could not do it. That happened when I was very young. Although I didn't have another experience of dream awareness for the next thirty years that dream memory has stayed in my head.

It was only in my later life that I managed to fathom the situation that could trigger those dreams. An earlier ordinary dream during the same night must have triggered the dream realisation during the following dream. That is because I was also able to remember an ordinary dream in which I had some lovely Indian sweets in a box. I had placed the box in a drawer for later consumption. Shortly after that, I had woken up I regretted not having eaten those sweets. I must have then immediately returned to my state of sleep in order that I could get to eat my sweets. That could have been the situation that must have put me into the dream of the mangoes in the market.

2 Walking along coastal path in a Devon town

During a walk with a colleague along a coastal path in the town of Torquay in Devon I suddenly realised that I was in a dream. I jumped up and shouted out to my friend that I was in a dream. Strangely, I then tried to find something to enable me to relate that dream to people when awake. We were walking slightly uphill along a wide footpath on the left side of the road. There was a railing on the side of the path and sea water below. There was nothing on the beach that provided me any evidence of being in a dream. Then I looked across the road at the buildings and saw a plaque at the entrance of a building. I rushed across the road to the building and read

272

the name on the plaque. There were four words on separate lines. I shouted these out to my friend and then ran back across the road in great delight.

One day in the café at Exeter College I was sitting with a college friend and was telling him about my experience of realising that I was dreaming during the dream. Just when I was finally describing my dream to him, one of the attendants happened to be passing by our table and gave me a puzzling look. I was puzzled at the look from the attendant. After I woke up in the morning, I realised that I had experienced two dreams during the same night. In the first one I had realised that I was in a dream. However, when I was relating that dream to a friend, I did not realise that I was in another dream. I cannot now recollect any of the words I had seen on the door plaque, but somehow, I had realised that I was in a dream when the thinking process is in explicable.

3 Walking by a small stream in the Exeter University ground

While walking on a footpath by a small stream in the grounds of the university near my house I realised that I was in a dream. I also felt that I must collect some positive identification of the dream. I started looking around to see what I could use to reveal the dream awareness. I looked towards the stream and looked at the plants I was walking by. I could not work out what I should be seeing to confirm that I was in a dream. Shortly afterwards, I gave up trying to look for some evidence of that dream and continued walking in dismay. When I woke up, I remember feeling very disappointed that I couldn't do anything during the dream to identify that I was dreaming. Although that was a boring experience, I still remember that it was another occasion of dream realisation during the dream.

4 My leap into flight

I was walking by a big stream on my own and suddenly realised that I was in a dream. I stepped into a most unusual activity without fear. From a large rock beside the stream, I put my arms out to the sides, crouched my legs and pushed myself up into the air. Wow, I was thrilled to be flying up. Then to my surprise the flying had stopped taking me up or forward when I was above the trees. My arms had to be moved to propel me forwards and ended up with me doing a breaststroke in the air. That took me forwards through the air towards a lake. That was all I experienced in my dream. I had been thrilled with that dream and it has remained in my head. That time I had initiated the activity of flying due to my awareness of dreaming.

The action of jumping up to go flying without any fear must have been triggered by some normal dream earlier. That must have occurred to remove any fear in my head in deciding to jump up and go flying when I became aware that I was dreaming. The ordinary dream preceding that must have been the one in which I was beside a hot air balloon in the grounds of the Mombasa transmitting station where I had been working. A large balloon was taking off from the field with people in the basket. When the balloon lifted off, I found that I was still beside the people although the balloon had lifted off the ground. When I looked around I saw that I was up in the air and not in the basket. The ground was below me. Although it was very unusual to be standing and floating in the air, it did not frighten me. Nor was I aware that I was in a dream. However, that is the experience that is most likely to have occurred earlier during the same sleep to trigger me to jump into the air for a flight without any fear. I had never realised that we can ignore gravity in our dreams because the dream uses only the mind and not the body.

5 An encounter with an elephant

I was standing outside a car on a dusty track somewhere in Kenya when a large elephant had appeared and was walking directly towards me. That scared me and made me run behind the car, down a slope and through the bushes to get away from the elephant. However, that elephant again appeared opposite me across the grass field, having descended through his side of the bushes. He was still coming towards me through the grass. That's when I strangely wondered if I was in a dream. Facing the elephant and pointing a finger at the elephant, I said to him, "Stop there." The elephant stopped. I then said to him "Turn around and go away." He turned around and moved away. It was a delight for me to have pushed him away and ran back to my car with a great feeling of joy.

Then at the car I thought "Why didn't I make him sit down and take me for a ride on its back?" That was a great relief for me. It was in a dream that I had told a wild elephant what to do and he did it. Not only that, the

African wild elephant understood English. That was the first time I managed to gain awareness that I was dreaming because of the fear I was sensing. In my earlier dreams in which I have been approached by lions or other creatures I had been woken out of the dream by the great sense of fear. In my elephant dream I somehow managed to stop the frightening experience by somehow realising that I was in a dream.

6 Space flight

While I was floating in space over the Earth and looking down at it, I realised that I was in a dream. I don't how I got there but had a thrilling view below me of some clouds and some unrecognisable land and the globe. I then did a somersault onto my back to look at the space above me. The first odd thing I felt was that I was being slightly supported by something underneath my back. I didn't expect to be feeling any gravity in space. Then I saw some layers of cirrus cloud above me. That also seemed to be odd. Still, I was delighted to be floating in space, but I don't know how I managed to get into space.

Me feeling gravity during my dream made me realise that dreaming only occurs in light sleep when a person could be experiencing some physical sensing. However, in a dream the brain can imagine something else. I had done a somersault in a dream, whereas in real life I must have done a sideways roll onto my back. That is why dreaming can be very strange.

7 Vertical take-off

I was coming down the stairs of a house that did not have any banisters beside the steps. When I was looking out through a side window, I suddenly realised that I was in a dream. I rushed down the stairs and ran past some family members. Outside the house I went to a slight mound on which I could stand for my launch. There was a young couple in front of me and there were some people and children to my right. The sight of the people around me then made me have another look around. That then made me feel that I was not in a dream and abandoned my plan to launch myself into space. I walked back into the house feeling disappointed.

Waking up in the morning I realised that I had missed my chance of a space launch in a dream because my brain did not have any images of what there is in sight in space when awake. The loss of continued awareness of the dream would have been my lack of preparation during my waking hours for my flight path into space and even my destination. That was the last time of my own awareness of being in a dream. I wondered if I would ever have such dream experiences again. However, I did experience something else about dreaming that had been unimaginable.

Dreaming when awake

It was in my later life that I had a couple of rare dream experiences; I had been dreaming when I was awake. I don't know if any other person has ever had that experience. There had been a ban on car driving for me when I suffered from a head problem in 2010. I spent a lot time cycling and found a lot of new routes that took cyclists away from car traffic. I enjoyed my trips to Dawlish Warren beach. I had parked my bicycle and walked along the beach away from the crowds towards the river Exe. It was during the weekdays that I came across very few people on the route. One day on a sunny afternoon, while walking on the empty beach on my own towards Exmouth, I recalled a dream. I could not figure out how an ordinary dream could be recalled a long time after being awake. I put that out of my mind. However, I did experience something similar again. Once again, I put that out of my mind. One day in the local library I had been doing some reading about dreaming and I realised that there is the possibility of a dream occurring even when we are awake. What had occurred in my head when I was walking on the beach in daylight was dreaming when awake, whereas I had been puzzled at remembering dreams that had occurred during the night when I was asleep. However, that experience then started making me ponder another major aspect of the human life.

Is God a dream?

During most of my life I had been involved in yoga exercises on my own at home and with other people during some evening sessions. When it came to be entering a state of meditation, I had found it to be very difficult, nor could I imagine what I was expecting to experience in that state. Then it dawned on me that the unusual dreams experienced by me could be related to the concepts of seeing or being with God when they were meditating. For meditation, the person must prepare the body to be locked out of existence to enable the mind to meditate. That results in the person entering a stage that is like going to sleep and dreaming. That made me realise that meditation experiences are no more than dreaming experiences. However, I still found yoga exercises to be very good for my body as well as my brain. Meditation could also be good for peace of mind. However, God during our meditation is nothing other than a dream. I decided that I would be able to fathom God only when I was fully awake and free to control my active thinking.

Chapter 20
Mysteries and delights in my life

Life Mysteries

All through my life there have been mysteries. And all through my life I had been solving mysteries. I never imagined that some of those mysteries would ever be solved. Those included:

- Where did the universe come from?
- Why is our planet only a speck in the universe?
- What started life on our planet?
- Why have humans failed to fathom the origin of life?
- What is God?
- Why is God allowing disasters on our planet?
- Where will we go after death?
- What on earth had brought me into existence?

Strangely, during the final stage of my existence I have solved all the mysteries that have been in my head during my life. That resulted in me deciding to place my explanations in my Autobiography Part II that is titled as Life Mysteries Solved. The book is for people with open minds. The contents of that book are shown in Addendum 4.

My music delights

Music had started giving me some delight during my young age. It was at my primary school that I had enjoyed doing some singing in English. At home the music on the gramophone and radio were mainly Indian cinema music and the singing was in Hindi. Listening to European classical music on the BBC overseas service was a delight. During the period of my higher education, pop and dancing music had been a delight. It was during my RAF life that I was introduced to the classical music. That delight then kept on increasing throughout my life. The recordings of music kept on advancing and discs allowed me to listen to music in the home and in the car. Indian classical music only entered my mind after coming to Britain.

Although there have been numerous composers who have been thrilling my life, there is a composer who became my favourite. The simple sound of *"dut dut dut daaa"* may be nothing of interest to a human mind. However, that sound did trigger the mind of a musical composer to create a fantastic symphony that is greatly stimulating for me. That is Beethoven's fifth symphony. That sound sequence also happened to have been used by British forces to signal the letter 'V' in Morse code and Beethoven's symphony became popular in Britain to proclaim victory. There may be only a limited number of people on our globe who might have heard that Beethoven symphony and liked it. To me, all of Beethoven's nine symphonies are delightful. His ninth symphony was composed when he was totally deaf and was unique as it integrated a hundred singers with the hundred musicians to produce the most wonderful music for the planet. Numerous other composers have produced delightful symphonies that usually have four movements. Symphonies use orchestras with multiple musical instruments, whereas other music compositions are made up of various numbers of movements and instruments. The concertos use an orchestra together with one or a few special instruments that lead the group. Those instruments could be the violin, piano, cello or bassoon. Another group of musical creations are called the sonatas that provide the music, using only some special instruments. In addition to that there are numerous other forms of music composition.

It was long after starting to listen to classical music that I started to learn about the notion of counterpoint in western classical music. In effect, a counterpoint is like using a male-female pair of dancers to perform a dance instead of a single dancer doing it. The use of two different tunes in the same music is what made the western classical music to become a great delight. In addition to that, there is the fantastic use of many different musical instruments played by a group of a hundred musicians in a single band. Only the creators of western music enabled humans to pass on delightful music to future generations by creating a method of writing down the music in a form of notes. That is something that does not seem to have been developed in any other part of our planet. Another delight of music has been that it can be produced by human voices doing various kinds of singing. Music created by humans and other life forms became a great delight to my life.

I know why the birds and other creatures create singing sounds, but I still don't understand how they select their sounds. Similarly, I feel that it does not matter if one does not understand the creation of the human music; it is the sound of music that is a delight to the listener. The creations by the composers may be based on some conceptions in their minds and may even be revealed in the titles for those creations, but I found that I had been enjoying the sounds, even if I had no conception of the title. *The Enigma Variations* produced by Elgar leave it to the listener to fathom what his tunes are based on. Composers created their music based on some conceptions in their heads, but the listeners do not need to know what the composers were thinking. Also, the listeners could even create their own concepts for the music they are hearing. Vivaldi has written some beautiful tunes in his creation of music called the *Four Seasons*. Beethoven's pastoral symphony includes the delightful sounds of a thunderstorm arriving and then passing away. Mozart created numerous music compositions for playing on instruments as well as with human singing. Gustav Holst has composed several delightful tunes for the different planets in our solar system. Vaughan Williams composed the lovely birdsong of the lark ascending. I also enjoy the Hebrides overture of *Fingals Cave* by Mendelssohn. When on holiday in the Hebrides in Scotland I missed seeing those caves, but I still enjoy the music. Human music is solely for human delights on our planet. I do not wish for any existence after life as I will be missing delightful human music that is only found on our planet.

Colours in our sky

Even the sky of our wonderful planet became a great delight in my life. We humans are certainly very privileged to be seeing the blue sky and the beautiful clouds, rainfalls and rainbows. These are very different to those of other planets. All humans will have experienced the delight of seeing the rainbow semicircle. There are not many people who have also seen the full circle rainbow. Those circular rainbows appeared for me when I have been flying and found them to be moving around with me. People looking at semi-circular rainbows are also likely to have noticed the sight of more than one rainbow on the same side. The normal sight of rainbows will often have a second rainbow that appears above the normal rainbow, which is slightly wider, in duller colours and will appear in reverse. However, sometimes two more rainbows can be seen attached to the bottom of the main rainbow.

In addition to the rainbow colours that we can see on the opposite side of the sun, there are rainbow colours in view even on the same side of the sun. The full circle of that rainbow mostly appears when there is a hazy atmosphere in line with the sun and the colours of those rainbows are in reverse to those in normal rainbows. During the periods of sunrise or sunset in some clouds on either side of the sun there may be seen only two parts of that reverse rainbow. Not many people seem to be aware that rainbow colours can be seen even when there is no rain falling.

Pink and turquoise colours appear in widespread layers on the side of the sun and are longer lasting. Those colours could appear on the slim edges of a cumulus cloud or over the whole layer of a thin stratus cloud or a cirrus cloud at very high level. The turquoise colour is a combination of the green and blue colours that are close together in their wavelengths and manage to go through small drops of water vapour forming the cloud. The pink colour is a combination of red and white lights. The very unusual sighting of proper rainbow colours can also appear in the clouds around the sun, even when there is no rain. Those fantastic sightings of rainbow colours and shapes can be seen beside the sun, even when there is no rain. What is even more unusual is the fact that rainbows with all their colours could also appear momentarily in the unusual shapes of the cloud edges that move past the sun.

Natural lifeforms

Ever since my childhood it has been a pleasure for me to associate with other life creatures on our planet. It was only in my later life that I realised that the numerous lifeforms on my planet are a unique existence in the universe. We humans may be the most advanced creatures on our planet, but we are unaware of the natural life around us. We humans are destroying natural life on our own planet. We are unaware of where our life path is taking us. Are we the most superior life?

Farewell folks

During my life I have experienced many delights and frights. After more than seventy-five years, I am still here and am leaving behind recollections of my life experiences. Unlike most humans, I am not afraid of the termination of my life, because I have been very close to losing my own life and survived. Most humans try to imagine some better existence after life termination. Instead of that, I am happy to be aware of my current existence on the most beautiful planet in the universe and to be associating with numerous other life forms with whom I am sharing my existence on a unique planet.

Goodbye

PHOTOGRAPHS
MY EARLY LIFE

1940   Me and my family in Mombasa

1945   A dhow similar to the one we sailed in

1946   Krishan, Krishna, me and Baldev

1948 My loving father

1948 Near his work location

1948 In my school uniform in our backyard

1954 With our doggy

1957 Selected for Jamboree in UK

1957   The Queen at Jubilee Jamboree, Sutton Coldfield

1959   Royal Technical College, Nairobi

1959 Kilimanjaro expedition

1959 Kilimanjaro peak

1965 RAF Air Electronics aircrew

1967 RAF crew in Aden on 37 Squadron Shackleton Mark 2

1965 Mt Kenya on RAF expedition

1968   Shackleton Mark 3 formation flight over Sharjah

1968   Shackleton crew at Sharjah

1975   Vulcan B2 at Midway Island in the Pacific Ocean

1975 Vulcan bomber XH558 beside oil rig, west of Shetland

Addendum 1

Auld Lang Syne

Should auld acquaintance be forgot,
And never brought to mind?
Should auld acquaintance be forgot,
And auld lang syne?

> For auld lang syne, my dear
> For auld lang syne,
> We'll tak a cup o' kindness yet,
> For auld lang syne.

And surely ye'll be your pint-stowp!
And surely I'll be mine!
And we'll tak a cup o' kindness yet
For auld lang syne.

> For auld lang syne, my dear,
> For auld lang syne,
> We'll tak a cup o' kindness yet,
> For auld lang syne.

We twa hae run about the braes,
And pu'd the gowans fine;
But we've wandered mony a weary foot
Sin' auld lang syne.

> For auld lang syne, my dear,
> For auld lang syne,
> We'll tak a cup o' kindness yet,
> For auld lang syne.

We twa hae paidled i' the burn,
Frae morning sun till dine;
But seas between us braid hae roared
Sin' auld lang syne.

> *For auld lang syne, my dear,*
> *For auld lang syne*
> *We'll tak a cup o' kindness yet,*
> *For auld lang syne.*

And there's a hand, my trusty fiere,
And gie's a hand o' thine!
And we'll tak a right guid-willie waught
For auld lang syne.

> *For auld lang syne, my dear,*
> *For auld lang syne,*
> *We'll tak a cup o' kindness yet,*
> *For auld lang syne.*

Robert Burns

Addendum 2

Daffodils

I wandered lonely as a cloud

That floats on high o'er vales and hills,

When all at once I saw a crowd

A host, of dancing daffodils;

Beside the Lake, beneath the trees,
Fluttering and dancing in the breeze.

Continuous as the stars that shine

And twinkle on the Milky Way

They stretch'd in never ending line
Along the margin of a bay:
Ten thousand saw I at a glance,

Tossing their heads in a sprightly dance.

The waves beside them danced, but they

Out-did the sparkling waves in glee:

A poet could not but be gay,

In such a jocund company:

I gazed - and gazed - but little thought

What wealth the show to me had brought:

For oft when on my couch I lie

In vacant or in pensive mood,

They flash upon that inward eye

Which is the bliss of solitude;
And then my heart with pleasure fills,
And dances in the daffodils.

William Wordsworth   *1807*

Addendum 3

Foreign words

Punjabi relatives

Male	Female	Relationships
Pitaji	Mataji	parents
Baaji	Maama	parents
Dadaji	Dadiji	grandparents, father's side
Nanaji	Naniji	grandparents, mother's side
Tayaji	Taiji	older than father, uncle/aunt
Chachaji	Chachiji	younger than father, uncle/aunt
Fufadj i	Puaji	father's sister and husband, uncle/aunt
Mamaji	Mamiji	mother's brother and wife, uncle/aunt
Masudji	Masiji	mother's sister and husband, uncle/aunt
Praji	Penji	older brother and sister or cousins
Papaji	Pabiji	brother or male cousin and wife
Jeejaji	Penji	sister or female cousin and husband
Pra / Jeeja	Pen / Pabi	younger relatives without the *'ji'*

Other languages

Amen is a European word made up with two sounds from the mouth to say 'so be it'.

Au revoir is a goodbye in French.

Bon Adieu is a farewell in French.

Auld lang syne is the Scottish way of saying 'old time song' in English.

Addendum 4

Life Mysteries Solved - Autobiography Part II   Contents